T0321963

Applying AI–Based IoT Systems to Simulation–Based Information Retrieval

Bhatia Madhulika
Amity University, India

Bhatia Surabhi
King Faisal University, Saudi Arabia

Poonam Tanwar
Manav Rachna International Institute of Research and Studies, India

Kuljeet Kaur
Université du Québec, Canada

A volume in the Advances in Computational Intelligence and Robotics (ACIR) Book Series

Published in the United States of America by
>	IGI Global
>	Engineering Science Reference (an imprint of IGI Global)
>	701 E. Chocolate Avenue
>	Hershey PA, USA 17033
>	Tel: 717-533-8845
>	Fax: 717-533-8661
>	E-mail: cust@igi-global.com
>	Web site: http://www.igi-global.com

Library of Congress Cataloging-in-Publication Data

Names: Bhatia, Madhulika, 1984- editor.
Title: Applying AI-based IoT systems to simulation-based information
    retrieval / Madhulika Bhatia, Surbhi Bhatia, Poonam Tanwar, and Kuljeet
    Kaur, editors.
Description: Hershey, PA : Information Science Reference, [2023] | "Topics:
    Internet of things, Big Data, Semantic web, Sensor data, Information
    retrieval, Representing data, Data Visualization, Data extraction,
    Handling sensor data, Tools and techniques, Big data, Algorithms for
    Data handling, Visualizing Big Data, Visualizing data with
    Graphs"--Preferatory pages. | Includes bibliographical references and
    index. | Summary: "This reference book is for readers seeking to learn
    and enhance their knowledge in the field of IoT, Artificial
    Intelligence, Handling IoT issue using AI, Deep Learning, Machine
    Learning, and related other AI techniques"-- Provided by publisher.
Identifiers: LCCN 2022033955 (print) | LCCN 2022033956 (ebook) | ISBN
    9781668452554 (hardcover) | ISBN 9781668452592 (paperback) | ISBN
    9781668452561 (ebook)
Subjects: LCSH: Internet of things. | Information visualization. | Big
    data. | Computer simulation. | Artificial intelligence.
Classification: LCC TK5105.8857 .A664 2023 (print) | LCC TK5105.8857
    (ebook) | DDC 004.67/8--dc23/eng/20220906
LC record available at https://lccn.loc.gov/2022033955
LC ebook record available at https://lccn.loc.gov/2022033956

This book is published in the IGI Global book series Advances in Computational Intelligence and Robotics (ACIR) (ISSN: 2327-0411; eISSN: 2327-042X)

British Cataloguing in Publication Data
A Cataloguing in Publication record for this book is available from the British Library.
All work contributed to this book is new, previously-unpublished material.
The views expressed in this book are those of the authors, but not necessarily of the publisher.
For electronic access to this publication, please contact: eresources@igi-global.com.

Advances in Computational Intelligence and Robotics (ACIR) Book Series

ISSN:2327-0411
EISSN:2327-042X

Editor-in-Chief: Ivan Giannoccaro, University of Salento, Italy

MISSION

While intelligence is traditionally a term applied to humans and human cognition, technology has progressed in such a way to allow for the development of intelligent systems able to simulate many human traits. With this new era of simulated and artificial intelligence, much research is needed in order to continue to advance the field and also to evaluate the ethical and societal concerns of the existence of artificial life and machine learning.

The **Advances in Computational Intelligence and Robotics (ACIR) Book Series** encourages scholarly discourse on all topics pertaining to evolutionary computing, artificial life, computational intelligence, machine learning, and robotics. ACIR presents the latest research being conducted on diverse topics in intelligence technologies with the goal of advancing knowledge and applications in this rapidly evolving field.

COVERAGE

- Machine Learning
- Synthetic Emotions
- Brain Simulation
- Artificial Life
- Agent technologies
- Adaptive and Complex Systems
- Artificial Intelligence
- Cyborgs
- Intelligent Control
- Cognitive Informatics

IGI Global is currently accepting manuscripts for publication within this series. To submit a proposal for a volume in this series, please contact our Acquisition Editors at Acquisitions@igi-global.com or visit: http://www.igi-global.com/publish/.

Titles in this Series

For a list of additional titles in this series, please visit:
http://www.igi-global.com/book-series/advances-computational-intelligence-robotics/73674

Multi-Disciplinary Applications of Fog Computing Responsiveness in Real-Time
Debi Prasanna Acharjya (Vellore Institute of Technology, India) and P. Ahmed Kauser (Vellore Institute of Technology, India)
Engineering Science Reference • © 2023 • 300pp • H/C (ISBN: 9781668444665) • US $270.00

Handbook of Research on AI and Knowledge Engineering for Real-Time Business Intelligence
Kamal Kant Hiran (Aalborg University, Denmark) K. Hemachandran (Woxsen University, India) Anil Pise (University of the Witwatersrand, South Africa) and B. Justus Rabi (Christian College of Engineering and Technology, India)
Engineering Science Reference • © 2023 • 359pp • H/C (ISBN: 9781668465196) • US $380.00

Applied AI and Multimedia Technologies for Smart Manufacturing and CPS Applications
Emmanuel Oyekanlu (Drexel University, USA)
Engineering Science Reference • © 2023 • 377pp • H/C (ISBN: 9781799878520) • US $270.00

Exploring Future Opportunities of Brain-Inspired Artificial Intelligence
Madhulika Bhatia (Amity University, India) Tanupriya Choudhury (University of Petroleum and Energy Studies, India) and Bhupesh Kumar Dewangan (School of Engineering, Department of Computer Science and Engineering, O.P. Jindal University, India)
Engineering Science Reference • © 2023 • 215pp • H/C (ISBN: 9781668469804) • US $270.00

Developments in Artificial Intelligence Creativity and Innovation
Ziska Fields (University of Johannesburg, South Africa)
Engineering Science Reference • © 2023 • 300pp • H/C (ISBN: 9781668462706) • US $270.00

For an entire list of titles in this series, please visit:
http://www.igi-global.com/book-series/advances-computational-intelligence-robotics/73674

701 East Chocolate Avenue, Hershey, PA 17033, USA
Tel: 717-533-8845 x100 • Fax: 717-533-8661
E-Mail: cust@igi-global.com • www.igi-global.com

Table of Contents

Detailed Table of Contents

Chapter 1
Hrithik Raj, Amity University, India
Ritu Punhani, Amity University, India
Ishika Punhani, University of Petroleum and Energy Studies, India

This chapter discusses the problems of project preparation, project planning, project execution, and monitoring of a real-world project. Emphasis is placed on MS Project – a software product designed to create plans, projects, and schedules as well as control and management of their implementation. It is discussed in a practical manner its ability to understand how much time and work developers are investing in a software project. As a result, the project management actions helped the project be delivered on time without compromising any time, budget, or resource constraints. The authors considered different scenarios related to project risk. They used the project crashing technique, and the time of the project was significantly reduced allowing the project to finish on time. The relations between the activities, the resources, and the time for their implementation are defined. The effectiveness of using different types of calendars—standard and continuous—specific to the continuous mining activities is evaluated.

Chapter 2

Divi Anand, Amity University, India
Isha Kaushik, Amity University, India
Jasmehar Singh Mann, Amity University, India
Ritu Punhani, Amity University, India
Ishika Punhani, University of Petroleum and Energy Studies, India

A blockchain is a growing list of documents, called blocks, that can be cryptographically related together. A cryptographic hash of the previous block, a timestamp, and transaction data are all protected in every block. The project's purpose is to supply a web app that demonstrates blockchain fundamentals that include transaction verification and hash generation. The reason of blockchain generation is to provide a chain of sequentially ordered data blocks that are stored in a decentralised manner through all community contributors (nodes). A block of facts is formed while the nodes solution, a complex mathematical assignment (evidence of labour) that is stipulated via a consensus strategy, is cryptographically blanketed. Because everything that happens on blockchain is encrypted, there's no doubt that it provides next-level encryption. Similarly, tampering with the data on the blockchain is impossible. To be safe, you can check file signatures on all nodes across all ledgers in the network to make sure they haven't changed.

Chapter 3

Jayanthi G., Sri Ramachandra Institute of Higher Education and
*   Research, India*
Purushothaman R., Siddartha Institute of Science and Technology, India

Highway traffic profiling is an essential service for the deployment of intelligent transport system (ITS) in Chennai metropolitan city. Recently, a traffic sequence mining framework was developed for the prediction of traffic flow on highways. Real-time traffic flow rate of the state highway SH-49 was collected under the authority and supervision of Tamil Nadu Road Development Corporation (TNRDC). The objective of this investigation is to deploy electronic traffic profiling with all essential services for highway traffic operations. The implementation of traffic sequence mining framework done earlier has highly motivated the authors to extend the present work to E-Traffic alert, a highway traffic profiling system that disseminates the dynamic traffic flow rate to commuters when deployed as mobile application and an interactive analytic tool for traffic operations when deployed as desktop web application.

Chapter 4

Anshika Gupta, Amity University, India
Shuchi Sirpal, Amity School of Engineering and Technology, Amity
University, India

The chapter describes the understanding and the application of the concept of the various AI algorithms that also include reinforcement learning algorithms, which is a great contribution to the decision-making of the AI agents/AI bots. The game consists of player and opponent AI competing with each other in which the goal is to kill the opponent. The game is basically an Action RPG game (real-time combat between the player and AI agents). Wherever the performer has the ability to focus and see on his own stats and the stats of the character, accordingly he can determine the health, mana, strength, XP, and other abilities. The AI bots on the other hand are programmed to follow the player, and depending on the state that it is in and the player's last attack, it makes decisions accordingly and tries to defeat the player. Application of the various AI algorithms on the software Unreal Engine are achieved by C++ programming and blueprint/visual scripting. The game contains player and adversary AI competing with each other in which the goal is to slay the opponent.

Chapter 5

Reet Kaur Kohli, Amity University, Noida, India
Seneha Santoshi, Amity University, Noida, India
Sunishtha S. Yadav, Amity University, Noida, India
Vandana Chauhan, Amity University, Noida, India

Drug discovery is the process in which healthcare is approached through identification of potential new therapeutic agents. CADD provides solutions at every stage of drug discovery including the leading challenges of cost and time. CADD has provided an effective solution to this challenge. AI has enabled multiple aspects of drug discovery, including the analysis of high content screening data and the design and synthesis of new molecules. The use of transparent methodologies like AI is crucial, particularly in drug repositioning/repurposing in rare diseases. An abundant variety of methods, in particular the concepts of deep learning, have been used for protein modelling and ligand-based drug discovery along with artificial neural networks for QSAR modelling. Structure-based ligand identification via AI modelling is also explored. AI presents the scientific community and the biopharma industry and its established processes for discovering and developing new medicines with new challenges.

It is necessary for human beings to undergo regular health check-ups, which all of us tend to ignore. As a result, late diagnosis of disease usually leads to ineffective treatment. To cater to this problem, the authors have developed a platform called Nakhasys, which is a smart AI-based application developed to diagnose a set of diseases like jaundice, anemia, etc. with the help of analysis of nail segmentation. This is based on the ancient Indian practice of Ayurveda. Initially a dedicated Android application will allow users to click a picture of their nails, which will be sent to the virtual machine hosted in Microsoft Azure cloud. This picture will be validated through Azure Custom Vision API. After successful validation, the same image will be sent to the custom ML model for further detection of the nail color, which will allow the application to predict the possible set of diseases. This diagnosis will alert the individual.

In order to reduce the unnecessary waste of the workforce, the proposed system has been developed. In this chapter, a secure environment from that future will secure and help increase motivation for intelligent things and productivity and enter newly grown markets, startups, and entrepreneurs. The significant contribution to knowledge was to improve the automatic boom barrier system, considering the low cost of the budget. This chapter is concerned with providing an automatic boom barrier, the gate operated by Raspberry Pi. Some of the features considered during this system's design were cost-effective and easy to use compared to existing systems. Security plays an essential role in making smart cities using the "automatic boom barrier system."

Chapter 8

Sreekanth T. G., PSG College of Technology, India
Senthilkumar M., PSG College of Technology, India
Manikanta Reddy S., PSG College of Technology, India

Glass and carbon fiber-reinforced plastics have become increasingly popular in engineering applications as relatively new materials, and it is expected that this trend will continue. E-glass laminates have become more common in aviation components such as wings, fuselages, and stabilizers as stronger, more durable, and tougher resins such as epoxies have evolved. A sudden breakdown of an engineering component like aircraft usually results in a significant financial loss, as well as posing a risk to human life. Vibration-based detection is one type of global damage identification method. Changes in physical qualities like damping, mass, and stiffness bring noticeable changes in the modal parameters in vibration-based damage detection approaches. This chapter demonstrates how vibration-based analysis can be used to forecast the severity and position of delamination in composites. The position and area of delamination in composite beams are determined using a supervised feed-forward multilayer back-propagation artificial neural network (ANN) in the MATLAB neural network toolbox.

Chapter 9

Manya Sangwan, J.C. Bose University of Science and Technology, India
Sapna Gambhir, J.C. Bose University of Science and Technology, India
Sumita Gupta, Amity School of Engineering and Technology, Amity
*   University, Noida, India*

Early detection that can be done to detect lung cancer is through radiological examination. Chest X-Ray or chest radiography is one of the tools that can be used to analyze lung diseases including pneumonia, bronchitis, and lung cancer. The image from the radiography will show the shape of the lungs difference between normal and abnormal lungs. In abnormal lungs, it will show nodules in the lungs on the results radiography image, but on the other hand, in normal lungs, it does not show nodules in the lungs on the radiographic image. This study to detect lung cancer using radiographic images using deep learning techniques. Therefore, by carrying out early revealing of lung cancer, it is hoped that this scheme will provide suitable action and directions for lung cancer patients and decrease lung cancer transience.

Rosy Madaan, CSE Department, FET, Manav Rachna International
Institute of Research and Studies, India

There is a large amount of data available on the web in form of opinions, which need to be accessed for mining opinions. This is an ever-growing field that brings together the reviews, blogs, discussions on forums, Twitter, microblogs, and social networks. A user may be looking for opinions on some commodity or product for making decision regarding purchase for which there is the need of a system based on question answering. This gives rise to a question answering (QA) system. This system works on all the aspects of question answering along with the mining of opinions. The chapter discusses all the modules of the question answering system along with how the opinions are mined. The details of implementation along with the performance analysis of the proposed system are given in the chapter. On performance evaluation, a high value of opinion accuracy has been found that shows that the system performs well.

Preface

OVERVIEW

The convergence of AI and IoT has resulted in a potent synergy that is revolutionizing many aspects of our daily lives. By leveraging the capabilities of AI-based IoT systems to collect, process, and analyze vast amounts of data from various sources, new opportunities have emerged for enhancing the efficiency, productivity, and safety of different industries.

Simulation-based information retrieval is one area that has significantly benefited from this technological revolution. While simulations are powerful tools for predicting and analyzing complex systems, they often generate massive amounts of data that can be challenging to analyze and interpret. The integration of AI-based IoT systems with simulation-based information retrieval can address these challenges and provide novel insights and solutions.

This book provides a comprehensive overview of the potential of AI-based IoT systems for simulation-based information retrieval. It covers the latest research and development efforts, practical applications, and emerging trends in this field.

The intended audience for this book includes researchers, engineers, and practitioners in AI, IoT, simulation, and information retrieval. It is also suitable for students and educators who want to gain a better understanding of this dynamic and rapidly evolving field.

We hope that this book inspires readers to explore the possibilities of AI-based IoT systems for simulation-based information retrieval and contributes to the progress of this field.

This work can be used as handbook for academics, developers, Industry persons, project/program managers, Postgraduate students, Undergraduate students and enthusiastic readers seeking to learn and enhance their knowledge in the field of IOT, Artificial Intelligence, Handling IOT issue using AI, Deep Learning, Machine Learning, and related other AI techniques.

TARGET AUDIENCE

The target audience includes researchers and practitioners working in the field of science and technology, academicians, research scholars, and IoT developers.

CHAPTERS

Chapter 1

A Practical Approach to Visualizing Different Phases of Project Management Using MSProject

This chapter discusses the problems of project preparation, project planning, project execution, and monitoring of a real-world project. Emphasis is placed on MS Project – a software product designed to create plans, projects, and schedules as well as control and management of their implementation. It is discussed in a practical manner its ability to understand how much time and work developers are investing in a software project. As a result, the project management actions helped the project be delivered on time without compromising any time, budget, or resource constraints. We considered different scenarios related to Project Risk. We used the project crashing technique, and the time of the project was significantly reduced hence allowing the project to finish on time. The relations between the activities, the resources, and the time for their implementation are defined. The effectiveness of using different types of calendars – standard and continuous - 24 hours specific to the continuous mining activities is evaluated.

Chapter 2

Visualisation of Blockchain Concepts

A blockchain is a growing list of documents, called blocks, which can be cryptographically related together. A cryptographic hash of the previous block, a timestamp, and transaction data are all protected in every block. The project's purpose is to supply a web-app that demonstrates blockchain fundamentals which include transaction verification and hash generation. The reason of Blockchain generation is to provide a chain of sequentially ordered data blocks which are stored in a decentralised manner through all community contributors (nodes). A block of facts is formed while the nodes solution a complex mathematical assignment (evidence of labour) that is stipulated via a consensus strategy this is cryptographically blanketed. Because everything that happens on blockchain is encrypted, there's no doubt that it provides next-level encryption. Similarly, tampering with the data on the blockchain is impossible. To be safe, you can check file signatures on all nodes across all ledgers in the network to make sure they haven't changed.

Chapter 3

Data Analytics With Selection of Tools and Techniques

Highway Traffic profiling is an essential service for the deployment of Intelligent Transport System (ITS) in Chennai Metropolitan City. Recently, traffic sequence mining framework was developed for the prediction of traffic flow on highways. Real time traffic flow rate of the state highway SH-49 was collected under the authority and supervision of Tamil Nadu Road Development Corporation (TNRDC). The objective of this investigation is to deploy electronic traffic profiling with all essential services for highway traffic operations. The implementation of traffic sequence mining framework done earlier has highly motivated us to extend the present work to E-Traffic alert, a highway traffic profiling system that disseminates the dynamic traffic flow rate to commuters when deployed as mobile application and an interactive analytic tool for traffic operations when deployed as desktop web application.

Chapter 4

AI in Gaming and Entertainment: Applying Artificial Intelligence Algorithms in a Game

The chapter's best describe the understanding and the application of the concept of the various AI algorithms that also include Reinforcement Learning algorithms which is a great contribution to the decision-making of the AI agents/AI bots. The game consists of player and opponents AI competing with each other in which the goal is to kill the opponent. The game is basically an Action RPG Game(real-time combat between the player and AI agents) wherever the performer has the ability to focus and see on his own stats and the stats of the character, accordingly he can determine the health, mana, strength, XP, and other abilities. The AI bots on the additional hand are programmed to follow the player and depending on the state that it is in and the player's last attack, it makes decisions accordingly and tries to defeat the player. application of the various AI Algorithms on the software Unreal Engine which is achieved by C++ programming and blueprint/visual scripting. The game contains of player and adversaries AI competing with each other in which the goal is to slay the opponent.

Chapter 5

Applications of AI in Computer-Aided Drug Discovery

Drug discovery is the process in which healthcare is approached through identification of potential new therapeutic agents. CADD with providing solutions at every stage of drug discovery including the leading challenges of cost and time. CADD has provided an effective solution to this challenge. AI has enabled multiple aspects of drug discovery, including the analysis of high content screening data, and the design and synthesis of new molecules. The use of transparent methodologies like AI is crucial, particularly in drug repositioning/repurposing in rare diseases. An abundant variety of methods, in particular, the concepts of deep learning have been used for protein Modelling and ligand based drug discovery along with artificial neural networks for QSAR modelling. Structure-based ligand identification via AI modelling is also being explored. AI is presenting the scientific community and the biopharma industry with new challenges and its established processes for discovering and developing new medicines.

Chapter 6

Nakhasys: An ML-Based Disease Diagnosing Application

It is necessary for human beings to undergo regular Health Check-ups which all of us tend to ignore more often. As a result late diagnosis of disease usually leads to ineffective treatment. To cater to this problem we have developed a platform called Nakhasys which is a smart AI based application developed to diagnose a set of diseases like jaundice, anemia etc. with the help of analysis of nail segmentation. This is based on ancient Indian practice of Ayurveda. Initially a dedicated android application will allow users to click a picture of their nails, which will be sent to the virtual machine hosted in Microsoft Azure cloud. This picture will be validated through azure custom vision API. After successful validation the same image will be sent to the custom ML model for further detection of the nail color which will allow the application to predict the possible set of diseases. This diagnosis will alert the individual for same.

Chapter 7

IoT-Based Automatic Boom Barrier for Enhancing Surveillance Security in Public Places

In order to reduce the unnecessary waste of the workforce, the proposed system has been developed. In this paper, we said about a secure environment, from that future will secure and help increase motivation for intelligent things and productivity and enter newly grown markets, startups, and entrepreneurs. The significant contribution to knowledge was to improve the automatic boom barrier system, considering the low cost of the budget. This paper is concerned about providing an automatic boom barrier, the gate operated by raspberry-Pi. Some of the features considered during this system's design were cost-effective and easy to use compared to existing systems. Security plays an essential role in making smart cities using our "automatic boom barrier system."

Chapter 8

Health Monitoring of Polymer Matrix Composites Using Vibration Technique

Glass and carbon fiber-reinforced plastics have become increasingly popular in engineering applications as relatively new materials, and it is expected that this trend will continue. E-glass laminates have become more common in aviation components such as wings, fuselages, and stabilisers as stronger, more durable, and tougher resins such as epoxies have evolved. A sudden breakdown of an engineering component like aircraft usually results in a significant financial loss, as well as posing a risk to human life. Vibration based detection is one type of global damage identification method. Changes in physical qualities like damping, mass and stiffness brings noticeable changes in the modal parameters in vibration-based damage detection approaches. This chapter demonstrates how vibration-based analysis can be used to forecast the severity and position of delaminations in composites. The position and area of delamination in composite beams are determined using a supervised feed-forward multilayer back-propagation Artificial Neural Network (ANN) in the MATLAB Neural Network Toolbox.

Chapter 9

Lung Cancer Detection Using Deep Learning Techniques

Early detection that can be done to detect lung cancer is through radiological examination. Chest X-Ray or chest radiography is one of the tools that be able to be used to analyze lungs diseases including pneumonia, bronchitis, and lung cancer. The image from the radiography will show the shape of the lungs difference between normal and abnormal lungs. In abnormal lungs, it will show nodules in the lungs on the results radiography image but on the other hand in normal lungs, it does not show nodules in the lungs on the radiographic image. This study to detect lung cancer using radiographic images using deep learning techniques. Therefore, by carrying out early revealing of lung cancer, it is hoped that this scheme will provide suitable action and directions for lung cancer patients and decrease lung cancer transience.

Chapter 10

Mechanism for Crawling, Filtering, and Presenting Opinionated Content on Online Products to the Customers

There is a large amount of data available on the web in form of opinions, which is need to be accessed for mining if opinions. This is an ever growing field which coincides the reviews, blogs, discussions on forums, Twitters, microblogs, and social networks. A user may be looking for opinions on some commodity or product for making decision regarding purchase etc. for which there is need of a system based on question answering. This gives rise to a Question Answering (QA) system arises. This system works on all the aspects of question answering along with the mining of opinions. The paper discusses all the modules of the Question Answering system along with how the opinions are mined. The details of implementation along with the performance analysis of the proposed system are given in the paper. On performance evaluation, a high value of Opinion Accuracy has been found which shows that the system performs well.

CONCLUSION

The long-standing objective of this book is finding patterns retrieving novel insights, predicting future behavior, etc. using this high amount of sensory data. Artificial Intelligence has an important role in facilitating analytics and learning in the IoT devices. This book covers the process of capturing and preprocessing IoT data and usage of different AI techniques – machine learning, deep learning, reinforcement learning, natural language processing, soft computing to build an high performance system. The purpose of this book is to enrich readers by the power of artificial intelligence to handle IoT sensor big data. The exposure of this AI-based IoT systems are needed in order to make IoT applications more intelligent.

Bhatia Madhulika
Amity University, India

Bhatia Surabhi
King Faisal University, Saudi Arabia

Poonam Tanwar
Manav Rachna International Institute of Research and Studies, India

Kuljeet Kaur
Université du Québec, Canada

Chapter 1
A Practical Approach to Visualizing Different Phases of Project Management Using MSProject

Hrithik Raj
Amity University, India

Ritu Punhani
Amity University, India

Ishika Punhani
University of Petroleum and Energy Studies, India

ABSTRACT

This chapter discusses the problems of project preparation, project planning, project execution, and monitoring of a real-world project. Emphasis is placed on MS Project – a software product designed to create plans, projects, and schedules as well as control and management of their implementation. It is discussed in a practical manner its ability to understand how much time and work developers are investing in a software project. As a result, the project management actions helped the project be delivered on time without compromising any time, budget, or resource constraints. The authors considered different scenarios related to project risk. They used the project crashing technique, and the time of the project was significantly reduced allowing the project to finish on time. The relations between the activities, the resources, and the time for their implementation are defined. The effectiveness of using different types of calendars—standard and continuous—specific to the continuous mining activities is evaluated.

DOI: 10.4018/978-1-6684-5255-4.ch001

INTRODUCTION

This project involves Developing a dashboard for Library Management in an application being developed for School ABC on the basis of Software Project Planning Techniques. This is accomplished in the context of a class framework which contains project preparation, project planning, project execution and monitoring, and project adaptation. In the project preparation phase, the Library Management Process included School ABC, Trusties, Project-team, Students, Suppliers as the major stakeholders, where School ABC, was internal stakeholder, Trustees were external stakeholders in an organization and Project-team, were external stakeholders. The objective of the project was to reduce the manpower and time spent on the library management process to make the system more manageable for a skeleton crew. The major funding was provided by Investors and Trustees and project was organized via dividing the dashboard into small parts such as Profile, Quick Links (consists of Accounts department, Uniform department etc.), Circulars, Cumulative Monthly Attendance, Images of student activities, Discussion Forums, Meeting Links. In planning, the critical milestones were Project Approval, Requirement Review, Design Approval and Final Approval which were successfully achieved. The coordination responsibilities were carried out by Project Manager, Functional Manager, Operational Manager, Internal Stakeholders which were further responsible for the schedule coordination respectively. Microsoft Project & MS Excel was used for the planning of project and evaluating risk respectively which involved Waterfall model as method which was the most efficient and accurate way suited for the project. In the third phase of execution and monitoring, for tracking the progress a number of metrices such as Formal code metrics, Developer productivity metrics, Agile process metrics, Operational metrics, Test metrics were used. Resource consumption was calculated with the help of Cost Variance, Resource capacity utilization, Group and project portfolio utilization, planned resources vs. resources in use, planned time vs Used time. Using project crashing technique, the Time of the project was significantly reduced hence allowing the project to finish on time. Initially the skill set of the staff was not taken into consideration hence to resolve that matter an early intervention was done by the management team so that the difficulties could be resolved in a timely manner without descoping the project, and hence there was no requirement for adding supplementary resources. As a result, the project management actions helped the project to be delivered on time without compromising with any of time, budget and resources constraints.

LITERATURE REVIEW

Investigating the Dynamics of Engineering Design Rework for a Complex Aircraft Development Project: Lessons Learned from a Soft Systems Thinking Lens

Organizations continue to have difficulty managing their intricate product development initiatives effectively (PDPs). The dynamics of engineering design rework (EDR), which must modify the product being created and disrupts the development process, are factors in subpar project performance. The aim of this study is to assess the EDR dynamics that have a detrimental effect on complex PDP performance and to recommend solutions. The research methodology is supported by the soft systems thinking paradigm. An aircraft development project's EDR dynamics were modeled using a causal loop model.

21st-Century General-Purpose Technologies and the Future of Project Management

General-purpose technologies (GPTs), usually referred to as platform technologies, are key economic activity catalysts. They are all-purpose in the sense that they support waves of cutting-edge goods and services and have several uses in a variety of industries. An industry can change dramatically from how it was before if new applications for the new GPT are identified. For instance, waves of creative destruction brought about by the printing press, steam engine, telephone, and computer have had a lasting impact on businesses and society (Schumpeter, 1976). The explanation of the extensive economic consequences brought on by GPTs serves as the foundation for the notion of Kondratiev cycles, which describe multi decade episodes of economic expansion (Rosenberg & Frischtak, 1984).

Navigating Tensions to Create Value: An Institutional Logics Perspective on the Change Program and its Organizational Context

Research has stressed the need of comprehending the value creation (VC) of change projects within their organizational context. This article uses institutional logics to examine how program management actors move around the interface between change programs and organizational context in order to generate value. In conjunction with the implementation of two public-sector municipal merger projects, a longitudinal comparison analysis was carried out. Findings demonstrate that viewpoints on VC may conflict by identifying change programs and settings as having different logics, which adds to the theory on change program VC. To ease the tensions and support program VC, we propose problematizing, creating, and team-building navigation methods.

Application of Career Ecosystems Theory and the New Psychological Contract to the Field of Project Management: Toward a Conceptual Model

In order to maintain a pool of project management employees with the knowledge, abilities, and skills necessary to support successful project delivery into the future, the goal of this article is to investigate how various players can function within a project management ecosystem. The interaction between project management employees and employers is mediated by professional associations, according to a new conceptual model that is provided together with a list of six propositions. The study contributes to knowledge of the new psychological contract and career ecosystems theory by applying it to a brand-new area of project management. Future research prospects and practical ramifications are also covered.

DETAILED IMPLEMENTATION

Problems with the traditional Library Management Process

1. It required a lot of manual paperwork, which was a time-consuming and resource-intensive process.
2. Lot of manpower was needed to manage trivial tasks.
3. It was difficult for students to get the books issued.
4. Data management was challenging, and the school management struggled to keep track of the details often including accounts, images, profiles, circulars, etc.
5. There was no quick access to information that was important such as links and discussion forums.

Major Stakeholders

1. Internal Stakeholders: School ABC, Project Team.
2. External within an organization Stakeholders: Trusties
3. External Stakeholders: Suppliers, Students.

4

Initial Objectives

1. To reduce the manpower & time spent.
2. Availability of proper information of books which gets recorded automatically.
3. Librarians can update the records like availability of books and its arrival status.
4. Ease of access for students & administration.
5. To make the overall framework manageable for a skeleton crew.

Milestones

1. Project Approval: Approval of the project blueprint. Project Phase milestones.
2. Requirements Review: Once all the requirements are gathered, they are reviewed and approved.
3. Design Approval: A plan of action is designed and approved that meets the requirements and fulfils the terms of the scope of work.
4. Final Approval: The final review session after testing and inspection where all the stakeholders agree that the work is finished and fulfills all the project requirements.

Coordination and Supervision

1. **Project Manager:** Develops a project plan, manage deliverables according to the plan, recruit project staff, lead and manage the project team, Determine the methodology used on the project, establish a project schedule and determine each phase, assign tasks to project team members and provides regular updates to upper management
2. **Functional Manager:** Assign project, discuss with the staff if they are satisfied with the work given and check the progress, gather information from other project managers to write the evaluation and works with the employee to set and coach on career goals
3. **Operational Manager:** Oversee production of goods or provision of services, makes sure the organization satisfies the requirements and expectations of the customers and clients
4. **Internal Stakeholders:** Take interests in the outcome of the project

Methods and Tools Used

MS Project

1. Always maintain control, be aware of, and accurately communicate project status on demand. Highlights the crucial path and retains conflict awareness through traffic signal execution and early warning markers.
2. Run what-if instances quickly to evaluate the consequences of various alternatives.
3. The ease of integration with certain other techniques facilitates communication with a wide range of stakeholders.
4. More time for business, the environment, and value additions.
5. Consistent yet another reporting at the appropriate level of detail at all tiers, from senior management to external stakeholders to team members.
6. Using a shared resource pool and effective use of different calendars, optimize resource utilization across projects in the organization.

Waterfall Model

1. **Ease of use:** This model is easy to understand and use. The division between the stages is easy to grasp regardless of prior experience.
2. **Structure:** The clear demarcation between stages helps organize and divide work.
3. **Documentation:** The emphasis on gathering and understanding requirements makes this model heavily reliant on documentation and makes it easier for new resources to move in and work on the project when needed.
4. **Risk:** There is very small scope of risk in this situation with this model because for this management system, all requirements are known beforehand and are very clearly specified. Moreover, this project is not a very long and complex project and that makes waterfall model an ideal choice.

Metrics for Project Execution and Monitoring

For Tracking Progress of the Project

1. Formal code metrics i.e., code complexity, lines of code, instruction path length.

2.   Developer productivity metrics include active days, assignment scope and efficiency. With the help of these metrics, it's easier to understand how much time and work developers are investing in a software project.
3.   Agile process metrics include lead time, cycle time and velocity that measure the progress of a dev team in producing working, shipping-quality software features.
4.   Operational metrics includes mean time between failures (MTBF) and mean time to recover (MTTR) which checks how software is running in production and how effective operations staff are at maintaining it.
5.   Test metrics comprises of code coverage, percent of automated tests, and defects in production helps us measure how a system is measured i.e., to test the quality of the software.
6.   Customer satisfaction contains Net Promoter Score (NPS), Customer Effort Score (CES) and Customer Satisfaction Score (CSAT), to measure how customers experience the software and their interaction with the software vendor.

For Resource Consumption

1.   **Cost variance:** measures the budgeted amount against the actual costs that were spent on a project or task
2.   **Resource capacity utilization:** this is the percentage of resource's work hours that is occupied by projects or tasks.
3.   **Group and project portfolio utilization:** a Group and project portfolio is how well groups of projects or your project portfolio is utilized.
4.   **Planned resources vs. resources in use:** Planned resources are the estimated number of resources used in a given task, project, or strategy. Resources in use are the actual resources being used.
5.   **Planned time vs used time:** Planned time is the estimated timeframe of the task, project, or strategy. Used time is the actual timeframe in which the task was accomplished.

Corrective Measures

1.   **Evaluate team's skill set:** An early to mid-project snapshot of the project technical needs may give a revised look at what is needed to get the job done and maybe that's not what the current team can offer.
2.   **Bring financials to the forefront:** If the project budget is becoming an issue, bring the team into management, making them aware of budget issues.

3. **Make collaboration happen:** To share the project schedule and make the team and customer own their tasks.
4. **Re-examine the risks:** Go back to the risks list and re-evaluate the current plans

Table 1. Analyzing different phases of the project

	Questions	Answers
Project Preparation	Why was the project initiated?	Problems with the traditional Library Management Process.
	Who were the major stakeholders?	A.V.B Public School, Trusties, Project-team, Students, Suppliers.
	What were the initial objectives?	Reduce the amount of workforce and hours spent, and make the system manageable with a skeleton crew.
	Where did the funding come from?	Investors and Trustees
	How was the project organized?	The five phases: initiation, planning, execution, monitoring, project close
Project Planning	What were the major critical milestones?	Project Approval Requirement Review Design Approval Final Approval
	How was the project schedule coordinated among the major contributors, suppliers, etc?	Duties of project manager, functional manager, operational manager, internal Trustees (internal stakeholder)
	Who had coordination responsibilities?	Project Manager Functional Manager Operational Manager Internal Stakeholders
	What planning techniques and tools were used?	MS Project MS Excel Waterfall Model
Project Execution and Monitoring	What metrics were used to track progress and resource consumption?	Track Progress -Formal code metrics -Developer productivity metrics -Agile process metrics -Operational metrics -Test metrics -Customer Satisfaction Resource consumption -Cost variance -Group and project portfolio utilization -Planned resources vs. resources in use -Planned time vs used time
	Was the project on track, technically, schedule wise, budget wise?	Yes, it was on track. Project Crashing could've been for Quality and cost.
Project Adaptation	What corrective measures were taken by management throughout the project?	-Evaluate team's skill set -Bring financials to the forefront -make collaboration happen -Re-examine the risks
	Was the project descoped?	No, the project was not descoped Project Crashing could've been for following parameters: -Scope and time
	Were resources added?	No resources added
	Did these management actions actually help or hurt the project?	-project delivered on time -Budget constraint met -Stressful atmosphere

Summary Assessment of the Project

Strategic Assessment

Used to assess whether a project fits in the long-term goal of the organization. The main aim of Library Management Dashboard is to increase efficiency, reduce labor, and make the service more accessible to their clients i.e., students. Thus, the solution fits in the long-term goal of the organization.

Strategic plan that clearly defines the objectives of the organization:

- Reduce the manual paperwork.
- Users should be able to update the information of books and manage availability and arriver record of the books/data.
- Save human efforts and time.
- Customer should be able to easily search and find the books.
- Immediate access to important information using "Quick Links" feature.
- Ease-of-Use: Single person should be able to manage the whole system.
- Evaluate individual projects against the strategic plan or the overall business objectives:
  - ○ **Program management:** suitable for projects developed for use in the organization.
  - ○ **Portfolio management:** suitable for project developed for other companies by software houses.

Program Management

Individual projects as components of a programmed within the organization. Programme as "A group of projects that are managed in a coordinated way to gain benefits that would not be possible were the projects to be managed independently.

Program Management Issues

Compared to other solutions/system that could have been used to solve the same problem, Library Management Dashboard is the best choice because of the following reasons.

- Reduce the manual paperwork.
- User should be able to update the information of books and manage availability and arriver record of the books/data.
- Save human efforts and time.
- Customer should be able to easily search and find the books.
- Immediate access to important information using "Quick Links" feature.

- Ease-of-Use: Single person should be able to manage the whole system.

Organization structure: How does the product affect the existing organizational structure? The existing workflow? The overall business model?

The organizational structure is definitely affected as the software is easy to use which in turn reduces the number of staff required to operate this software thus, reducing the man-power to do the same task. Also, making the workflow much more efficient.

Q1: What Information does the Product Provide?

1. User Profile Info
2. Quick Links (consists of Books on Shelves, Accounts, Class Classification, Books Classification etc)
3. Circulars
4. Images of student activities
5. Discussion Forums
6. Meeting Links

Q2. To Whom is the Information Provided?

- ABC's Students and Staff.

Q3. What are the Staff Implications?

- Before: The staff size was small and because there was a lot of manual work, school had appointed individual staff for trivial task which can be automated. The manual registration of book and other data/info often included human error. Often there were conflicts.
- After: Now there's synergy among the staff. The info. on the LMS is upto date. The Quick Links saves time.

Q4. What are the Impacts on the Overall Policy on Staff Development?

With LMS, now being replaced with traditional system, unnecessary, human resources can be avoided. Also, there's improvement in staff efficiency and stress level.

Q5. How does the Product Affect the Image of the Organization?

The staff and data are much more organized and up-to-date with the latest information. Thus, their clients i.e., students are satisfied. Also, there's a synergy among staff.

- **Technical Assessment:** Functionality against hardware and software

Economic Assessment

Why?

Consider whether the project is the best among other options. Following options were considered by the A.V.B Public School to solve the current problem with the library management system.

- **Option 1**: Hire more professional people that can handle the task better.
  - **Reason 1:** This could have solved the problem but could've increased school's budget.
- **Option 2**: Hire more staff so that task can be distributed across many hence getting the work done quicker.
  - **Reason 2:** This could have solved the problem but too many people working at the same place on same thing could've have resulted in conflicts thus impacting the image of the organization/school.
- **Option 3**: Develop a dedicated application that solves the problem.
  - **Reason 3**: The reason A.V.B Public School settle on this solution is because given the budget this project is the best solution in long run.

How?

- **Cost-benefit Analysis**
  - A standard way to assess the economic benefits. There are two steps to assess the benefits.
  - Identify and estimate all the costs and benefits of carrying out the project
  - Express the costs and benefits in a common unit for easy comparison (e.g., $)
  - Costs:
    § Development costs: $10,000
    § Setup costs: $2,300
    § Operational costs: $6,600

- Benefits:
  - § Direct benefits: $39,080
  - § Assessable indirect: $5,000
  - § Intangible benefits: $8,577
- **Cash Flow Forecasting**
  - Estimation of the cash flow over time
  - Reasons why it is required is due to the following:
    - § An excess of estimated benefits over the estimated costs is not sufficient
    - § Need detailed estimation of benefits and costs versus time
    - § Need to forecast the expenditure and the income
    - § Accurate forecast is not easy
    - § Need to revise the forecast from time to time
- **Cost-benefit Evaluation Techniques**
  - Net profit = 52,657 - 18,900 (Total income – Total costs) = $33,757
  - Payback period = Time taken to break even
  - Return on Investment (ROI) = average annual profit
  - _____ X 100% total investment
  - <u>Net present value (NPV):</u>
    - § It is the sum of the present values of all future amounts. Present value is the value which a future amount is worth at present. It takes into account the profitability of a project and the timing of the cash flows.
    - § Let n be the number of year and r be the discount rate, the present value (PV) is given
    - § by

value in year n

$$PV = \frac{\text{_____}}{}$$

$(1+r)\,^n$

  - **Issues in NPV:**
    - § Choosing an appropriate discount rate is difficult
    - § Ensuring that the rankings of projects are not sensitive to small changes in
    - § discount rate
  - **Guidelines Used:**
    - § We used the standard rate prescribed by the organization
    - § We used interest rate + premium rate
    - § We used a target rate of return
    - § We ranked the projects using various discount rates

     ○   **Disadvantages Noted:**
- § May not be directly comparable with earnings from other investments or the costs of borrowing capital
- § <u>Internal Rate of Return (IRR):</u>

❖ The percentage discount rate that would produce a NPV of zero. It is a relative measure.

- **Advantages:**
  - § It is convenient as it is directly comparable with the rate of return on other projects and with interest rates.
  - § It is useful as a project could get dismissed due to its small IRR value and it indicates further precise evaluation of a project.
  - § Supported by MS Excel and Lotus 1-2-3.
- **Estimation:**
  - § Why? – to define the project budget and to 'refine' the product to realize the budget
  - § Who? – the manager
  - § What? – size and cost
  - § When? – always
  - § How? – techniques and models
- **Issues related to Estimation:**
  - § It was difficult for us to make accurate estimation.
  - § We had previous data and analyzed the actual values against the estimates so that we know how accurate we were.
  - § Also, we had previous data of the whole organization so that we know how accurate the estimation method, if any, used within the organization were.
- **Positive Attitude Towards Estimation:**
  - § We used our estimation as a guide to manage our project.
  - § From time to time, we needed to revise our estimation based on the current status of the project.
- **Estimation Approaches:**
  - § Expert judgement: Asked the knowledgeable experts
  - § Estimation by analogy: Used the data of a similar and completed project.
  - § Pricing to win: Used the price that was low enough to win the contract.
  - § Top-down: An overall estimate was determined and then broken down into each component task.
  - § Bottom up: The estimates of each component task are aggregated to form the overall estimate.

§ Algorithmic Model: Estimation was based on the characteristics of the product and the development environment.
- **Size Estimation:**
  § Problems related to size estimation
  § Size Estimation Model
  § Function Point Analysis (FPA)
- **Problems related to size estimation:**
  § Nature of software
  § Novel application of software
  § Fast changing technology
  § Lack of homogeneity of project experience

COST-BENEFIT ANALYSIS

Cost/benefit analysis is comparing the expected costs and expected benefits

- Issues:

  ◦ Estimating costs
  ◦ Estimating benefits

  Use of financial models to evaluate.

Cost-Benefit Analysis: (Two Steps)

1. Identified and estimated all of the costs and benefits of carrying out the project and operating the delivered application.
2. Expressing the costs and benefits in common units

Cost-Benefit Analysis - Cost Estimation

1. Estimate costs to compare with benefits/other investment options
2. Overall estimation is based on:
   a. Estimation of required activities (structure)
   b. Estimation for each activity
   c. Estimation of installation/setup cost
   d. Estimation of operational cost
   e. Difficult, as a lot of these are `estimates'; estimation errors cascade

Cost-Benefit Analysis - Cost Category

1. Development costs
   a. Salaries (base, incentives, and bonuses)
   b. Equipment for development
      i. Hardware
      ii. Software
2. Setup costs
   a. Hardware and software infrastructure
   b. Recruitment/staff training
   c. Installation and conversion costs.
3. Operational costs
   a. Costs of operating the system once it has been installed
      i. Support costs
      ii. Hosting costs
      iii. Licensing costs
      iv. Maintenance costs
      v. Backup costs

BENEFIT ESTIMATION

Estimate benefits of new system based on the:

- Estimation of cost savings and money generation when deployed
- Value of information obtained for objective driven project
- Value of intangibles

Benefit Types

- Direct benefits

  ○ Directly accountable to new system
    § Cost savings (e.g., less staff, less paper, quicker turnaround)
    § Money generation (e.g., new revenue stream, new markets)

❖ Measurable after system is operational
   ❖ Have to be estimated for cost/benefit analysis

- Indirect benefits
- Intangible benefits
  - Positive side effects of new system
  - External system (e.g., increase branding, entry to new markets)
  - Internal system (increased interest in job for users, enabler for other systems)
  - Often very specific to a project; not measurable even after a system is operational
  - Part of strategic decision rather than cost/benefit analysis

Cash Flow Forecasting

Indicates when expenditure and income will take place.

Cash Flow Analysis

Typically, there are outgoing payments initially and then incoming payments. There might be additional costs at the end of the project life. Cash flow considerations.

- **Is initial funding for the project available?**
  - Answer: Yes, the initial funding was available.
- **Is timing of incoming/outgoing cash flow in line with financial plans?**
  - Answer: Yes.
- **If cash flow is critical, forecasting should be done quarterly or monthly?**
  - Answer: Neither, we used weekly cash flow forecast instead.
  - Reasons:
    § Forces discipline through "cash is king" mentality

❖ Operators cannot hide behind accounting tricks to hide underperformance.

❖ Focusing on the near- and medium-term time frames can uncover potential issues quickly and can help businesses subject to seasonality get through off-seasons.

§ Enhances understanding of customers and suppliers

❖ The customer and supplier stratification process provides insights into key customers and suppliers, depending on the situation:

❖ If a customer is paying slowly: It can be used as an excuse to call a customer. Instead of simply demanding payment, it can be another revenue generating opportunity—assuming your company still wants business from this customer

❖ If certain suppliers offer early pay discounts: Having a handle on cash flow can enable a company to take advantage of these discounts and increase profitability

❖ If certain vendors are relaxed on the enforcement of their terms: A company can stretch some of their flexible suppliers to decrease net working capital and increase cash

❖ Helps businesses understand the cost of growth. Growing companies are often cash-constrained because capital expenditures and inventory investments must be made ahead of the revenue associated with the growth. Understanding near-term liquidity needs enables a company to plan for this growth and raise the appropriate financing. It thus also helps a company avoid failure to deliver or worse, major financial distress.

§ Reduces cost of capital

❖ By understanding liquidity, a company can minimize borrowing on credit to fund interim payments like payroll and rent. In other cases, a company can reduce the amount of cash kept on hand and instead deploy the capital through re-investment into the business, debt reduction or dividends.

§ Increases communication with other departments

❖ In order to properly complete the cash flow forecast, the finance team must communicate with colleagues in sales, purchasing, accounts payable, accounts receivable, human resources, etc. It forces the finance forecasting experts to gain a fuller understanding of the business and how it operates.

§ Risky/expensive projects might be funded using venture capital.

Cost-Benefit Evaluation Techniques

- Costs and benefits have to be expressed using the same scale to be comparable. It is usually expressed in payments at certain times (cash flow table).
- Payments at different points in time are not comparable based only on the amount, time of payment should be considered.
- Techniques:
  - Net profit: Difference between total cost and total income
    § **Pros:** Easy to calculate
    § **Cons:** Does not show profit relative to size investment (e.g., consider Project 2), Does not consider timing of payments (e.g., compare

Projects 1 and 3), Not very useful other than for "back of envelope" evaluations
- ○ Payback period: Time taken to break even
  - § **Pros**: Easy to calculate, gives some idea of cash flow impact
  - § **Cons**: Ignores overall profitability, not very useful by itself, but a good measure for cash flow impact
- ○ Return on investment: It is also known as the accounting rate of return (ARR). It provides a way of comparing the net profitability to the investment required.

The common formula– ROI = (average annual profit/total investment) X 100

- § **Pros**: Easy to calculate
- § **Cons:** Does not consider the timing of payments, misleading: does not consider bank interest rates, not very useful other than for "back of envelope" evaluations
  - ○ Net present value: It is a project evaluation technique that takes into account the profitability of a project and the timing of the cash flows that are produced. Sum of all incoming and outgoing payments, discounted using an interest rate, to a fixed point in time (the present).

Cost-Benefit Evaluation Techniques-Net Present Value

Present value = (value in year t)/(1+r) ^t
r is the discount rate
t is the number of years into the future that the cash flow occurs
(1+r) ^t is known as discount factor
- ○ In the case of 10% rate and one year
  - ▪ Discount factor = 1/ (1+0.10) = 0.9091
  - ▪ In the case of 10% rate and two years
  - ▪ Discount factor = 1/ (1.10 x 1.10) = 0.8294
- § **Pros**: Takes into account profitability, considers timing of payments, considers economic situation through discount rate
- § **Cons**: Discount rate can be difficult to choose, standard measure to compare different options
  - ○ Internal rate of return: Internal rate of return (IRR) is the discount rate that would produce an NPV of 0 for the project. It can be used to compare different investment opportunities. It is a standard way to compare projects
    - ▪ **Pros**: Calculates figure which is easily comparable to interest rates

- **Cons**: Difficult to calculate (iterative)

RISK

Technical Risks

There was no conceptual threat, but these types of risk jeopardize the quality and timeliness of the software. If they become a reality, they may make implementation difficult or impossible.

Business Risks

There was no business risk, but it could have compromised the survival of the software being developed. If they become real, they jeopardize the project or the product.
   Sub-categories of Business risks:

1.   Market risk – we could've built an amazing product or framework that hardly anyone wants
2.   Strategic risk – we could've built a business model that no longer belongs into the firm's business
3.   Sales risk – we could've built a service that the sales representatives doesn't fully comprehend how to sell
4.   Management risk – we could've lost the support of key stakeholders due to variation or a change in people
5.   Budget risk – we could've working capital or personnel obligation

Known Risks

Those risks that can be identified through a thorough examination of the project management plan, the organizational and functional environment in which the project is being designed, and other reliable data sources. (e.g., unrealistic delivery date). Following a thorough review of the project plan, we found out that there were no known risk and for example, the delivery date was realistic, and the budget was also enough.

Predictable Risks

These were the risk that are extrapolated from past project experience (e.g., past turnover)

Unpredictable Risks

These were the risk that can and do occur, but are extremely difficult to identify in advance

Reactive versus Proactive Risk Strategies

Reactive Risk strategies

- "Don't worry, I'll think of something"
- Our majority of software teams and managers didn't rely on this approach
- In this approach nothing is done about risks until something goes wrong
- The team then flies into action in an attempt to correct the problem rapidly (firefighting)
- Crisis management is the choice of management techniques

Proactive Risk Strategies (the One we Followed)

- Steps for risk management were followed
- Primary objective was to avoid risk and to have a contingency plan in place to handle unavoidable risks in a controlled and effective manner
- Following were the steps followed for Risk Management:
  - Identify possible risks; recognize what can go wrong
  - Analyze each risk to estimate the probability that it will occur and the impact (i.e., damage) that it will do if it does occur.
  - Rank the risks by probability
    § Impact may be negligible, marginal, critical, and catastrophic and impact
  - Develop a contingency plan to manage those risks having high probability and high impact

Risk Identification

Generic Risks

- Risks that are a potential threat to every software
- Budget Risk
- Resistance to Change

- Resource Risk
- Sponsor Support
- Schedule Risk
- Stakeholder might not fulfill any commitments to the project.
- Legal Risk

Product-specific Risks

Risks that can only be recognized by those who have a thorough understanding of the concept, people, and surroundings that will be used to design the product. This necessitates a review of the project plan and the scope statement.

- "What special characteristics of this product may threaten our project plan?"

  - Integration Risk
  - Scope Risk
  - Project Dependencies
  - Architecture Risk
  - Operations Risk
  - Project Estimates
  - Design Risk

Known and Predictable Risk Categories

Product Size

Risks associated with overall size of the software to be built A.V.B Public School LMS was indeed a complex and big software.

Business Impact

Risks associated with constraints imposed by management or the marketplace. Since the budget was enough it didn't affect the development of the software in any way.

Customer Characteristics

Risks associated with sophistication of the customer and the developer's ability to communicate with the customer in a timely manner. This is one of the most common risks but the requirement listed by A.V.B Public School was specific and the SDLC model chosen didn't require too much customer intervention.

Process Definition

Risks associated with the degree to which the software process has been defined and is followed:

- **Development environment** – risks associated with availability and quality of the tools to be used to build the project
- **Technology to be built** – risks associated with complexity of the system to be built and the "newness" of the technology in the system. The software to be built was not new but the software was complex on its own.
- **Staff size and experience** – risks associated with overall technical and project experience of the software engineers who will do the work. The developers were highly qualified, and the team was small.

Questionnaire that we considered related to Project Risk

- Have top technology and customer executives formally agreed to back the project? Yes
- Are end-users incredibly passionate about the project and the framework that will be built? Yes
- Are the software engineering team and its customers fully aware of the needs? Yes
- Have customers been involved fully in the definition of requirements? No
- Are the expectations of end users reasonable? Yes
- Is the project's scope consistent? Yes
- Is the software engineering team's skill set diverse enough? Yes
- Are the project's specifications consistent? Yes
- Is the project team familiar with the technology that will be used? Yes
- Is the project team's size sufficient to complete the work? Yes
- Is everyone in the customer/user community on board with the project's importance and the system/requirements? Yes

Risk Components and Drivers

- The project manager identified the risk drivers that could affect the following risk components
  - ¡ **Performance risk** - the degree of uncertainty that the product will meet its requirements and be fit for its intended use

¡ **Cost risk -** the degree of uncertainty that the project budget will be maintained

¡ **Support risk** - the degree of uncertainty that the resultant software will be easy to correct, adapt, and enhance

¡ **Schedule risk** - the degree of uncertainty that the project schedule will be maintained and that the product will be delivered on time

- The impact of each risk driver on the risk component is divided into one of four impacts levels
  ¡ Negligible, marginal, critical, and catastrophic
- Risk drivers can be assessed as impossible, improbable, probable, and frequent

Risk Projection (Estimation)

- Risk projection (or estimation) attempts to rate each risk in two ways:
  ◦ The probability that the risk is real
  ◦ The consequence of the problems associated with the risk, should it occur
- The project planner, managers, and technical staff perform four risk projection steps
- The intent of these steps is to consider risks in a manner that leads to prioritization
- Be prioritizing risks, the software team can allocate limited resources where they will have the most impact

Risk Projection/Estimation Steps

- Establish a scale that reflects the perceived likelihood of a risk (e.g., 1-low, 10-high)
  ◦ Budget Risk (2)
  ◦ Resource Risk (4)
  ◦ Schedule Risk (2)
  ◦ Stakeholder might not fulfill any commitments to the project. (5)
  ◦ Legal Risk (1)
  ◦ Integration Risk (6)
  ◦ Scope Risk (3)
  ◦ Project Dependences (4)
  ◦ Architecture Risk (2)
  ◦ Operations Risk (2)

- ◦ Project Estimates (4)
- ◦ Design Risk (2)
- Estimate the impact of the risk on the project and product
  - ◦ Budget Risk: If we fall short on budget quality and resources can be compromised.
  - ◦ Resource Risk: If we fall short on resources a lot of tasks will be distributed among small team thus increasing the time. Also, increasing stress on an individual developer.
- Schedule Risk (2):
  - ◦ late delivery
- Stakeholder might not fulfill any commitments to the project. (5):
  - ◦ Internal stakeholder might change the req. at very last moment.
  - ◦ Ext. w/ Org. might reduce/withdraw budget thus affecting the whole project.
  - ◦ External Stk. might fall short on resources.
- Integration Risk (6):
- Student, staff, admin Dashboard should work with LMS. If it doesn't the whole ecosystem might fail/affect.
- Scope Risk (3)
- The protect may be descoped.
- Project Dependences (4)
- Student, staff, admin Dashboard should work fine in order for our application to function well.
- Architecture Risk (2)
- The arch. should be designed in such a way that its extendable and scalable.
- Project Estimates (4)
- We might under/over-estimate the project.
- Design Risk (2)
- App might not be user-friendly.
- Note the overall accuracy of the risk projection so that there will be no misunderstandings
- The assumptions were quite accurate.

Table 2. Developing a risk table

SNO	RISK DRIVER	PROBABILITY (%)	IMPACT (out of 5)
1.	Budget Risk	20	2
2.	Resource Risk	40	3
3.	Schedule Risk	20	1
4.	Stakeholder Risk	50	3
5.	Integration Risk	60	4
6.	Scope Risk	30	4
7.	Project Dependences	40	3
8.	Architecture Risk	20	3
9.	Operations Risk	20	2
10.	Project Estimates	40	3
11.	Design Risk	60	5

Assessing Risk Impact

1. Three factors affect the consequences that are likely if a risk does occur
   a. Its nature – This indicates the problems that are likely if the risk occurs
   b. Its scope – This combines the severity of the risk (how serious was it) with its overall distribution (how much was affected)
   c. Its timing – This considers when and for how long the impact will be felt
2. The overall risk exposure formula is RE = P x C
   a. P = the probability of occurrence for a risk
   b. C = the cost to the project should the risk actually occur
3. Example
   a. P = 80% probability that 18 of 60 software components will have to be developed
   b. C = Total cost of developing 18 components is $25,000
   c. RE = .80 x $25,000 = $20,000

Risk Mitigation, Monitoring, and Management

- An effective strategy for dealing with risk must consider three issues
- (Note: these are not mutually exclusive)
  ¡ Risk mitigation (i.e., avoidance)
  ¡ Risk monitoring

    ¡ Risk management and contingency planning
- Risk mitigation (avoidance) is the primary strategy and is achieved through a plan

    ¡ Example: Risk of high staff turnover
- Seven Principles of Risk Management Maintain a global perspective

    ¡ Viewed software risks within the context of a system and the business problem that was intended to solve

    ¡ Take a forward-looking view

    ¡ Thought about risks that may arise in the future and established contingency plans

    ¡ Encourage open communication

    ¡ Encouraged all our stakeholders and users to point out risks at any time

    ¡ Integrate risk management

    ¡ Integrated the consideration of risk into the software process

    ¡ Emphasize a continuous process of risk management

    ¡ Modified identified risks as more becomes known and add new risks as better insight were achieved.

    ¡ Develop a shared product vision

    ¡ A shared vision by all stakeholders facilitated better risk identification and assessment.

    ¡ Encourage teamwork when managing risk

    ¡ Pooled the skills and experience of all stakeholders when conducting risk management activities.

Q1. Was it an Unqualified Success?

Since we clearly stated the requirement, budget was enough, developers were experienced enough and there was little to no risk. Hence, we can say that the project was unqualified success.

Q2. Was it a Failure?

No, as we were able to deliver the project on time and the development was finished within the budget constraints.

Q3. What are the Lessons Learned for Future Projects?

This project was an ideal one because we had enough time and the budget was given. The developers were experienced and the requirements were clearly stated. And also, there was no customer intervention needed.

Following were the lessons learned:

- Avoidance of mistakes
- Reduced risks
- Seizing of opportunities
- Increased project quality

Q4. Were there Follow-up Projects?

No, there were no follow up projects related to LMS.

Q5. Is the project still on-going?

Although the project is completed the maintenance of the project is still going on.

Q6. What makes this project unique?

Enough time and budget, experienced developers and clear statement of requirements are few things that make this project unique. No customer intervention was needed and no risk was encountered. Also, we don't get to see all these things at once in a project thus making it an ideal one.

CONCLUSION

The objective of the Library Management System was fulfilled which was to provide the easiness to students or visitors that they can easily take/find the book according to their choice and read it in the better way. It's the responsibility of the Library Management System that they provide such a peaceful environment that everyone learns without disturbance. The first charter for the project and the objectives is to complete the first version of the software for the instrument in 6 months, and also design the project within given constraints.

Library management system decreases the deferral time for response time to the customers so the association can adjust to advertise and ask genuinely without any loss of customers. Their principal objective is to effectively execute the framework system to manage the number of books, their types as well as journal articles. The Library management system can now do the following:

1. To develop as well as to maintain Books database and their types whether Management, Science, Research etc.

2. The system will help to implement a computerized framework that will help to track the particular record and it will save time.
3. To carry out the charging as well as releasing functions of the course area more effectively.
4. To provide various search options to know the availability of books in the library.
5. To generate the list of books due by a particular part and furthermore the overdue charges.

REFERENCES

Rosenberg, N., & Frischtak, C. R. (1984). Technological innovation and long waves. *Cambridge Journal of Economics*, *8*(1), 7–24.

Schumpeter, J. A. (1976). II. Capitalism. *Socialism and Democracy*, 1942.

ADDITIONAL READING

de Melo, É. S., Vieira, D., & Bredillet, C. (2022). Investigating the Dynamics of Engineering Design Rework for a Complex Aircraft Development Project: Lessons Learned From a Soft Systems Thinking Lens. *Project Management Journal*, *53*(6), 625–640. doi:10.1177/87569728221118342

Farid, P., & Waldorff, S. B. (2022). Navigating Tensions to Create Value: An Institutional Logics Perspective on the Change Program and its Organizational Context. *Project Management Journal*, *53*(6), 547–566. doi:10.1177/87569728221111321

Steen, J., Klein, G., & Potts, J. (2022). 21st-Century General-Purpose Technologies and the Future of Project Management. *Project Management Journal*, *53*(5), 435–437. doi:10.1177/87569728221125095

APPENDIX

Project Charter

Table 3.

PROJECT IDENTIFICATION		
Project Name	Library Management System	
Description	Design, develop and implement Library Management System	
Sponsor	A.V.B Public School	
Project Manager	Librarian	
Project Start and End date	02/06/2021	03/12/2021

Table 4.

PROJECT DESCRIPTION
The objective of the Library Management System is to provide the ease to students or visitors that they can easily take/find the book according to their choice and read it in a better way. It's the responsibility of the Library Management System that they provide such a peaceful environment that everyone learns without disturbance. The first charter for the project and the objectives is to complete the first version of the software for the instrument in 6 months, and also design the project within given constraints.

Table 5.

PROJECT OBJECTIVES (PURPOSE)
This development of the library management system will decrease the deferral time for response time to the customers so the association can adjust to advertise and ask genuinely without any loss of customers. Their principal objective is to effectively execute the framework system to manage the number of books, their types as well as journal articles. The main objective of developing library management system is as following: 1. To develop as well as to maintain Books database and their types whether Management, Science, Research etc. 2. The system will help to implement a computerized framework that will help to track the particular record and it will save time. 3. To carry out the charging as well as releasing functions of the course area more effectively. 4. To provide various search options to know the availability of books in the library. 5. To generate the list of books due by a particular part and furthermore the overdue charges.

Table 6.

4. PROJECT SCOPE
1. Provide book information. 2. Provide borrower's information. 3. Provide library card information. 4. Provide return and penalty information. 5. Provide attendance information. 1. Provide inventory information.

Table 7.

COMMUNICATION MANAGEMENT PLAN
Communication Management Is Essential "Openness is of the utmost importance" might be a platitude, yet it remains constant. Indeed, even at the most significant level, a slight misstep in correspondence can be the distinction between project achievement and undertaking disappointment. Experienced directors will disclose to you that it is so critical to dodge informative mistakes during project execution. As an undertaking administrator, you should have sharp situational mindfulness and speak with your group and customers obviously and adequately. This can keep any misconception from occurring among you and your group/customer. Correspondence is essential to project achievement. On the off chance that there's an absence of open correspondence in your group, it will be hard for you to recognize the underlying driver of an issue, when things turn out badly. At the point when things begin going downhill, some undertaking supervisors may reprimand others for it. Such a conduct prompts further issues. Try not to look for someone else to take the blame and assume liability for your and your group's exhibition. In a perfect world, you need to put your time in setting up a reasonable correspondence plan with your group ready. Keep in mind, without legitimate correspondence, it's difficult to manage project issues viably.

Table 8.

RISK AND ISSUE MANAGEMENT PLAN		
RISK	**DESCRIPTION**	**STRATEGY**
Too much in scope	Have we included too much in the project scope for the time we have? If so, do we abandon features or do we go over schedule?	Project Charter approval, and Change Management Plan
Unspecified or insufficient time	Can I count on a specific number of hours per week from the Dev team? Can this be formalized (particular days/ times per week). If not, a risk is that other project will take immediate priority.	Apply techniques, and strategies to more flexibly share the workload across all members of the team, allowing developers to take on some system administration roles
Overschedule	What if we can't get it done by December 2021.	Project Charter approval, and Change Management plan
Budget	Insufficient Budget or over budget issue	Maintaining a budget plan in the beginning like balanced budget, surplus budget, deficit budget.

Chapter 2
Visualisation of Blockchain Concepts

Divi Anand
Amity University, India

Isha Kaushik
Amity University, India

Jasmehar Singh Mann
Amity University, India

Ritu Punhani
Amity University, India

Ishika Punhani
University of Petroleum and Energy Studies, India

ABSTRACT

A blockchain is a growing list of documents, called blocks, that can be cryptographically related together. A cryptographic hash of the previous block, a timestamp, and transaction data are all protected in every block. The project's purpose is to supply a web app that demonstrates blockchain fundamentals that include transaction verification and hash generation. The reason of blockchain generation is to provide a chain of sequentially ordered data blocks that are stored in a decentralised manner through all community contributors (nodes). A block of facts is formed while the nodes solution, a complex mathematical assignment (evidence of labour) that is stipulated via a consensus strategy, is cryptographically blanketed. Because everything that happens on blockchain is encrypted, there's no doubt that it provides next-level encryption. Similarly, tampering with the data on the blockchain is impossible. To be safe, you can check file signatures on all nodes across all ledgers in the network to make sure they haven't changed.

DOI: 10.4018/978-1-6684-5255-4.ch002

INTRODUCTION

A blockchain is a shared distributed database or ledger between computer network nodes. A blockchain serves as an electronic database for storing data in digital form. The most well-known use of blockchain technology is for preserving a secure and decentralised record of transactions in cryptocurrency systems like Bitcoin. The innovation of a blockchain is that it fosters confidence without the necessity for a reliable third party by ensuring the fidelity and security of a record of data.

Blockchain is significant because information is the lifeblood of business. It is best if it is received quickly and is accurate. Blockchain is the best technology for delivering that information because it offers real-time, shareable, and entirely transparent data that is kept on an immutable ledger and accessible exclusively to members of a permissioned network. Among other things, a blockchain network can track orders, payments, accounts, and production. Additionally, because everyone has access to the same version of the truth, you can see every aspect of a transaction from beginning to end, increasing your confidence, and opening new prospects.

A normal database and a blockchain differ primarily in the way that the data is organised. In a blockchain, data is gathered in groups called blocks that each include sets of data. A chain of data known as the blockchain is created by blocks, each of which has a specific amount of storage and is linked to the block that was filled earlier. A blockchain, as its name suggests, arranges its data into pieces (blocks) that are strung together, whereas a database typically organises its data into tables.

The purpose of Blockchain Technology is to supply a series of sequentially ordered records blocks that are stored in a decentralized way employing all network participants (nodes). A block of records is formed when the nodes solve a complex mathematical undertaking (evidence of labour) this is stipulated by using a consensus approach this is cryptographically covered.

With the development of blockchain technology, it has fused with various of latest statistics technologies, such as IoT, cloud computing, and large facts, and is now serving as infrastructure help. Meanwhile, it contributes extensively to the development of next-technology facts technology. With the help of the blockchain, regular IoT devices can acquire navy-grade security. Furthermore, several studies have been conducted to peer if it's miles nicely desirable to the IoT. They additionally display how blockchain and IoT are carefully included, which includes facilitating the sharing of offerings and resources, establishing a service market between gadgets, and allowing customers to automate the encryption and authentication procedure inside the time-eating workflow of numerous current units, and they display that the aggregate of blockchain and IoT is constructive. The aggregate can boost the boom of a ramification of groups, power great reforms and improvements throughout numerous industries, and pave the manner for brand new enterprise models and distributed packages.

Despite the reality that most of the people trust one of its blessings is cybersecurity's inherent robustness, it's far nonetheless now not a fully comfy and cyber-assault-loose technical platform. Because privateness and records integrity is so essential, blockchain is increasingly getting used to making sure the safety of cloud settings, which might be especially at risk of antagonistic assaults that would compromise facts. They've already been utilized in the diffusion of programs as decentralized fraud-resistant computing tactics that do not depend on a trusted authority. Several industry sectors have visible ways to include blockchain technology's abilities into their operations in latest years, exhibiting its adaptability.

Several extraordinary ways and inputs had been added to decorate the blessings of the blockchain era and make the process method less complicated. The introduction of a new era of blockchain-based groups has coincided with a growth in token usage, necessitating greater studies into what blockchain tokens represent and how they relate to their underlying business model. Tokens have evolved because of the artifact of choice within the blockchain world to represent belongings, software, or a claim on anything specific to a sure blockchain challenge.

LITERATURE REVIEW

Blockchain is gaining traction in educational studies and industrial packages due to the fact it is idea to have the potential to disrupt business practises in a ramification of industries. The residences of blockchain packages (safety, immutability of record maintaining, performance, and disintermediation) offer answers to a diffusion of troubles that companies and businesses face (Sharma, Jindal, and Borah, 2022). Due to its decentralised, persistency, anonymity, and auditability characteristics, it has attracted quite a few interests from both industry and academia. Blockchains have recently gotten a variety of attention because they allow decentralised alternatives to value manufacturing and control. To growth the security, scalability, and efficiency of their offerings, many banks, Internet companies, car manufacturers, and even governments at some stage in the sector have implemented or are exploring blockchains (Mohanta et al., 2019).

Blockchain, frequently called the Internet of Value, is a tremendously new generation. There is not any consensus on its capacity well worth, as there's with different new era, with some claiming that it will bring extra disruptive adjustments than the Internet and others disputing its significance. Despite dire predictions, there's proof that blockchain is a super, revolutionary era so one can rework the manner transactions are carried out, thanks to its capability to offer confidence amongst unknown events, make certain the immutability of data, and take away the need for intermediaries (Chen et al., 2018). The interest in virtual forex, the large number of posted blockchain studies, and MDPI's journal Future Internet, which solely publishes blockchain articles, along with this unique problem protecting modern-day and destiny blockchain difficulties, all factor to the relevance of blockchain.

Over the previous couple of years, teachers and groups have conducted great studies on using blockchain technologies for a diffusion of programs. Due to its decentralised, everlasting, anonymous, and auditable traits, the blockchain model has gotten lots of interest. Blockchains are currently in the headlines all around the international (Makridakis and Christodoulou, 2019). They've already been utilized in a spread of programs as decentralised methods to fraud-resistant computing that do not rely upon a relied-on authority. In latest years, quite a number of market sectors have observed techniques to include blockchain generation's abilities into their operations, demonstrating its versatility.

While the financial offerings enterprise has received the public of the attention thus far, numerous initiatives in other carrier-associated fields, like as healthcare, show that that is starting to exchange. This research makes a speciality of a diffusion of beginning points for Blockchain technology within the healthcare industry. This article attempts to highlight diverse influences, aims, and potentials related to this disruptive generation via the use of examples from public healthcare administration, consumer-oriented scientific studies, and medication counterfeiting in the pharmaceutical zone (Michael, Cohn, and Butcher, 2018).

The goal of Blockchain technology is to create a series of sequentially ordered information blocks that are saved in a decentralised way throughout all community participants (nodes). When the nodes solve a complex mathematical mission (evidence of labour) this is prescribed by way of a consensus approach this is safeguarded cryptographically, a block of statistics is generated.

Each time a transaction is accomplished within the network, these blocks of statistics are generated and saved in a decentralised ledger maintained by all taking part nodes, in place of in a single database. This is also known as Distributed Ledger Technology (DLT), and it affords the inspiration for blockchain applications. Competing nodes are paid with tokens when they create a block verifying the transaction, which may be used in a diffusion of approaches both outside and inside the community, consisting of a technique of transaction or for alternate with cryptocurrencies or fiat currencies (Casino, Dasaklis, and Patsakis, 2019). The range and possession of those tokens with the aid of a participating node can't be changed due to the fact the rest of the network's nodes have information in their ownership. Transactions are established instantly, securely, and anonymously in this manner; they are efficient and immutable on account that no intermediaries are required, and issues such as double-spending and conflicting transactions are prevented.

Decentralized nature and operation, transparency of information statistics, open source get admission to, autonomy and believe, immutability, and anonymity are all characteristics of blockchain (Antoniadis, Kontsas, and Spinthiropoulos, 2019). As a result of these developments, security and auditability have advanced dramatically, and disintermediation has increased accept as true with in the gadget even as lowering transaction costs for all events worried. Furthermore, the network's decentralised structure and the manner records are stored lessen the probabilities of the network collapsing or dropping statistics because of malicious attacks or technological problems, that is a primary problem with traditional relevant database structures.

Finally, smart contracts, which might be software programmes that describe agreement phrases the usage of logical expressions, are a vital a part of blockchain. If the provisions of the settlement are completed in an automatic manner without the use of intermediaries, those programmes are run inside the blockchain (like legal professionals, administrators and so forth.). In this manner, transaction costs are decreased, moral hazard is reduced, believe between the engaged events is built, and approaches in every factor of the firm or corporation are computerized, ensuing in Distributed Autonomous Organizations (DAO) that lessen transaction charges even more and construct accept as true with (Mohanta et al., 2019).

The deployment of blockchain is positive to provide a spread of advantages, and it'll no longer update existing loyalty programmes, however, instead revitalise them, making them less complicated to use and amplifying their impact on brand loyalty. Consumers will hold to apply their playing cards, or even better, their smart telephones, but instead of gathering factors that can most effective be used at a particular store or institution of outlets, they'll earn tokens that may be used at a variety of outlets or organizations, or maybe exchanged for cryptocurrencies that may be exchanged directly between consumers or converted into real foreign money (Makridakis and Christodoulou, 2019). This technique, in addition to the new token marketplace, will advantage groups financially by means of reducing liabilities because of delayed sales in their financial accounts.

Tokenization may also make it viable to combine all of a agency's loyalty programmes (consisting of present playing cards) right into a unmarried interactive platform that can accommodate all styles of interactions between a logo and its clients, aside from purchases, which include a customer's engagement with the emblem's social media debts, digital advertising and marketing, contents and giveaways, opinions, and so forth. As a end result, blockchain-primarily based loyalty programmes can provide a better and greater comprehensive client enjoy and cost, because all client interactions with the brand company could be recorded, taken into consideration, and rewarded in an obvious and smooth-to-monitor manner for all customers who participate within the blockchain.

Patients, medical doctors, and medication departments inside the healthcare region ought to embody present day technology to present higher carrier to stop clients. One of the most vital issues that desires to be addressed within the healthcare sector is privateness. The traits of blockchain reveal a way to address the situation that has arisen. A digital database may be shared amongst several customers even as shielding privacy the usage of Blockchain.

Smart contracts, the following-technology community infrastructure aimed at resolving economic troubles, have the potential to upend traditional borrowing agreements. In an average lending courting, the lender now not handiest lends cash however also accepts risks, which ends up in excessive loan hobby and items mortgages, with the price of products mortgages frequently exceeding the loan amount. Borrowers can utilise virtual belongings as collateral in clever contracts, not just to keep away from discounts on bodily matters, but additionally to lower mortgage charges (Yaga et al., 2019). There is no want to provide the lender with a credit score or employment records, as well as several papers. The belongings are stored at the blockchain and can be accessed by using all and sundry.

MATERIALS AND METHODS OF LEARNING

JAVASCRIPT: JavaScript is a client-side scripting language that may be used to program and create how web pages react when an event occurs. JavaScript is a scripting language that is both simple to learn and powerful, and it is commonly used to control the behavior of online pages. Moreover, it is very lightweight, cross platform as well as interpreted language. The programs written in it are called "scripts". It can be abbreviated as JS. There are also complex server-side JavaScript versions, such as Node.js, that allow you to add more functionality to a website than simply downloading files (such as real-time collab between many systems). JavaScript can be attached to the objects of its environment inside a host environment (for example, a web browser) to allow programmatic control over them. The project has extensive use JavaScript to write scripts/ programs for various pages.

NODE.JS: Node.js is an open source, server side, free server environment. It may run it on several platforms including Linux, Windows, Mac OS, Unix to name a few. Node.js uses JavaScript on the server. Most importantly Node.js is asynchronous, non-blocking single threaded programming which make it very desirable and efficient. It can engender dynamic page content. It may even be used to open, create, write, read, close and update files on the server therefore managing your database. The platform is based on JS engine in Google Chrome also called V8 engine. One of the important features of Node.js is that it uses even driven programming and builds fast and scalable network applications. Never taking time for buffering data, the application sends out data in chunks (output). Node.js is the runtime environment for JavaScript in our project as well.

HTML/CSS: HTML stands for HyperText Markup Language and CSS refers to Cascading Style Sheet. These are used to build web application and effects. CSS helps you save time and effort. It can control the layout of numerous web pages at the same time. CSS is basically used to format the layout of our webpage. The HyperText Markup Language, or HTML is the universal markup language used for designing that's presented in a web browser. HTML holds of a series of many elements. Summarising, HTML and CSS will always operate together, and one can use both while building your website or learning more about them.

PUG.JS: A JavaScript library PUG is used for easy-to-code template engine used for coding in HTML in an even more readable way. Codes written in PUG gets converted into standard programs of HTML. It's a very high-performance template. It was earlier termed as JADE. Install it using NPM. For the project which used PUG for beautifying html programs in easy-to-read manner. In most cases, the template engine will accept data from an external source and inject it into the template it is constructing. The graphic below illustrates this point. Moreover, it supports JavaScript natively, allowing a user to format HTML code with JavaScript expressions. One can reuse the static web pages with dynamic data using this method.

SHA-256: For hashing, SHA (Secure Hash Algorithm) 256 cryptographic hash algorithm is used. Hashing is a process of converting data into a particular hash so that only intended people can access it using for instance, private and public keys. SHA 256 isn't an encryption as it cannot be decrypted back to original text which is a feature of hashing. Whereas it is a kind of signature for any kind of file in this case our string of data. SHA-256 produces a unique 256- bit (32-byte) signature for all data. It is a successor to SHA-1, and together called SHA-2. The Project uses SHA-256 because it is the strongest hash functions available. Regarding our project, utilised hashing for the process of mining. NPM is two main things: first, it's an online repository for open-source Node.js projects; second, it's a command-line application for interacting with that repository that helps with installation of packages, version control, and dependency management. On using npm, you'll find a plethora of Node.js modules and apps, with more being added each day. Once one has selected a package to install, can do so with a single command in command-line prompt. It's a nice companion function for AES because of the 256-bit key.

HASHING: The process of transforming a given key into a smaller value for O (1) retrieval time is known as hashing (Zhai et al., 2019). This is accomplished by using a function or technique known as a hash function to translate data to an encrypted or simplified possible result known as a "hash code" or "hash." This hash is used as the index to narrow down search criteria and swiftly retrieve data.

Applications

- Hashing is the most frequent method for creating hash tables. A hash table is a list that maintains key/value pairs and allows you to access any entry by its index.
- A hash function is used to map the keys to the size of the table since there is no limit on the amount of key/value pairs; the hash value becomes the index for a given element.
- Data encryption also employs hashing. Passwords can be saved as hashes, preventing plaintext passwords from being accessed even if a database is hacked. Popular cryptographic hashes include MD5, SHA-1, and SHA-2.
- Retrieval of data: hashing maps object data to a representative integer value using functions or algorithms. When searching for these objects on the object data map, a hash can be used to narrow down queries.
- In hash tables, for instance, developers record data in the form of key and value pairs, such as a customer record. The key aids data identification and serves as an input to the hashing function, with the hash code or integer being mapped to a fixed size after that.
- Digital Signatures: Hashing aids in the encryption and decryption of digital signatures, which are used to validate message senders and recipients. In this case, the digital signature is transformed by a hash function before the hashed value (also known as a message digest) and the signature are provided to the receivers in separate communications.
- The same hash function computes the message digest from the signature upon reception, which is then compared to the sent message digest to guarantee they are same. The hash function indexes the original value or key and allows access to the data associated with a particular value or key that is obtained in a one-way hashing process (Chen et al., 2018).
- Cryptography: To safeguard data, cryptography employs numerous hash functions. The following are some of the most often used cryptographic hashes:
  - Secure Hash Algorithm 1 (SHA-1) is a hashing algorithm that is both secure and fast.
  - Secure Hash Algorithm 2 (SHA-2) is a second version of the Secure Hash Algorithm
  - Secure Hash Algorithm 3 (SHA-3) is the third version (Oliveira et al., 2018). Hash functions of Message-digest like MD2, MD4 and MD5 help hash digital signatures. The signature is hashed and then converted into a shorter value known as a message digest.

DIGITAL SIGNATURES

It is a mathematical approach that verifies the integrity and authenticity of a communication, software, or digital document. It helps us to authenticate the message contents and verify the author's name, date, and time of signatures. A digital signature is a mathematical approach that verifies the integrity and authenticity of a communication, software, or digital document. It helps us to authenticate the message contents and verify the data, author's name, and time of signatures. It assists with data authentication, non-repudiation, and integrity.

A digital signature consists of three algorithms:

- **Key   generation   algorithm**
  The key generation algorithm chooses a private key at random from a list of possibilities. This algorithm generates the private key and the public key that corresponds to it.
- **Signing algorithm** A signing algorithm produces a signature for the document.
- **Signature verifying algorithm** A signature verifying algorithm either accepts or rejects the document's authenticity.

WORK DONE

A blockchain is a growing list of documents, known as blocks, that are cryptographically linked together. A cryptographic hash of the preceding block, a timestamp, and transaction data are all included in each block. The project's purpose is to produce a web-app that demonstrates blockchain fundamentals such as transaction verification and hash generation.

The project will assist us in better understanding blockchains and verifying transactions before they are finalised. Taking advantage of blockchain technology's automated capabilities, particularly in digital payments, in a timely manner, minimising delays and lowering third-party service costs. The user would be able to input values, which may be data or transactions, through the web-interface. App's Data would be hashed by the web app, and we'd be able to validate it by comparing different hashes.

This would also give a user interface for maintaining records of different transactions and calculating whether accurate financial transactions from various accounts are taking place by displaying them through Coinbase. While performing live simulations, the user will be able to grasp blockchain ideas.

Following are some of the running webpages from our web application:

The Home Page

The following is the home page of our web-application that provides the user with some general information on blockchain, it's leveraging and its usage as shown below.

Figure 1. Home Page

Figure 2. Home page information

INTRODUCTION TO BLOCKCHAIN
A blockchain is a growing list of records, called blocks, that are linked together using cryptography. Each block contains a cryptographic hash of the previous block, a timestamp, and transaction data. is the most popular digital currency in which such transactions are conducted. There is no physical transfer of money; just a record of the transaction. This makes blockchain one of the safest and most secure information-recording and financial transaction mechanisms today.

WHAT IS LEVARAGING BLACKCHAIN?
Organizations are leveraging the blockchain technology to create smart contracts that remove the need for third-party administrators and evaluators. For executing smart contracts, a computer code is run on top of the blockchain whereby the parties set pre-defined rules beforehand. When these rules are met, the agreement is completed, and it is automatically enforced.

The Hash Page

A hash looks like a bunch of random numbers. It is like a fingerprint of some digital data. Now coming to the hash page, the Hash will give the fingerprint of anything that we type in the Data box. The hash changes every time we write a letter. For example, if I type "Hello", the hash becomes 185f8db32271fe25f561a6fc938b2e264306ec304eda518007d1764826381969. If we type the same data, we'll get the same hash. Even if we type nothing and the box is blank, that also has a different hash. We'll always get a hash. Now we have extended this idea of hash and built a block page.

Figure 3. Hash Page

The Block Page

The Block page is just like the Hash page. We have just broken the Data box from Hash page into 3 sections – Block, Nonce and Data.

- The Block Box specifies the block number
- The Nonce Box refers to the "number only used once"
- The Data Box is where we enter our data.

So, when the Data box is empty, the hash we get starts with 4 zeroes which means it's valid. The green background tells us that it's signed. Now if we type a word, the hash will change, and the background will turn red which signifies that the hash is not valid (Yuan, Xu, and Si, 2017).. That's when the "Nonce" plays an important role. Now I can change the nonce many times to check which number in Nonce gets the ash to start with 4 zeroes. To save time and effort, we have introduced a mine button. This mine button will run through all the nonce numbers to try to find the one where the Hash starts with 4 zeroes. This process is called mining. After clicking the mine button, we'll get a number in the Nonce Box that hashes out to a number that starts with 4 zeroes and therefore satisfying our definition of what a signed block is.

Figure 4. Block Page with signed data

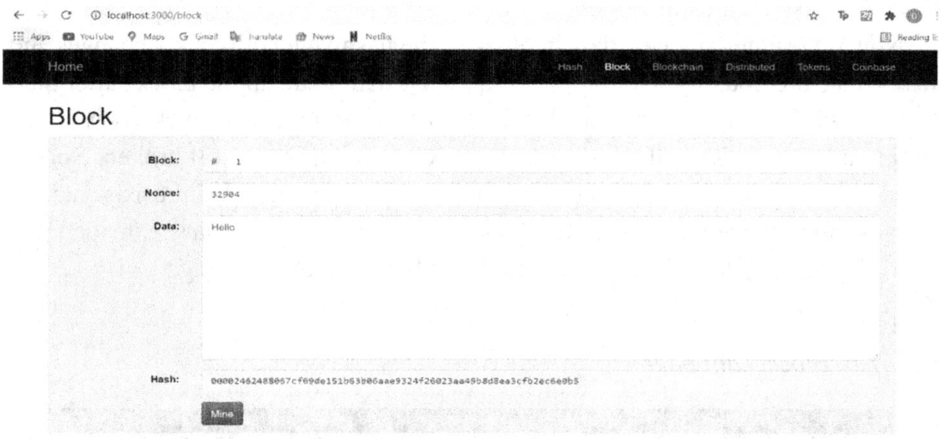

Figure 5. Block page after changing text

The Blockchain Page

Blockchain is basically a chain of these blocks. But how do we do that? Now all the blocks in a blockchain have block numbers, nonce, data, hash and a previous box. We have discussed about everything in the hash and block page but what is this previous box? Now what happens is that each block points back to the one before it. The hash value of block 1 goes in the previous value of block 2 and the hash value of block 2 goes in the previous value of block 3 and so on. The previous value of block 1 is just a bunch of zeroes.

Now if we enter any new data in block 2, the hash value of block 2 changes and so does the previous value of block 3 and thus it will break all the blocks after that. Now to avoid this, if we write any data in a block, we remine it and pick a new nonce so that it becomes signed. However, the blocks after this are still broken. So, we must remine the data in all blocks after it. That's how a blockchain resists change.

Now how do we know that our blockchain is remined? We have extended this idea of remining blockchain and built a Distributed blockchain page.

Figure 6. Blockchain page

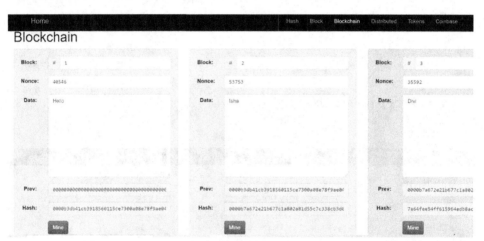

The Distributed Blockchain Page

It looks exactly like the previous blockchain. We have peers in this page like Peer A, Peer B and so on. All these peers are identical. Now if we enter some data in peer B and remine the data in all blocks of Peer B, it becomes signed. But we can see that the hashes in the latest blocks of Peer A and Peer C are same but that of Peer B are different (Thompson, 2017). Now we know there is something wrong with peer B. So, the point is that blockchains can have thousands of blocks very easily but rather than checking through them all, we just need to check the hashes of the latest block and we can tell if any data was altered in the previous blocks.

Figure 7. Distributed Blockchain page with Peer A

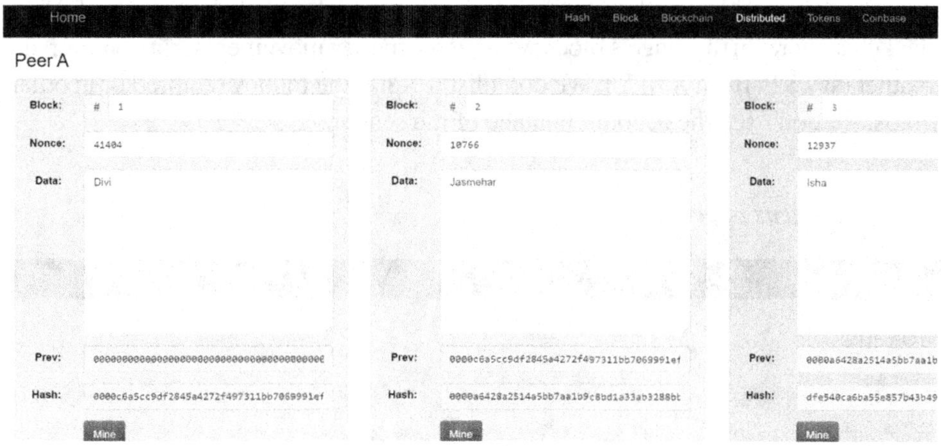

Figure 8. Distributed Blockchain with Peer B

The Functions being used for SHA-256 Hashing, mining is as shown below. We have called these functions several times throughout the application.

Tokens Page

In this page we add tokens in the form of a currency and replace data that was being seen in previous pages with certain transactions. And like previous pages there are several blocks and peers. If we change anything in a particular block the color of our blocks would change to red alerting us to check transactions (Nakamoto, 2009). Doing so one would never lose track of the money which is the whole point of using blockchain here. In this page's block we only see money movements from one person to other (say $25 from X to Y). We don't list if X has the money required or in other words, we don't see the account balance of the sender.

Figure 9. Tokens page

Coinbase Page

To overcome the problem stated above in Tokens page, the Coinbase page has an addition of Coinbase transaction in the given blocks. Here a certain amount of money is being invented and given to the concerned person (sender) so that person can carry forward transactions. Her dispersion is controlled. Using this we can track transactions and check if the money being sent exists in an account by going backwards. If one adds inappropriate transaction amounts the blocks will turn red. Therefore, it resists tampering. This provides an efficient way to handle agreement on what has happened in past in the form of immutable history.

Figure 10. Coinbase page

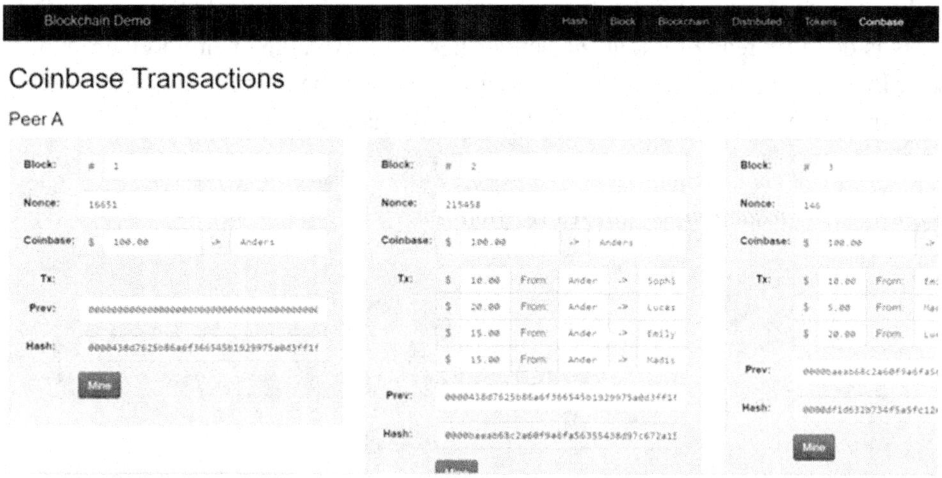

Public/ Private Keys Page

A problem that occurs in our previous pages, that there is nothing to stop somebody from adding a transaction that creates abnormalities and there seems to be no protection. To overcome this situation. We look at another cryptographic primitive: Public and Private key pairs (Mohanta et al., 2019). The Keys page allows one to create a private key that is kept confidential and public key which is told to all intended people.

Figure 11. Public and Private keys generation

Public / Private Key Pairs

Private Key

65645124001427200769618650116875726431131717237126312693843499695125187055170

Public Key

0433d43659db98f64ea8809ee0e4a8a2a28882b95cc3f052505adc88b738ec8af49570651186759421fa554ff5f8bcacc208bedb19e8

Transaction Signatures Page

In signatures transaction page, it allows one to type in a transaction and enter a private key that only the sender has and once 'Sign' is hit a message signature is generated.

This signature is sent to intended person who passes it into given area as well as the public key. One would be able to verify if the message is valid if block turns green. This is done by realizing that the sender has the private key behind given public key. In verifying one can understand that the amount mentioned is correctly being sent from one public key to another by the legitimate person.

Figure 12. Transaction Signatures verification

RESULT

The web application is a demonstration of blockchain concepts including verification of transactions over its path and how hashes are created, how it's used in blocks and blockchains as well as add another cryptographic primitive: public & private key pair used for signatures. There is no physical transfer of money, just a record of the transaction. This makes blockchain one of the safest and most secure information-recording and financial transaction mechanisms today. The record of transactions is kept in a peer-to-peer network. There are no central authority needs to confirm the transactions. The transactions are verified by the participants in peer-to-peer networks.

In future project work, we will be removing data box and will add tokens that will show all the transactions between people. It will not show the bank account statements but only the money movements. We will also add a Coinbase transaction box to our blocks. It will show the amount of money that a person has and then the transactions made with that amount. It will show all the transactions made between multiple people after that first transaction that the user will enter. To make it more secure and not just anyone can create these transactions, we've added the feature of private key, public key, and message signatures. Private key is to be kept private and public key can be shared with anyone. The block when turns green, tells us that it's a valid message. It verifies that whoever came up with the message signature has access to the private key behind the public key (Van Saberhagen, 2013). All of this will happen in a blockchain so we will have to keep remining the data to make the blocks signed and then check if the hashes in the peers are identical. This web-app will help us to check all the previous transactions and will warn us with an unsigned block if there's any error. The user would be able to understand blockchain concepts while doing live simulations.

CONCLUSION

We learnt some new languages like HTML and CSS, Javascript, Node.js and Pug.js. We used Javascript for any reaction on the webpage after an event occurs. We used node.js so that our code runs in an asynchronous, single thread and no waiting is done for transactions or hashes to be shown and remining of data. For the layout of our pages and for adding more styles to it, we have used HTML, CSS and Pug.js. For hashing in our project about Blockchain we have used the SHA 256 cryptographic hash algorithm. We faced difficulty in writing the code of our hashing algorithm. Regarding our project, we have utilised hashing for the process of mining. We have understood these blockchain concepts while doing live simulations.

REFERENCES

Antoniadis, I., Kontsas, S., & Spinthiropoulos, K. (2019). Blockchain and brand loyalty programs: A short review of applications and challenges. In *International Conference on Economic Sciences and Business Administration* (Vol. 5, No. 1, pp. 8-16). Spiru Haret University.

Casino, F., Dasaklis, T. K., & Patsakis, C. (2019). A systematic literature review of blockchain-based applications: Current status, classification and open issues. *Telematics and Informatics*, *36*, 55–81.

Chen, W., Xu, Z., Shi, S., Zhao, Y., & Zhao, J. (2018, December). A survey of blockchain applications in different domains. In *Proceedings of the 2018 International Conference on Blockchain Technology and Application* (pp. 17-21). 10.1145/3301403.3301407

Chen, W., Xu, Z., Shi, S., Zhao, Y., & Zhao, J. (2018, December). A survey of blockchain applications in different domains. In *Proceedings of the 2018 International Conference on Blockchain Technology and Application* (pp. 17-21). Academic Press.

Makridakis, S., & Christodoulou, K. (2019). Blockchain: Current challenges and future prospects/applications. *Future Internet, 11*(12), 258. doi:10.3390/fi11120258

Michael, J., Cohn, A., & Butcher, J. R. (2018). Blockchain technology. *The Journal, 1*(7), 1–11.

Mohanta, B. K., Jena, D., Panda, S. S., & Sobhanayak, S. (2019). Blockchain technology: A survey on applications and security privacy challenges. *Internet of Things, 8*, 100107.

Nakamoto, S. (2009). *Bitcoin: A peer-to-peer electronic cash system Bitcoin: A Peer-to-Peer Electronic Cash System.* https://bitcoin. org/en/bitcoin-paper

Oliveira, L., Zavolokina, L., Bauer, I., & Schwabe, G. (2018, December). *To token or not to token: Tools for understanding blockchain tokens.* ICIS.

Sharma, P., Jindal, R., & Borah, M. D. (2022). A review of blockchain-based applications and challenges. *Wireless Personal Communications*, 1-43.

Thompson, S. (2017). The preservation of digital signatures on the blockchain. *See Also*, (3).

Van Saberhagen, N. (2013). *CryptoNote v 2.0.* Academic Press.

Yaga, D., Mell, P., Roby, N., & Scarfone, K. (2019). Blockchain technology overview. *arXiv preprint arXiv:1906.11078*.

Yuan, C., Xu, M. X., & Si, X. M. (2017). Research on a new signature scheme on blockchain. *Security and Communication Networks*.

Zhai, S., Yang, Y., Li, J., Qiu, C., & Zhao, J. (2019, February). Research on the Application of Cryptography on the Blockchain. *Journal of Physics: Conference Series, 1168*(3), 032077.

ADDITIONAL READING

Asokan, N., Shoup, V., & Waidner, M. (2000). Optimistic fair exchange of digital signatures. *IEEE Journal on Selected Areas in Communications, 18*(4), 593–610.

Blum, M., Feldman, P., & Micali, S. (2019). Non-interactive zero-knowledge and its applications. In *Providing Sound Foundations for Cryptography* (pp. 329–349). On the Work of Shafi Goldwasser and Silvio Micali.

Boneh, D., Gentry, C., Lynn, B., & Shacham, H. (2003). Aggregate and verifiably encrypted signatures from bilinear maps. In *Advances in Cryptology—EUROCRYPT 2003: International Conference on the Theory and Applications of Cryptographic Techniques, Warsaw, Poland, May 4–8, 2003 Proceedings 22* (pp. 416-432). Springer Berlin Heidelberg. 10.1007/3-540-39200-9_26

Du, X., Shayman, M., & Rozenblit, M. (2001, May). Implementation and performance analysis of SNMP on a TLS/TCP base. In *2001 IEEE/IFIP International Symposium on Integrated Network Management Proceedings. Integrated Network Management VII. Integrated Management Strategies for the New Millennium (Cat. No. 01EX470)* (pp. 453-466). IEEE.

Du, X., Xiao, Y., Guizani, M., & Chen, H. H. (2007). An effective key management scheme for heterogeneous sensor networks. *Ad Hoc Networks*, *5*(1), 24–34.

Eyal, I. (2015, May). The miner's dilemma. In *2015 IEEE Symposium on Security and Privacy* (pp. 89-103). IEEE.

Gentry, C. (2009, May). Fully homomorphic encryption using ideal lattices. In *Proceedings of the forty-first annual ACM symposium on Theory of computing* (pp. 169-178). 10.1145/1536414.1536440

Joux, A., & Vitse, V. (2013). Elliptic Curve Discrete Logarithm Problem over Small Degree Extension Fields: Application to the Static Diffie–Hellman Problem on. *Journal of Cryptology*, *26*(1), 119–143. doi:10.100700145-011-9116-z

Koblitz, N., Menezes, A., & Vanstone, S. (2000). The state of elliptic curve cryptography. *Designs, Codes and Cryptography*, *19*(2/3), 173–193. doi:10.1023/A:1008354106356

Micali, S., Ohta, K., & Reyzin, L. (2001, November). Accountable-subgroup multisignatures. In *Proceedings of the 8th ACM Conference on Computer and Communications Security* (pp. 245-254). ACM.

Nayak, K., Kumar, S., Miller, A., & Shi, E. (2016, March). Stubborn mining: Generalizing selfish mining and combining with an eclipse attack. In *2016 IEEE European Symposium on Security and Privacy (EuroS&P)* (pp. 305-320). IEEE.

Sapirshtein, A., Sompolinsky, Y., & Zohar, A. (2017). Optimal selfish mining strategies in bitcoin. In *Financial Cryptography and Data Security: 20th International Conference, FC 2016, Christ Church, Barbados, February 22–26, 2016, Revised Selected Papers 20* (pp. 515-532). Springer Berlin Heidelberg.

Sasson, E. B., Chiesa, A., Garman, C., Green, M., Miers, I., Tromer, E., & Virza, M. (2014, May). Zerocash: Decentralized anonymous payments from bitcoin. In 2014 IEEE symposium on security and privacy (pp. 459-474). IEEE.

Singh, A., Rumantir, G., South, A., & Bethwaite, B. (2014, August). Clustering experiments on big transaction data for market segmentation. In *Proceedings of the 2014 International Conference on Big Data Science and Computing* (pp. 1-7). Academic Press.

Xiao, Y., Chen, H. H., Du, X., & Guizani, M. (2009). Stream-based cipher feedback mode in wireless error channel. *IEEE Transactions on Wireless Communications*, *8*(2), 622–626.

Yao, X., Han, X., Du, X., & Zhou, X. (2013). A lightweight multicast authentication mechanism for small scale IoT applications. *IEEE Sensors Journal*, *13*(10), 3693–3701.

Chapter 3
Data Analytics With Selection of Tools and Techniques

Jayanthi G.
Sri Ramachandra Institute of Higher Education and Research, India

Purushothaman R.
ⓘD https://orcid.org/0000-0002-8129-5298
Siddartha Institute of Science and Technology, India

ABSTRACT

Highway traffic profiling is an essential service for the deployment of intelligent transport system (ITS) in Chennai metropolitan city. Recently, a traffic sequence mining framework was developed for the prediction of traffic flow on highways. Real-time traffic flow rate of the state highway SH-49 was collected under the authority and supervision of Tamil Nadu Road Development Corporation (TNRDC). The objective of this investigation is to deploy electronic traffic profiling with all essential services for highway traffic operations. The implementation of traffic sequence mining framework done earlier has highly motivated the authors to extend the present work to E-Traffic alert, a highway traffic profiling system that disseminates the dynamic traffic flow rate to commuters when deployed as mobile application and an interactive analytic tool for traffic operations when deployed as desktop web application.

DOI: 10.4018/978-1-6684-5255-4.ch003

INTRODUCTION

In our recent work, 2017 – 2020 (Jayanthi and Jothilakshmi, 2019, 2021; Jayanthi and García Márquez, 2021a, 2021b; Jayanthi, García Márquez, and Ragavendra Prasad, 2022, Jayanthi, 2023) travel time based traffic information sequence was formulated and implemented in a traffic information sequence mining framework. The framework shown in Figure.1.(b) was developed for the prediction of traffic flow on highways using the data set recorded at the centralized toll center shown in Figure.1.(a). Real time traffic volume data for 52 weeks is collected at a centralized toll system comprising all toll collection centers at three different sites in Chennai city, namely, (i) Site-1: Perungudi- Seevaram, the entry Toll Plaza (ii) Site-2: ECR link Road, and (iii) Site-3: Egattur, the exit toll plaza. The data services of these three sites are under the authority of TNRDC. The research findings reported that traffic volume on highways can be predicted by mining travel time based traffic information sequence and it is feasible to deploy the framework in any suitable location.

Figure 1. (a) TNRDC Centralized Toll Center (b) Traffic Sequence Mining Framework

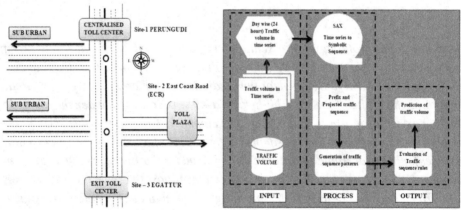

The availability of historical traffic flow rate and connectivity of sites has motivated authors to formulate highway traffic profiling system that has following objectives.

1. To capture the dynamics of physical traffic flow by an Extract-Transform-Load (ETL) data pipeline design for the representation of raw traffic count.
2. To design a machine learning pipeline that augments the traffic sequence mining framework with vehicle speed based on multi-criteria decision making support for profiling the highway traffic.

3. Design an analytic pipeline to disseminate dynamic traffic information in successive time instances and operate the vehicular traffic with the help of interactive dashboard.

Urban transport system is a time varying network. Traffic congestion induces unpredicted delay in travel time. The traffic flow rate on highways at temporal scales contributes in travel time computation in successive time instances. Formulation of Sequence Convolution based auto-encoder Long Short term Memory (SCAE-LSTM) network aims at sequencing the temporal traffic flow rate in preceding time instance to estimate the traffic flow in successive time instances. Given origin and destination (OD) pair, temporal traffic sequence helps in estimating traffic flow rate on highways. Hence, Spatial-TemporAl Reconnect (STAR) algorithm is proposed. The performance of STAR is investigated by conducting extensive experimentation on real traffic network of Chennai Metropolitan City.

The computational complexity of the algorithm is empirically analyzed. The proposed STAR algorithm is found to estimate traffic flow during peak hour traffic with reduced complexity in computation compared to other baseline methods in short term traffic flow predictions like LSTM, ConvLSTM and GRNN. Finally, conclusions on results are presented with directions for future research.

Figure 2. Highway Traffic Profiling System

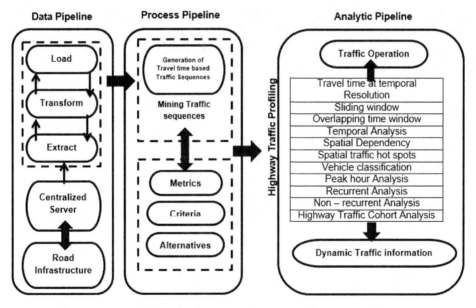

The various stages of pipeline involved in this project are shown in Figure.2. The data pipeline design is needed to capture the dynamics of the physical traffic flow from road side infrastructure and transform to a representational form for processing the traffic information. The process pipeline essentially performs the task of travel time based traffic sequence generation. The evaluated traffic patterns are the source of information for deciding the criteria and alternatives. The resulting patterns will be streamed to the analytic pipeline for profiling the highway traffic based on travel time at temporal resolution, sliding window, overlapping time window, temporal analysis, spatial dependency, spatial traffic hot spots, vehicle classification, peak hour analysis, recurrent, and non – recurrent congestion analysis when deployed as mobile and desktop application. The following section explains the recent developments in transport data analytics.

BACKGROUND

Travel information is dynamic traffic information used to developed software enabled services for traffic control, traffic monitoring, operation and management. This dynamic traffic information in real time operational settings is used in transportation planning, infrastructure development, and smart cities thereby forms a source of data asset of a nation (Wei, Wu, and Ma, 2019). The two inevitable real time components of a physical traffic flow are space and time. The temporal component of traffic flow is time indexed while flow of traffic on uplink and downlinks of road segments forms the spatial components of traffic flow (Ermagun & Levinson, 2018; Ermagun, Chatterjee, and Levinson, 2017). The concept of Artificial Intelligence (AI) theory is recently established in transport analytics.

Figure 3. ITS deployable services

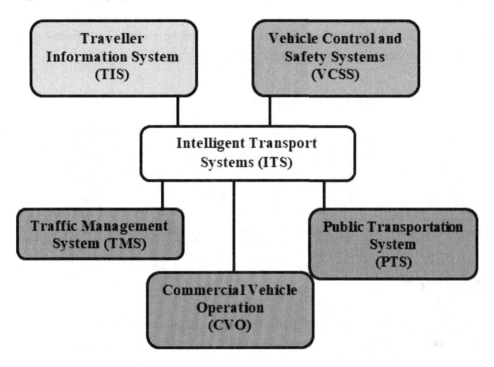

National highway authority of India (NHAI) has taken steps to deploy ITS services all over the nation for safe and secure travel. The specific achievements are location based system for freight management, vehicle tracking, stop signal and speed violation detection, passenger information services, electronic ticket vending, public surveillance through cameras, emergency response management for reducing causalities and rescue from accidents, mass rapid transit, metro rail transport, and electronic toll collection through prepaid tag named FASTag that was deployed in 523 toll plaza all over India by NHAI. Recently, traffic information service of ITS was established on Eastern Peripheral Expressway facility in Dasna, Ghaziabad, Uttar Pradesh. Thus, the world-wide objective of ITS is to ensure safe, and secure travel with the help of information and communication technologies. The recent advancements and ITS deployment services in India are given in Table.1. However, highway traffic profiling is an essential ITS service that can be deployed for sustainable mobility and transport in Chennai city. The objectives and methodologies with phasing of the E-Traffic Alert project are as follows.

Objective 1

To capture the dynamics of physical traffic flow by an Extract-Transform-Load (ETL) data pipeline design for the representation of raw traffic count.

Table 1. Methodology: Experimental Design

Cloud Space	:	Google Cloud Space configuration in the range of 5 -10 TB per month
Data Store	:	Formatted store of categorical (Text), image (Unstructured), Discrete numeric, and Continuous numeric.
Technologies	:	Streaming real time traffic data using Kafka connect. Apache Kafka, an open-source component that works as a data hub for simple for centralized data integration between data sources.
Programming Language	:	Apache Spark and Python – Pandas data processing module.

Objective 2

To design a machine learning pipeline that augments the traffic sequence mining framework with vehicle speed based on multi-criteria decision making support for profiling the highway traffic.

Table 2. Methodology: Experimental Design

Cloud Space	:	Configuration of Google Cloud Space for 10 TB per month.
Data Store	:	Database design Postgres SQL (Open Source)
Multi-Criteria Decision Making (MCDM)	:	Augmenting TOPSIS, AHP, BWM with Traffic Sequence mining framework
Technologies	:	Apache Spark, PySpark, SQL
Programming Language	:	Python with Web App development

Objective 3

Design an analytic pipeline to disseminate dynamic traffic information in successive time instances and operate the vehicular traffic with the help of interactive dashboard.

Table 3. Methodology: Experimental Design

Cloud Space	:	Configuration of Google Cloud Space for 10 TB per month.
Data Store	:	Database design Postgres SQL (Open Source)
Machine Learning Modules	:	Sklearn, tensor flow, Keras Module
Web Development	:	Streamlit, Machine Learning
Technologies	:	Geographical Information System (GIS), Tableau for visualization with traffic cohort Study
Programming Language	:	Python – Apache Spark Full stack Web development

The experimental design and methodologies stated above have been grouped in to three phases as follows:

The phases of this project are,

1. Design of Extract-Transform-Load data Pipeline
2. Augmenting traffic sequence mining framework with multi-criteria decision making support,
3. Analytic pipeline for dissemination of dynamic traffic information.

The total duration of 24 months is divided into three phases each of 8 months' timeline for design, development, testing and validation of software units. The flow of work in each of the above phases is shown in Figure 2 and timeline for completion of tasks in each phases are shown in detail in Table.2.

RESEARCH OUTCOME

Highway traffic profiling is a deployable Intelligent Transport System (ITS) service. The proposed E-Traffic alert is an automated software unit developed for profiling the highway traffic for disseminating dynamic traffic information in successive time instances. The system is proposed to deploy both mobile and desktop web application. This software system assists commuters in planning their travel for work and other trips. The significant outcomes and their social relevance at each phase of the project are detailed as follows.

1. The outcome of Phase 1 is the representation of physical flow rate as traffic flow on highways is dynamic and unprecedented at times. This representation framework is essential in gaining insight of traffic flow rate that would reach

out to public commuters as traffic pattern when queried at various temporal resolutions ranging from minutes to hours.

2. The outcome of Phase 2 is a proactive decision-making tool for the travelers to choose their mode of transport for mobility with diverse alternatives when augmented with travel time based traffic sequences.

3. The outcome of Phase 3 is a dashboard to visualize temporal and spatial behavior of physical traffic flow which is crucial for routing the vehicular flow in different operational settings. Moreover, the traffic profiling leads to proactive travel time plan rather than reactive with existing facility and road side infrastructure.

4. Highway traffic cohort study in this investigation will track the temporal and spatial traffic indicators whose outcome will assist in identifying the trending of traffic flow and their incidence rate with environmental pollution causing road traffic noise, stroke, myocardial infarction, exposure to traffic-borne air pollutants and other such effects causing pollution.

Significance of Transport Data Analytics

Disseminating dynamic traffic information in successive temporal resolutions will enable proactive congestion management when devised in following ways.

- Highway traffic profiling service is essential for Emergency Vehicle (EV) operations when reaching a designated location has multiple alternative routes considering the spatial and temporal behavior of traffic flow rate.
- Commuters availing multi – modal transportation will benefit from travel time based traffic sequence considering successive temporal resolutions with respect to spatial location and vice versa.
- E-Traffic alert system deployed as mobile and desktop application will devise sustainable mobility of freight units which can be accessed by common people.
- Sectors like travel, tourism, consignment shipping, and logistics (parcel and food delivery services can essentially develop their business by using the highway traffic profiling system.

REFERENCES

Ermagun, A., Chatterjee, S., & Levinson, D. (2017). Using temporal detrending to observe the spatial correlation of traffic. *PLoS One, 12*(5), e0176853. doi:10.1371/journal.pone.0176853 PMID:28472093

Ermagun, A., & Levinson, D. M. (2019). Development and application of the network weight matrix to predict traffic flow for congested and uncongested conditions. *Environment and Planning. B, Urban Analytics and City Science, 46*(9), 1684–1705. doi:10.1177/2399808318763368

Jayanthi, G. (2023). Multi Criteria Decision Making Analysis for sustainable Transport. In F. P. García Márquez & B. Lev (Eds.), *Sustainability: Cases and Studies in Using Operations Research and Management Science Methods* (pp. 1–8). Springer International Publishing.

Jayanthi, G., & García Márquez, F. P. (2021a). Travel time based traffic rerouting by augmenting traffic flow network with temporal and spatial relations for congestion management. In *Proceedings of the Fifteenth International Conference on Management Science and Engineering Management:* Volume 1 *15* (pp. 554-565). Springer International Publishing.

Jayanthi, G., & García Márquez, F. P. (2021b). Data mining and information technology in transportation—a review. In *Proceedings of the Fifteenth International Conference on Management Science and Engineering Management:* Volume 2 *15* (pp. 849-855). Springer International Publishing.

Jayanthi, G., García Márquez, F. P., & Ragavendra Prasad, M. (2022, May). Routing Vehicles on Highways by Augmenting Traffic Flow Network: A Review on Speed Up Techniques. *International Conference on Intelligent Emerging Methods of Artificial Intelligence & Cloud Computing Proceedings of IEMAICLOUD, 2021*, 96–105.

Jayanthi, G., & Jothilakshmi, P. (2019). Prediction of traffic volume by mining traffic sequences using travel time based PrefixSpan. *IET Intelligent Transport Systems, 13*(7), 1199–1210. doi:10.1049/iet-its.2018.5165

Jayanthi, G., & Jothilakshmi, P. (2021). Traffic time series forecasting on highways-a contemporary survey of models, methods and techniques. *International Journal of Logistics Systems and Management, 39*(1), 77–110. doi:10.1504/IJLSM.2021.115068

Jayanthi, G., & Jothilakshmi, P. (under review). Deep learner for traffic flow assessment on highways based on spatial - temporal traffic sequences. *IETE Journal of Research.*

Wei, W., Wu, H., & Ma, H. (2019). An autoencoder and LSTM-based traffic flow prediction method. *Sensors (Basel)*, *19*(13), 2946. doi:10.339019132946 PMID:31277390

Chapter 4
AI in Gaming and Entertainment:
Applying Artificial Intelligence Algorithms in a Game

Anshika Gupta
Amity University, India

Shuchi Sirpal
Amity School of Engineering and Technology, Amity University, India

ABSTRACT

The chapter describes the understanding and the application of the concept of the various AI algorithms that also include reinforcement learning algorithms, which is a great contribution to the decision-making of the AI agents/AI bots. The game consists of player and opponent AI competing with each other in which the goal is to kill the opponent. The game is basically an Action RPG game (real-time combat between the player and AI agents). Wherever the performer has the ability to focus and see on his own stats and the stats of the character, accordingly he can determine the health, mana, strength, XP, and other abilities. The AI bots on the other hand are programmed to follow the player, and depending on the state that it is in and the player's last attack, it makes decisions accordingly and tries to defeat the player. Application of the various AI algorithms on the software Unreal Engine are achieved by C++ programming and blueprint/visual scripting. The game contains player and adversary AI competing with each other in which the goal is to slay the opponent.

DOI: 10.4018/978-1-6684-5255-4.ch004

INTRODUCTION

Computer Games have been a great source of entertainment for the young generations and even adults. They have been a part of people's daily life and with an increase in technology, there is also an increase in the quality of the games. Gaming has evolved with time as it started as early as the 1950's when the chess and checker games were written on the computer program. The games gave opponents a run for their money, but the real onset of video games came with the game pong and space wars in the '70s. Back then, these games worked on discrete logic and had two players' concepts. This gave rise to single-player games, where the developer would have to make use of non-Player characters, just to make the game more interesting. These Non-Player characters were not controlled by the player or the user who was playing the game and to do this the developers used stored patterns to decide the action of the non-player character. These stored patterns were the pre-decided outcomes of the user input in the game. The concept of single-player concepts connected the gaming industry with artificial intelligence. Developers used artificial intelligence tools to create more advanced games for example the Pacman introduced air patterns in the maze game, which was a genre usually used by journalists at the time (*Sign in Page,* n.d.).

Nowadays, the advancement of games has increased and even the non-player characters are much more sophisticated and even comes with certain difficulty to win the game. The players and non-Player characters are designed quite precisely as we see the opponents in the games are stronger. Most importantly, the opponents perform according to the behavior of the player instead of following the pre-decided patterns. Artificial intelligence concepts like virtual reality and augmented reality have improved the feel and look of the players and opponents in the game along with achieving the foremost goal of user experience for the users. These concepts have also made room for research and the development of applications altogether. The non-player characters have become more intelligent with artificial intelligence, and they can provide answers according to the user's behavior. An example of this is Watson developed by IBM, a question-answering computer that can provide answers to the users in natural language. This has also led to an increase in user engagement towards the games with time. If we look back now, there is a huge change in the gameplay of the games in the '70s and that of now. The opponents are much more intelligent, and it is difficult to win the game. The computer as the opponent has been trained previously on data based upon the patterns, therefore the player needs to know better than the patterns that have been used. Artificial Intelligence helps to create a real-world environment, that has characters that exhibit human intelligence and behaviors. Apart from the graphics, sounds, and animations, the human-like intelligence and decision-making ability of the opponents provide a great deal of user engagement and experience for the users. This is achievable because of the artificial intelligence components. It has provided room for advanced computer games in the gaming industry nowadays.

Now let us see, how is Artificial intelligence used in games. In computer games, artificial intelligence is seen as the brain of the game. Certain algorithms help to generate responses based on the user inputs. As we all know that every user is different and everyone responds to a particular situation differently, therefore the artificial intelligence in the game will make an intelligent response based on the set of inputs provided by the user. The two criteria on which we determine the component or non-player characters who respond to the inputs supplied are the user's inputs in the game and the difficulty level. There are several popular fighting games on the market; in these games, if a player kicks an opponent, the intelligent response is to block the kick. This is how artificial intelligence handles the game by responding to the player in a human-like manner. When Artificial intelligence and game come together it focuses on providing an engaging user experience to gain profits in the industry. However, AI has influenced gaming in numerous ways over the last few years, and it is much more than simply the experience (Zang et al., 2007).

To begin with, the game's bots have gotten pretty clever. Bots are similar to the non-player characters that we discussed before. In terms of intelligence, these bots have evolved significantly. In addition, the game's difficulty levels may be adjusted, and the user's reaction can be predicted at each stage. Let's use an example to try to grasp it from the standpoint of a game. For example, if you're playing a football game on a gaming console, the computer is your opponent. Now that you're always passing the ball ahead, the bot is expecting the pattern in the game to figure out how to take the ball away from you. The bots will be able to score a goal utilizing their intelligence after they have figured out the patterns. As a result, the bots employ intelligence to plan their games in response to the user's inputs/moves. Second, using ideas such as augmented reality and virtual reality, artificial intelligence has improved the user experience of these games. The capacity of users to engage or interact better with the interfaces improves the quality of the experience. The better feel and appearance of non-player characters has been a very effective development for the gaming business in attracting new customers. This also gives the gaming experience a competitive edge and heralds the entrance of next-level gaming. The hardware console that was utilized to give augmented and virtual reality has completely transformed the experience and added value to the way games are now developed. The games are emulated on augmented reality platforms to improve the quality of the user experience, which is exactly what the developers wanted.

Artificial intelligence in games has long been a source of opportunity for researchers to better understand the psychological aspects of how an AI bot would behave to a user and vice versa. As consumers engage with artificial intelligence, a large amount of data is created, and this gives us the chance to learn more about how people interact with machines in general. When we examine the data gathered when the user interacts with the bots in a certain gaming environment, we may learn more about how the human brain functions in various simulations and situations. Similarly, the bot's reaction behavior is investigated to discover how it would respond to a set of user inputs. The emergent gaming phenomena revolves around the creation of a set of complicated systems that offer you an image and gameplay where the outcome is determined by the user's engagement. Overall, AI has aided a great deal, and it has even sparked the mobile gaming experience. It has also improved the user experience for mobile users (*Logout Page,* n.d.).

ARTIFICIAL INTELLIGENCE ALGORITHMS USED IN GAME AI

AI has been used by Developers and scientists for a very long time probably more than 50years. It gives intelligent life to the characters in the game that are not being controlled by the players themselves but actually, it has its own thinking mechanism. Everything about a Non-Player Character from decision making, controlling actions to learning and acquiring knowledge continuously is done by implementing various AI algorithms. Tasks like pathfinding, pattern movement, neural networks, genetic algorithms, collision detection, simple chasing, and evading, are all small parts of AI and are pretty much similar to weak AI that developers add in the game.

AI Techniques in Gaming are of Two Types: Deterministic and Nondeterministic

Deterministic behavior or performance is defined and predictable like it will work and behave just like it is told and will have no uncertainty. Just for an example like a simple chasing algorithm. The algorithm works in a way as the code described to make a Nonplayer character move forward at some or toward a target point by advancing the x and y coordinate axes until the character's x and y coordinates with the target location. This technique is fast, easy to implement, understand, test, debug, and at times they become predictable because it follows a certain pattern (might be complicated to understand).

Nondetermininstc behavior or performance is just the opposite of that of deterministic behavior. This behavior has a degree of uncertainty and is somewhat and is somewhat unpredictable. The non-player character learns to play on its own, it even adapts by learning the other player's behavior whether it includes fighting tactics or skills or making new strategies for winning chess games. The techniques and methods don't require developers to explicitly code all the behaviors and actions to be performed during any scenarios. These methods can learn and extrapolate on their own and promotes a kind of behavior that emerges without explicit instructions i.e. unpredictable. Reinforcement Learning, Neural networks, decision trees, probabilistic methods, genetic algorithms, finite state machines, fuzzy logic for fuzzy state machines, and Bayesian algorithms are used to solve this purpose. A-life techniques also exhibit natural behaviors and have been a great success in creating video games and in robotic applications. These natural behaviors are also instantaneous on the basis of real-time systems and developed as a result of the combined effect of lower-level algorithms (Hammond, 1990).

Algorithms and Techniques that are used to implement Game AI are-

Navigation

A*

For pathfinding, about how to get a character from one place to another on a map considering the various obstacles, terrain, algorithms such as A" are applied. It acts like a navigation agent and helps to determine to take the next possible best step which is closer to the target place.

Figure 1. Conditional Probabilities Different Events

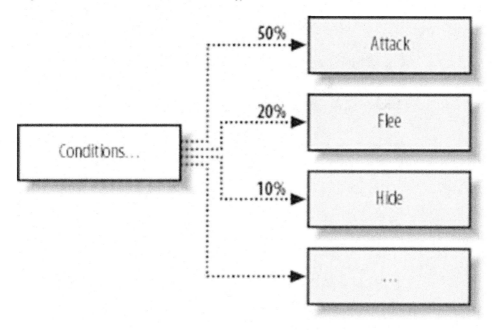

Genetic Algorithms

These algorithms are adaptive heuristic search algorithms that are based on the facts and ideas of genetics and natural logical optimal selection for a problem to find a solution.They generates and find best and high quality solutions for optimization and search problems to find the best possible path. Since these algorithms deal with the entire scene along with the location of the objects present in the Game scene, so it has to work over large space state.

NEURAL NETWORKS

Artificial neural networks, or simply neural networks or networks that consist of a few layers- input, hidden, and output layers, attempt to mimic our brain's processing capability, more like on a far smaller scale.

Figure 2. Human Brain

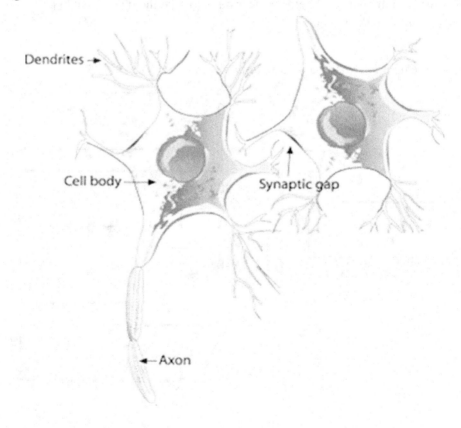

Neural networks make the game's AI to adapt as the game which is being played.

Assembled massive neural networks are used to handle the most common and general AI tasks where a given game creature or character could encounter. The neural network acted as the entire AI system—the whole brain, so to speak.

Neural networks often are combined with other techniques such as fuzzy systems, genetic algorithms, and probabilistic methods.

CONTROL

Neural networks often are used as neural controllers for robotics applications. In these cases, the robot's sensory system provides relevant inputs to the neural controller, and the neural controller's output, which can consist of one or more output nodes, sends the proper responses to the robot's motor control system (Aamodt and Plaza, 1994).

For example, a neural controller for a robot tank might take three inputs, each indicating whether an obstacle is sensed in front of or to either side of the robot. (The range to each sensed obstacle also can be input.)

Figure 3. Neural Controller for carrying out Actions

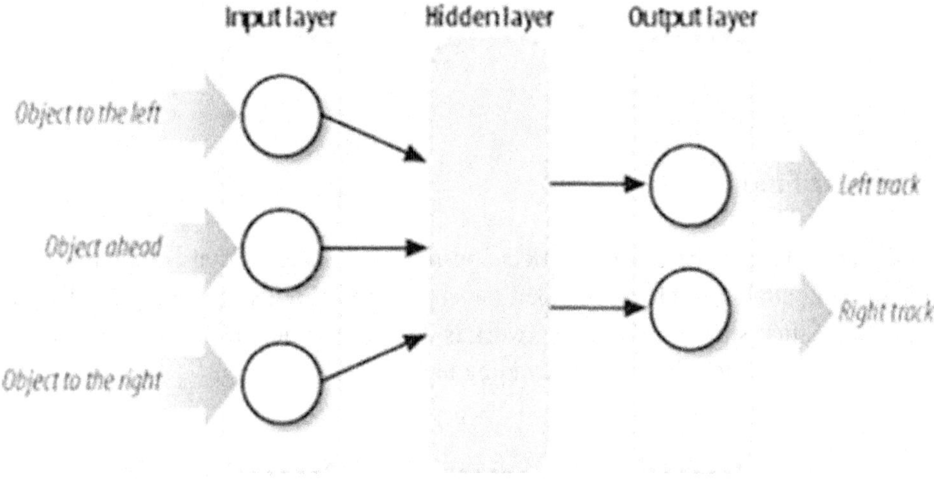

THREAT ASSESSMENT

This approach requires in-game training and validation of the network but potentially can tune itself to the playing style of the player. It is used in a Strategy simulation-type game in which the player has to build technology and train units to fend off or attack the computer-controlled base (Bourg and Seemann, 2004).

It can be used for predicting the type of threat presented by the player at any given time during gameplay.

Figure 4. Neural Network's Decision Making

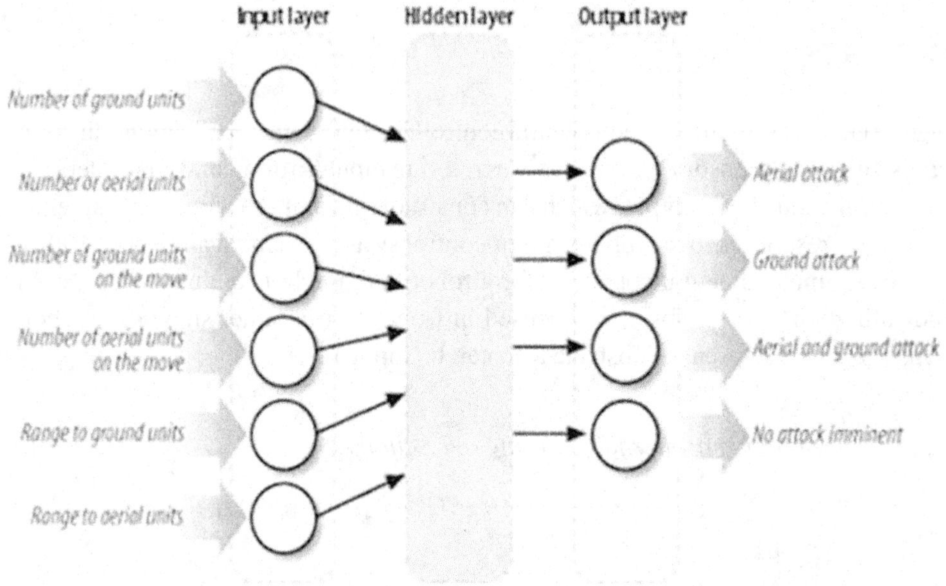

Attack or Flee

It justifies handling the creature's decision-making process—that is, whether the creature will attack, evade, or wander, depending on whether an enemy (a player) is in the creature's proximity. the network is designed to decide whether to attack, evade, or wander, not chasing and evading techniques.

Figure 5. Deciding whether to Attack/Flee/Evade

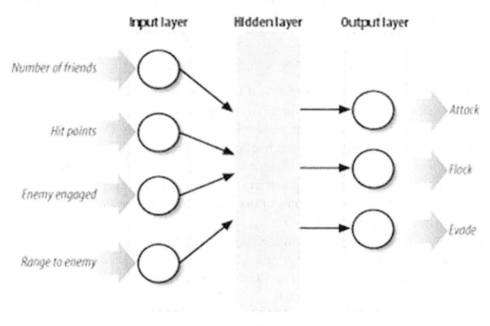

This way, the players will find it as if they are playing with real people because these methods lead to more intelligent decision-making and make playing with a real opponent. These smart, easy AI techniques make it more fun and interactable to play (Newton and Fang, 2016).

These techniques can also be said as smaller and easy ways to design and implement an AI robot, since application and going to through the pathway of creating and implementing the algorithms is very much similar. Indeed, the entire software would be 70% similar. The only difference is to add physics and electric mechanisms on the robot's body structure.

DECISION MAKING

Fuzzy Logic

Reasoning method or techniques that is much similar to the human reasoning. It helps in making decisions in a real time mode while playing game. It works in a way where there are intermediate possibilities between digital values 1(Yes) or 0(No). The numerical values lie between 0 and 1 and are LP (Large Positive), MP(Medium

Positive), S(Small), MN(Median Negative), LN(Large Negative). This method may not give an accurate reasoning but definitely gives an acceptable reasoning.

Decision Trees

Decision trees are one of the Supervised Learning algorithms since we feed lots of data that includes facts and values. To configure the rules and knowledge with the behavior system of the AI non player character, DECISION TREE algorithms are mostly used. To build a decision tree for each npc, states of the game must be defined accordingly, states like distance to the target or enemy bot, distance to all weapon status or enemy weapon status, or a particular fighting technique that the bot previously did, health status of the enemy or the player. With the states a decision tree can be created to govern the bot decision at a given state with certain probability. These rules, knowledge of states is configured with decision trees, based on data and the decisions that were made in the past conclusions are made by assigning values, and these values decide the next best course of action to be taken (Aha, Molineaux, and Ponsen, 2005).

AGENTS AND FINITE STATE MACHINES

An agent's job in a computer game is to make decisions and perform tasks to achieve some set of goals, as does a human player.

Agents in games are sets of FSMs that work on their particular problems and send messages to each other. Alternatively, an agent could be a set of fuzzy state machines, neural networks, genetic algorithms or any combination of some or all of these techniques.

But here, I have applied Finite State Machine, since I found it to be one of the easiest to understand and implement among all the other algorithms.

A finite state machine is an abstract machine that can exist in one of several different and predefined states. A finite state machine also can define a set of conditions that determine when the state should change. The actual state determines how the state machine behaves.

Figure 6. Finite State Machine

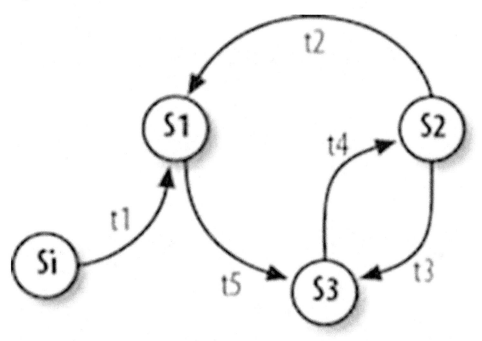

They can roam freely, chase the player, or evade the player. In each state they behave differently, and their transitions are determined by the player's actions.

Figure 7. Ghost finite state machine diagram

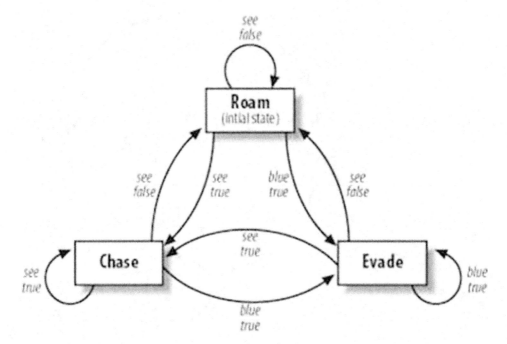

THE SENSORY SYSTEM

In real-time game playing, the AI has to understand the current along with a continuous change in the environment to make sure that it seems realistic to the opponent that is the player. The sensory systems help us with that, it provides us with critical details such as the nearby players, nearby covers, sound levels, and many other variables of the environment that can alter movement. A sensory system usually consists of several modules, such as sight, sound, and memory, to help the AI capture information about the environment. The use of memory will allow the bot to avoid an area where it remembers seeing a severe threat or rush back to an area where it last saw its group. Creating a sensory system in the case of an enemy player is heavily based on the environment where the AI fights the player. It needs to be able to find cover, evades the enemy, get ammo, and other features that you feel create immersive AI for your game. A game with AI that challenges the player creates a uniquely individual experience (*Logout Page,* n.d.). "

In this project, we have used the sensory system to detect the pawns that the AI can see. We have also used functions to check for the line of sight of the enemy. We have checked whether there is another pawn in the way of our path. We can check for cover and other resources within the area. Steering is one of the techniques to achieve realistic movements for the player AI. It basically influences the movement of the AI to its next destination. For example, Avoidance is used for avoiding the collide between the different AIs. And on the other hand, flocking is the movement of an entire group of AIs having the same mindset of intelligence. The goal stays just the same about giving a realistic movement.

REINFORCEMENT LEARNING

RL approach is used to train a numerous amount of AI strategic behaviors such as NPC attack or defence, pathfinding and almost every behavior a human player is capable of performing while playing. Reinforcement Learning works on the basis of the ability of an agent to make changes and learn from its surrounding environment.

The environment contains all the possible data or knowledge about the agent's particular state or about a particular setting. The AI agent interacts with the environment in discrete time steps. And at each unit of time, the agent gains or receives a reward (positive feedback) or penalty (negative feedback) and so it learns automatically without any labelled data, but experience. The motive and the purpose of the algorithm is to improve its performance over time and experience by getting maximum rewards and minimum penalties. In Game AI, the agent continues keep performing and doing like take actions, change states, or remain in the same state and get feedback whether a positive or negative and keeping the values and results into account, and according to the previous data, it decides and take the next best possible action or state.

Q-Learning algorithm is a value-based learning algorithm in Reinforcement Learning that is widely used in implementing in navigating to new places in the most efficient path from the initial to the target point in the game scene. The algorithm works as a lookup table, or some may say a python dictionary or java hash tables. It calculates maximum expected future rewards for action and guides at each state, this iterative process improves over time by repeating over and over again by gaining rewards and penalties. It works over a Q function that uses a Bellman equation and takes inputs such as states and actions (Aamodt and Plaza, 1994).

REFERENCES

Aamodt, A., & Plaza, E. (1994). Case-based reasoning: Foundational issues, methodological variations, and system approaches. *AI Communications*, 7(1), 39–59.

Aha, D. W., Molineaux, M., & Ponsen, M. (2005). Learning to win: Case-based plan selection in a real-time strategy game. *Case-Based Reasoning Research and Development: 6th International Conference on Case-Based Reasoning, ICCBR 2005, Chicago, IL, USA, August 23-26, 2005 Proceedings, 6*, 5–20.

Bourg, D. M., & Seemann, G. (2004). *AI for game developers*. O'Reilly Media, Inc.

Hammond, K. J. (1990). Case-based planning: A framework for planning from experience. *Cognitive Science, 14*(3), 385–443.

Logout Page. (n.d.). Epic Games. https://www. unrealengine.com/id/logout?redirectUrl=https%3A% 2F%2Fwww.unrealeng ine.com%2Fen-US%2F

Newton, P. L., & Feng, J. (2016). *Unreal Engine 4 AI Programming Essentials*. Packt Publishing Ltd.

Sign in Page. (n.d.). Epic Games. Retrieved from https:// www.unrealengine.com/id/login?client_id=17ce2d286483 4898ab71847859286c81&response_type=code

Zang, P., Mehta, M., Mateas, M., & Ram, A. (2007, January). Towards Runtime Behavior Adaptation for Embodied Characters. *IJCAI, 7*, 1557–1562.

Chapter 5

Applications of AI in Computer–Aided Drug Discovery

Reet Kaur Kohli
Amity University, Noida, India

Sunishtha S. Yadav
Amity University, Noida, India

Seneha Santoshi
https://orcid.org/0000-0001-8893-2221
Amity University, Noida, India

Vandana Chauhan
Amity University, Noida, India

ABSTRACT

Drug discovery is the process in which healthcare is approached through identification of potential new therapeutic agents. CADD provides solutions at every stage of drug discovery including the leading challenges of cost and time. CADD has provided an effective solution to this challenge. AI has enabled multiple aspects of drug discovery, including the analysis of high content screening data and the design and synthesis of new molecules. The use of transparent methodologies like AI is crucial, particularly in drug repositioning/repurposing in rare diseases. An abundant variety of methods, in particular the concepts of deep learning, have been used for protein modelling and ligand-based drug discovery along with artificial neural networks for QSAR modelling. Structure-based ligand identification via AI modelling is also explored. AI presents the scientific community and the biopharma industry and its established processes for discovering and developing new medicines with new challenges.

DOI: 10.4018/978-1-6684-5255-4.ch005

INTRODUCTION

Computer Aided Drug Discovery and design is an arena of Computational Biology that is being explored more and more with major improvements being made in the past decade. The amalgamations of AI and ML with existing CADD technologies has led to the numerous successful outcomes of CADD. Before delving into the concepts of CADD and its applications with AI, it is important to gain an understanding of what AI and ML are as follows.

Artificial Intelligence and Machine Learning

It is essentially the development of such machines and models that are "intelligent". What one means by this is that these machines and models use deduction processes inspired from the way a human thinks. AI which is often erroneously confused with Machine Learning is a method derived from the concepts of ML and deep learning to enable the user to understand problems rationally and to come up with possible solutions. One may define Machine Learning as a subset of AI, fundamentally the generation of such analytical models which accepts enormous data as input and can successfully sort through this data to establish the presence of any patterns and make decisions based on this. As mentioned above, AI is the development of such machines and models that are "intelligent". When the avenue of artificial intelligence was first explored, researchers had aimed to essentially duplicate the way humans think through a machine. Over the years, scientists have adopted new definitions and explored new arenas of AI and aim at developing systems that don't just think like humans but can have deduction powers personalised for a number of simulated conditions to come up with optimum solutions for the given problem. (Leighton et al., 2022)

These AI systems use the concepts of ML and neural networks to do what might be understood as mimicking human decision-making patterns in a way that these decisions are a series of yes or no questions. The aforementioned concept of Machine Learning and AI finds its application in many spheres. Biology and Life Sciences is one such field that has significantly benefited from AI and ML. Biological and Life Sciences research has led to an abundance of biological data that has been generated (omics data). AI and ML has enabled researchers to analyse the vast amount of biological data and draw inferences from the patterns recognized in the data using AI and ML. AI and ML has enormous applications in a very important are of life sciences which deals with medicine and healthcare. Some of the noteworthy examples that have been highlighted further. Antibody Discovery and Antibody selection is a notable example of AI in healthcare (Artificial intelligence turns to antibody selection, 2022). ML has also been used to design antibodies by recognizing appropriate epitopes and paratopes. Deep Learning models have also been utilized for identifying paratopes for a set of particular epitopes (Narayanan et al., 2021). Precision Medicine is another ingenious application of machine learning that suggests possible prognosis and treatment options taking into account the patients' history and ongoing treatments (if any). How this is actuated by machine learning can be understood by gaining a proper understanding of the concept. This can be facilitated by grasping the concepts of ML by classifying it under supervised learning, unsupervised learning and reinforcement learning (Ow et al., 2016). Another such example of AI and ML being used in the healthcare industry is the use of wearable devices to monitor and record the enormous range of vital measurable signals, for example, heartbeat, temperature, spo2 levels in blood, etc. The tracking of this data has helped develop technologies that can successfully indicate the occurrence of atrial fibrillation in a patient (Yu et al., 2018). With the rapid development of new strains of pathogens and in turn the increasing rate with which scientists are encountering new diseases, in particular COVID-19, the demand for an efficient solution to the problem of discovering new and possible drugs for the treatment of these diseases considering that the typical time frame and cost of discovering a possible drug for a disease is exorbitant. CADD (Computer Aided Drug Design) is an evident solution for this predicament. It is complementary to if not a substitute for the high throughput screening step in drug discovery. It involves the use of computational tools (in-silico) to enhance and systematize the process of drug discovery and design, the enhancement of novel drugs owing to preexisting knowledge about the chemicals and their biological functional implications. CADD has been successfully used to design and discover drugs for ailments like Cancer, COVID-19, malaria, etc. (Arya & Coumar, 2021; Anwar et al., 2021). Various tools of AI have been combined with the process of computer aided drug discovery. The advantages of this amalgamation are plenty, from screening drugs and identifying the suited set of drugs for a particular ailment, to quantifying the safety and efficacy of compounds that may then be selected as possible drugs (Danani, 2019).

This chapter further discusses the use of AI and ML at the various levels of drug discovery especially its involvement in computer aided drug discovery.

CADD: AN OVERVIEW

Computer aided drug design is a method of discovering and designing drugs in silico, saving on the time and cost that are generally foreseen for the experimental alternatives (in-vitro). There are several approaches adopted in CADD, however the most promising and widely accepted approaches are structure-based drug design and ligand-based drug design.

(Surabhi & Singh, 2018). The integrations of the concepts of computational tools like AI, ML, DL, etc. with the concepts of CADD have enabled the development of more precise methods of drug design and discovery. These concepts and approaches are discussed further in the following sections.

DRUG TARGET IDENTIFICATION USING AI AND ML

The identification and selection of a suitable drug target is the first and one of the most crucial steps in drug discovery (Target Selection, 2022). It is the recognition of genes and/or proteins that are imperative to the pathogenicity of a disease. It also includes examining information obtained from genomics (functional and structural), proteomics, and in-vitro and in-vivo research. AI and ML are used in drug target identification to analyse this information obtained as well as information pertaining to protein-protein interaction (drug and target), gene expression data, possible drug molecules, and information acquired by clinical experiments (if any). AI and ML are also used to understand the structures of the drug and target molecules (proteins), as well as the structure of the drug target complex by using models that are trained on cryo-EM microscope data. Moreover, AI and Reinforcement Learning models can be used to infer measurements related to potential energy, molecular bonds, molecular fragments, etc. (Bala, 2022). Subsequently, either of the CADD methods (structure-based or ligand-based) is applied to further the process of drug discovery.

Use of Deep Learning in Protein Modelling

Proteins are the functional molecules of life. The various functions that a protein performs is highly influenced by its structure. The molecular targets listed in public repositories and literature are majorly known to be proteins. Hence, modelling the structures and in turn understanding the functions of the involved proteins is quintessential to the process of computer aided drug discovery. Limitations of the wet lab (experimental data based on XRD, NMR, etc.) have led to a position where we do not have experimental evidence for all the discovered proteins. Computational modelling of biomolecules, especially proteins has enabled the research community to study the possible functions of a protein and even build new biomolecules possessing the desired functions using the predicted 3D structures of proteins and other biomolecules that interact with these proteins. (Gao et al., 2020). The protein models generated using computational techniques (e.g., homology modelling) are knowledge-based methods that require a threshold level of similarity to exist between the template and target sequences. This necessitates the existence of such proteins as well as experimental structural information of these template proteins. However, this criterion cannot be fulfilled for a lot of proteins, affecting the quality of models created. Deep Learning has enabled researchers to create superior models for proteins where homology modelling becomes difficult owing to lack of significantly similar template protein sequences.

Deep learning is an extension of AI that is increasingly being used to identify and understand the drug targets and their interaction (Jing et al., 2018). Deep learning is a technique that has been used to successfully create three dimensional models of proteins using domain specific features based on techniques of SNN and ML applied at large to available datasets. As reported by CASP13, effective models of proteins that do not currently have an experimental backing can be made using DL. Moreover, these models were found to be more reliable than the models produced using more traditional computational techniques. Using DL algorithms, models generation can be automated based on inferences gathered from studying previous data (training sets) and to analyse the hypotheses of the existence of a relation between the data fed into the algorithm versus the generated output (Gao et al., 2020).

CADD and AI Algorithms

Molecular Docking is one of the key methods used in computer aided drug discovery (Yu & Chen, 2021). It has been used thereafter in amalgamation with AI and other computational tools to develop algorithms like the ant colony algorithm. Most recently, this algorithm which is a probabilistic algorithm has been used for the segmentation of images of brain obtained via magnetic resonance. The segmentation of these images aids the detection and diagnosis of several neurological ailments that have shown correlation to the size and the volume of the brain. It has also helped in deducing surgical plans for such ailments (Khorram & Yazdi, 2018).

Another noteworthy example of AI being used in CADD is in the infamous method known as virtual screening. Various Deep Docking platforms facilitate researchers to screen through enormous libraries of chemical compounds to find and select suitable ligands to be then taken forward for either structure-based drug discovery or ligand-based drug discovery depending on the knowledge base available for a particular target (Gentile et al., 2022).

STRUCTURE BASED DRUG DESIGN

Structure based drug design is the identification or generation of ligands with a particular set of physico-chemical attributes with high drug-ligand binding affinity, utilizing structural data obtained via experiments and/or homology-based tools. Structure based drug design utilises existing 3D structures or modelled structures of proteins and drug molecules to identify the necessary ligand binding sites on the protein. SBDD methods like pocket detection are some of the pioneering techniques used to predict ligand binding sites and to investigate the functions of identified proteins. (Laurie & Jackson, 2006). Once a comprehensive list of these possible ligands and ligand binding sites is obtained, chemical structures of potential interacting compounds are created. Following this, a proper evaluation of the characteristics of the compounds is done (affinity, potency, half-life, etc.). The 3-dimensional structure for these compounds as well as their interactive complex with the ligand is then modelled. This creates headway for the process of introducing desired modifications in the compounds or to essentially mould such compounds that would have increased affinity and show improved drug action.

A limitation of classical SBDD is the side effects of drugs observed during post-delivery phase. This is overcome by using computational tools like AI and ML to predict the possible adverse effects (involves the use of models that are trained on reliable and relevant datasets that improve with subsequent iterations) (Dutta & Bose, 2021). This approach of CADD finds its application in a vast variety of computer aided healthcare applications. Most notably, it is used in drug repurposing and de- novo drug discovery (Ferreira et al., 2015).

Another important advancement in the process of drug discovery owing to the conceptualisation of AI being used in CADD is its use in screening massive repositories of chemical compounds that may be suitable drugs based on various physical, chemical, and biological (functional) properties that the molecule inherently possesses. These properties can be studied and analysed at mass using AI. It has also found its use in finding a suitable compound as a possible drug from known compounds i.e., repurposing (Ayers et al., 2022).

Drug Repurposing

Understanding the enormous allocation of resources required for drug design and discovery without in silico interventions, an ingenious solution of repositioning already approved drugs as possible drugs for other diseases is currently on the rise. The standard method of drug repurposing involves the following stages: (A) Selection of a particular drug as a possible drug for an indication. (B) Systematic analysis for drug efficacy. (C) Phase 2 clinical trial efficacy tests. (Pushpakom et al., 2018)

AI, molecular visualization tools and big data analytics are crucial in drug repurposing. These computational techniques have made it possible to not only model 3D structures of drug target molecules and potential drugs (with precise molecular positioning) but to compare possible drugs using publicly available repositories of current drugs (Mohanty et al., 2021). These tools enable researchers to successfully understand drug-target interactions in simulations of the environment the molecules are typically present in which further facilitate the evaluation of possible drugs for a particular target (Zhou et al., 2020). These AI based techniques have been used by various companies like BenevolentAI, Innoplex, Deargen, GSK, etc. to establish whether drugs of the likes of barcitinib, hydrochloroquine can be repurposed to be a remedy for COVID-19. (Mohanty et al., 2020)

Ligand Based Drug Discovery

Drug discovery has also been approached through ligand based in silico techniques like SAR, QSAR modelling, and Pharmacophore (Ligand-based Drug Discovery | Jubilant Biosys, 2022). It is adapted in place of SBDD when sufficient information regarding target structure is not available. It does require structural information of existing molecules that are known to control to target molecule (Aparoy et al., 2012). QSAR modelling and the application of ANNs in QSAR modelling is explored further in this chapter.

AI IN QSAR MODELLING

QSAR (Quantitative Structure Activity Relationship) works on the principle that structurally and chemically similar molecules are bound to have similarities in their function. These methods are used to draw precise relations between the structural properties and in turn their biological significance. QSAR modelling requires the researcher to first identify existing molecules with the desired function, a key requirement at this stage being the availability of structural data for that molecule. Once this is done, the molecular descriptors that contribute towards the desired function are identified and correlations are drawn between the function and the molecular structure to replicate this with the novel drug. The model is then generated and assessed for accuracy. (Acharya et al., 2011)

QSAR modelling uses various chemometrics like MLR and PLS to draw mathematical relations between structure and function that can be used in CADD to design novel drugs or improve the effectivity of an existing drug (Luo et al., 2011). Here MLR or Multiple linear regression is a statistical method to understand the extent and impact of a statistical correlation between a dependent and an independent variable (Peter et al., 2019). A plethora of tools derived from the concepts of AI and ML are applied in QSAR to enhance the quality of the model thus generated. These are RNN, CNN, SVM, ANN, etc. ANN based modelling is a simulation of human neural interactions in the form of binary questions. The application of ANN in QSAR modelling is seen in many software packages like MOPAC, Dragon, etc. These integrations of the concepts of ANN with QSAR enable the involved calculations on the molecular level to be more precise and in turn aid in generating a 3D structure model that is more precise. These integrated applications of ANN and QSAR provide accurate results in shorter spans of time with lower resource cost allocations as compared to experiments run to determine the same. This integration is also known to improve the prediction and description capabilities of regular QSAR models. (Montañez-Godínez et al., 2014)

DE NOVO DRUG DESIGN

De novo drug design is a CADD method that is used to engineer specific novel drug molecules based on the target. The phases of de novo drug design are- a description and analysis of the ligand binding site, generation of the desired molecules based on the biding site, validation of the novel drug molecule. The key methods that are utilised in de novo drug design are ligand based and structure-based drug design which have been described in the sections above. For unknown target or ligand binding site structure, homology modelling of proteins is a method that is adopted frequently in de novo drug design. Currently, CADD methods involving the concepts of Artificial Intelligence. CNNs, RNNs, Aes, GANs are the various applications of AI that are seen as crucial tools for de novo drug discovery and design. (Mouchlis et al., 2021)

Tools like RL, i.e., reinforcement learning and DRL are crucial to the process of de novo drug design. These tools normally develop models of drug molecules and target molecules in SMILES format. (Blaschke et al., 2020)

Success Cases

Integrated solutions of traditional experiments, CADD and AI and ML technologies have been used increasingly to find quick and effective solutions for instance in the case of vaccine development for COVID-19 (Floresta et al., 2022). COVID-19 and other success cases of CADD have been discussed in this section. The sudden onset and spread of the SARS-COV2 virus necessitated haste in the production of a cure or a preventive drug. However, this does not entail ignoring efficiency and outcome percentages. AI based methods in CADD and de novo drug design have proven essential in the in-silico design of vaccines and possible drugs. Vaccines using this method have been proven safe for use during clinical trials and are currently out in the market. These vaccines were designed based on the structure of spike proteins and epitopes. These were initially modelled computationally reducing the time that went into performing experimental analysis (Keshavarzi Arshadi et al., 2020; Floresta et al., 2022). Apart from this, there is immense ongoing research on novel drugs as well as new combination therapy mixture drugs that can help cure cancer

(Agrawal, 2018). Various pharmaceutical companies and technological companies like Microsoft are expanding into the realm of AI medicine. Table 1 mentions some examples of applications of artificial intelligence in drug discovery.

Table 1. List of applications of AI in CADD

Name of the application	Use
TOX21	Tool used to predict toxicity of compounds (Arabi, 2021).
DeepSite	Used to determine the quality of sites in a protein target (Arabi, 2021).
RANC	Made by Aspuru-Gudzik and Zhavoronkov's team for de novo drug discovery (Zhavoronkov, 2018).
XCON	Application created in 1985 used for AI based drug discovery. It was one of the pioneering tools that catered a million dollar industry (Agrawal, 2018).

CONCLUSION

The process of developing a new drug typically involves an extensive five step process. This process encompasses the drug design and discovery stage, the underlying preclinical research, the clinical trials, the regulatory approval stage, and the post-launch monitoring (Phases of Drug Development Process, Drug Discovery Process | NorthEast BioLab, 2022). As established, the entire process necessitates the disposal of enormous amounts of resources in the aspects of time and money. To reduce the amount of resources in terms of both time and money, in-silico processes and tools have been accepted and unified with the standard process of drug discovery and design. CADD (Computer Aided Drug Design) is such a method that can be implemented to replace certain steps of the standard discovery process, as well as effectively cut down certain steps (like in the case of drug repositioning).

The amalgamation of the techniques of CADD with other useful computational tools like Artificial Intelligence, Deep Learning, Machine Learning, etc. has enabled scientists to not just refine the process of drug discovery, but to explore a new arena of computational biology integrated with medical and pharmaceutical sciences.

REFERENCES

Acharya, C., Coop, A., & Polli, J., & MacKerell, A. (2011). Recent Advances in Ligand-Based Drug Design: Relevance and Utility of the Conformationally Sampled Pharmacophore Approach. *Current Computer-aided Drug Design*, 7(1), 10–22.

Agrawal, P. (2018). Artificial Intelligence in drug discovery and development. *Journal of Pharmacovigilance*, *6*(2). https://doi.org/10.4172/2329-6887.1000e173

Anwar, T., Kumar, P., & Khan, A. (2021). *Modern Tools and Techniques in Computer-Aided Drug Design*. Molecular Docking for Computer-Aided Drug Design.

Aparoy, P., Kumar Reddy, K., & Reddanna, P. (2012). Structure and Ligand Based Drug Design Strategies in the Development of Novel 5- LOX Inhibitors. *Current Medicinal Chemistry*, *19*(22), 3763–3778.

Arabi, A. A. (2021). Artificial Intelligence in Drug Design: Algorithms, applications, challenges and Ethics. *Future Drug Discovery, 3*(2). doi:10.4155/fdd-2020-0028

Arya, H., & Coumar, M. (2021). Lead identification and optimization. The Design & Development of Novel Drugs and Vaccines, 31-63.

Ayers, M., Jayatunga, M., Goldader, J., & Meier, C. (2022). *Adopting AI in Drug Discovery*. https://www.bcg.com/en-in/publications/2022/adopting-ai-in-p harmaceutical-discovery

Bala, M. (2022). *4 Application Areas of Artificial Intelligence in Drug Discovery*. https://www.wipro.com/holmes/4-application-areas-of-artifici al-intelligence-in-drug-discovery/

Berger Leighton, B., Daniels, N., & Yu, Y. (2022). *Computational biology in the 21st century*. https://dspace.mit.edu/handle/1721.1/116419

Blaschke, T., Arús-Pous, J., Chen, H., Margreitter, C., Tyrchan, C., Engkvist, O., Papadopoulos, K., & Patronov, A. (2020). REINVENT 2.0: An AI Tool for De Novo Drug Design. *Journal of Chemical Information and Modeling*, *60*(12), 5918–5922.

Cavasotto, C., & Orry, W., A. (2007). Ligand Docking and Structure-based Virtual Screening in Drug Discovery. *Current Topics in Medicinal Chemistry*, *7*(10), 1006–1014.

Danani, A. (2019). *Artificial Intelligence and Computer Aided Drug Design*. https://www.mdpi.com/journal/ijms/special_issues/computer_ai ded_drug_design

Dutta, S., & Bose, K. (2021). Remodelling structure-based drug design using machine learning. *Emerging Topics in Life Sciences*, *5*(1), 13–27.

Ferreira, L., dos Santos, R., Oliva, G., & Andricopulo, A. (2015). Molecular Docking and Structure-Based Drug Design Strategies. *Molecules (Basel, Switzerland)*, *20*(7), 13384–13421.

Floresta, G., Zagni, C., Gentile, D., Patamia, V., & Rescifina, A. (2022). Artificial Intelligence Technologies for COVID-19 De Novo Drug Design. *International Journal of Molecular Sciences, 23*(6), 3261.

Gao, W., Mahajan, S., Sulam, J., & Gray, J. (2020). Deep Learning in Protein Structural Modeling and Design. *Patterns, 1*(9), 100142.

Gentile, F., Yaacoub, J. C., Gleave, J., Fernandez, M., Ton, A.-T., Ban, F., Stern, A., & Cherkasov, A. (2022). Artificial Intelligence–enabled virtual screening of ultra-large chemical libraries with deep docking. *Nature Protocols, 17*(3), 672–697. https://doi.org/10.1038/s41596-021-00659-2

Hunter, W. (2009). Structure-based Ligand Design and the Promise Held for Antiprotozoan Drug Discovery. *The Journal of Biological Chemistry, 284*(18), 11749–11753.

Jing, Y., Bian, Y., Hu, Z., Wang, L., & Xie, X. (2018). Deep Learning for Drug Design: An Artificial Intelligence Paradigm for Drug Discovery in the Big Data Era. *The AAPS Journal, 20*(3).

Jubilant Biosys. (2022). *Ligand-based Drug Discovery.* https://www.jubilantbiosys.com/services/ligand-based-drug-di scovery/#:~:text=Ligand%2Dbased%20drug%20discovery%20(LBDD,known%20 to%20modulate%20the%20target

Keshavarzi Arshadi, A., Webb, J., Salem, M., Cruz, E., Calad-Thomson, S., Ghadirian, N., Collins, J., Diez-Cecilia, E., Kelly, B., Goodarzi, H., & Yuan, J. (2020). Artificial Intelligence for COVID-19 Drug Discovery and Vaccine Development. *Frontiers in Artificial Intelligence, 3*.

Khorram, B., & Yazdi, M. (2018). A new optimized thresholding method using ant colony algorithm for Mr Brain Image Segmentation. *Journal of Digital Imaging, 32*(1), 162–174. https://doi.org/10.1007/s10278-018-0111-x

Kinnings, S., & Jackson, R. (2011). ReverseScreen3D: A Structure-Based Ligand Matching Method To Identify Protein Targets. *Journal of Chemical Information and Modeling, 51*(3), 624–634.

Laurie, A., & Jackson, R. (2006). Methods for the Prediction of Protein-Ligand Binding Sites for Structure-Based Drug Design and Virtual Ligand Screening. *Current Protein & Peptide Science, 7*(5), 395–406.

Luo, J., Hu, J., Fu, L., Liu, C., & Jin, X. (2011). Use of Artificial Neural Network for a QSAR Study on Neurotrophic Activities of N-p-Tolyl/phenylsulfonyl L-Amino Acid Thiolester Derivatives. *Procedia Engineering*, *15*, 5158–5163.

Mohanty, S., Harun, A. I., Rashid, M., Mridul, M., Mohanty, C., & Swayamsiddha, S. (2020). Application of Artificial Intelligence in COVID-19 drug repurposing. *Diabetes & Metabolic Syndrome: Clinical Research & Reviews*, *14*(5), 1027–1031.

Mohanty, S., Rashid, M., Mohanty, C., & Swayamsiddha, S. (2021). Modern computational intelligence based drug repurposing for diabetes epidemic. *Diabetes & Metabolic Syndrome: Clinical Research & Reviews*, *15*(4), 102180.

Montañez-Godínez, N., Martínez-Olguín, A., Deeb, O., Garduño-Juárez, R., & Ramírez-Galicia, G. (2014). QSAR/QSPR as an Application of Artificial Neural Networks. *Methods in Molecular Biology (Clifton, N.J.)*, 319–333.

Mouchlis, V., Afantitis, A., Serra, A., Fratello, M., Papadiamantis, A., Aidinis, V., Lynch, I., Greco, D., & Melagraki, G. (2021). Advances in De Novo Drug Design: From Conventional to Machine Learning Methods. *International Journal of Molecular Sciences*, *22*(4), 1676.

Narayanan, H., Dingfelder, F., Butté, A., Lorenzen, N., Sokolov, M., & Arosio, P. (2021). Machine Learning for Biologics: Opportunities for Protein Engineering, Developability, and Formulation. *Trends in Pharmacological Sciences*, *42*(3), 151–165.

Nature.com. (2022). *Artificial intelligence turns to antibody selection*. https://www.nature.com/articles/d42473-019-00331-0

NorthEast BioLab. (2022). *Phases of Drug Development Process, Drug Discovery Process*. https://www.nebiolab.com/drug-discovery-and-development-process

Ow, G., Tang, Z., & Kuznetsov, V. (2016). Big data and computational biology strategy for personalized prognosis. *Oncotarget*, *7*(26), 40200–40220. doi:10.18632/oncotarget.9571 PMID:27229533

Perkin Elmer. (2022). *Target Selection*. https://www.perkinelmer.com/category/target-selection?utm_source=Google&utm_medium=cpc&utm_campaign=LSC-DDS-2022-EMEAI-PaidSearch-SCH-EGM-ZZ&sfdc_id=7014V000002EBvr&LS=PPC&adgroup=135555101655&ad=591153414423&keyword=target%20discovery%20and%20validation&gclid=CjwKCAjwv-GUBhAzEiwASUMm4oFRT6A0G1e76cp6QlVOeJlwTsxVwTUQTzcCXOsmN-DLFml4swI2EBoC7JoQAvD_BwE

Peter, S., Dhanjal, J., Malik, V., Radhakrishnan, N., Jayakanthan, M., & Sundar, D. (2019). Quantitative Structure-Activity Relationship (QSAR): Modeling Approaches to Biological Applications. Encyclopedia of Bioinformatics and Computational Biology, 661-676.

Pushpakom, S., Iorio, F., Eyers, P., Escott, K., Hopper, S., Wells, A., Doig, A., Guilliams, T., Latimer, J., McNamee, C., Norris, A., Sanseau, P., Cavalla, D., & Pirmohamed, M. (2018). Drug repurposing: Progress, challenges and recommendations. *Nature Reviews. Drug Discovery*, *18*(1), 41–58.

Śledź, P., & Caflisch, A. (2018). Protein structure-based drug design: From docking to molecular dynamics. *Current Opinion in Structural Biology*, *48*, 93–102.

Surabhi, S., & Singh, B. (2018). Computer aided drug design: An overview. *Journal of Drug Delivery and Therapeutics*, *8*(5), 504–509.

Vyas, V., Bhati, S., Patel, S., & Ghate, M. (2021). Structure- and ligand-based drug design methods for the modeling of antimalarial agents: A review of updates from 2012 onwards. *Journal of Biomolecular Structure & Dynamics*, 1–26.

Yu, K., Beam, A., & Kohane, I. (2018). Artificial intelligence in healthcare. *Nature Biomedical Engineering*, *2*(10), 719–731. doi:10.103841551-018-0305-z PMID:31015651

Yu, W., & Chen, Z. (2021). Computer aided drug design based on Artificial Intelligence algorithm. *Journal of Physics: Conference Series*, *2066*(1), 012012. https://doi.org/10.1088/1742-6596/2066/1/012012

Zhavoronkov, A. (2018). Artificial Intelligence for drug discovery, Biomarker Development, and generation of novel chemistry. *Molecular Pharmaceutics*, *15*(10), 4311–4313. https://doi.org/10.1021/acs.molpharmaceut.8b00930

Zhou, Y., Wang, F., Tang, J., Nussinov, R., & Cheng, F. (2020). Artificial intelligence in COVID-19 drug repurposing. *The Lancet Digital Health*, *2*(12), e667–e676.

Chapter 6
Nakhasys:
An ML–Based Disease Diagnosing Application

Poonam Tanwar
Manav Rachna International Institute of Research and Studies, India

ABSTRACT

It is necessary for human beings to undergo regular health check-ups, which all of us tend to ignore. As a result, late diagnosis of disease usually leads to ineffective treatment. To cater to this problem, the authors have developed a platform called Nakhasys, which is a smart AI-based application developed to diagnose a set of diseases like jaundice, anemia, etc. with the help of analysis of nail segmentation. This is based on the ancient Indian practice of Ayurveda. Initially a dedicated Android application will allow users to click a picture of their nails, which will be sent to the virtual machine hosted in Microsoft Azure cloud. This picture will be validated through Azure Custom Vision API. After successful validation, the same image will be sent to the custom ML model for further detection of the nail color, which will allow the application to predict the possible set of diseases. This diagnosis will alert the individual.

INTRODUCTION

Machine learning (ML) is used to automate the diagnostic modeling. Ml based system can learn from the historical data to identify patterns and make the automated decisions. Complex mathematics may be used in background to handle the huge data as faster as possible by Mente and Marulkar (2017), Gandhat et al. (2016), Madaan

DOI: 10.4018/978-1-6684-5255-4.ch006

and Goyal (2020), Anjali. (2020) and Fawcett, Linford, and Stulberg (2004). ML can be used as an extra capability of computers as discussed by Ananth (2020). The ML model is used for validation on sample data by Ananth (2020) using null hypothesis as ML uses an iterative learning from data until useful pattern is not found. Kraus & Drass (2020) proposed the algorithm for automatic nail detection in regular color images to reduce the influence of illumination and occlusion. In this method, the Histograms of Oriented Gradients (HOG) used the Support Vector Machine as a classifier. By Kraus & Drass (2020) With time-to-time detection of nails we can treat the disease more effectively as we have to train our AI based application through machine learning and deep learning concepts and with timely detection we can collect more data which helps in better treatment of the disease by Funde and Thepade (2016), Sharma and Tanwar (2020, 2021, 2011), and Pathak et al. (2020).

LITERATURE REVIEW AND EXISTING SYSTEM

This section is used to present the survey or background methods of systems which are based on nail image analysis for different disease detection are given below.

- Hardik and Shah (2012) proposed a method for extracting a section of a known image using color processing and palm image were used for analysis and experimental work. Noriaki et. al. in 2013 used fingernail detection using hand images including pal and distribution density, color continuity has been used to improve accuracy by Mente and Marulkar (2017).
- Sharma and Shrivastava (2015) worked on nail color and texture and segmented images on the basis of texture and further used for analysis on the basis of color and texture.
- In 2016, Gandhat et al. proposed the method for analysis of nail images using Haar Transforms Matrix to generate features. Row mean method has been used to reduce feature vector and then compare a query feature vector stored in template dataset using similarity measures like MSE, absolute difference. And then they find out matching and calculate GAR (Genuine acceptance ratio) and produced result.
- The early stage disease detection system which process nail image has been proposed by Indi and Gunge in 2016 to extract the feature from sample data. The Weka tool has been used for training dataset using patients nail images. Using color detection algorithm and decision tree by C4.5 used for experimental work and achieved 65% results which correctly matched with training data set by Indi and Gunge (2016) and Singal and Arora (2015).

- Saranya and Ranichitra (2017) used the image segmentation technique to detect nail abnormality. Median and average filters were used for preprocessing and converted into gray scale to improve the efficiency. Watershade, Thresholding and k-means segmentation techniques have been used to identify the nail shape and will be used for diagnosis purposed.
- Thakare, Meshram, and Baradkar (2017) presented the medical support system for detecting human health conditions using Decision tree, Neural network and support vector machine. Based on nail color and texture analysis Bicolor algorithm and GLCM algorithm was also used.

Existing System

Much advancement is already done in the field of disease detection, but this ancient technique usually used by ayurvedic doctors was somehow lagging behind. The methods widely used for disease prediction are usually done using heavy machinery by labs, which is not easily accessible by all. The latest technology like smart watches, portable sensors are also playing a good role in monitoring health on a day-to-day basis. The major drawback which has been mentioned in this research is that the existing system is either too costly or too inconvenient to use. After the integration of our proposed technology with the existing ones, it could definitely give an edge to modern diagnosis for this relentless world.

Feasibility Study

Financial Feasibility

Being a standalone system, the project does not have any hardware costs. Resources required for the successful testing and implementation is readily available. Source codes are created taking reference from open-source materials. Hence no costs required in terms proprietary licensing. Further implementation may raise costs if we wish to apply the project in the market or open it for public use. Hardware costs may arise including but not limited to cloud space renting, faster processing units as well. Machine Learning model usually require more computing resources than traditional application and handling images as large scale also need more storage so due to this while implementing this at large scale we need virtual machines with more computing power and storage which are costly but not much when compared to traditional servers. Furthermore, if the project is to be combined with any proprietary application additional licensing cost might be required. From this it is clear that the project is financially feasible.

Technical and Time Feasibility

The project is solely developed in PYTHON 3.0 using open-source libraries having free support from the developers and friendly online forums. Algorithms such as OpenCV are highly synchronized to be used without hindrances. Time factor has already been accessed beforehand keeping in mind the errors and obstacles that usually arise while handling image processing projects. The project can be completed in finite time. From this it is clear that the project is technically feasible.

Resource Feasibility

Resources required for implementing the project successfully are:

- Programming Device (Laptop) with specification enough to handle image processing.
- Android Smartphone with a camera of descent specs which is used to capture image.
- Internet Connection to establish connection with server.
- Programming Tools (Open source and freely available) Programmers (Team members)
- It is quite clear from the above points that the project meets the required resource feasibility.

Risk Feasibility

Risk feasibility for the project can be defined in the following points:

- **Risk associated with size:** Since the project is dealing with images, the size is an issue but for the current state it is doable without undergoing any risks. The whole project can be fit under 500MB for now. But once we open the project to the public, we might need databases and storage management software to store the dataset.
- **Technical Risks: Is the technology new or obsolete?** The technology is a mixture of both new and old but not obsolete. The technology has extensive support from the developers and engaging online developer's forums. Hence no risk in implementing the technology.
- **Does the project demand beta or unstable version usage of any software/ algorithm?** No such concern will be raised while implementing this project as all the tools and algorithms to be used in the project has been already running successfully in already existing applications. As discussed above it

is clear has that the project has the required risk feasibility to be implemented successfully.

Social/Legal Feasibility

The projects use free development tools and provide the system as an open-source implementation for final year submission. Till date there is no charges applicable for reusing this system in further development or research and analysis. Since this project eliminates the roadblocks identified in the existing systems as stated above, it will have great value in enhancing the development of casual health care diagnoses that can predict the disease with which individual might be suffering. Hence the project has the required social and legal feasibility to start implementation.

Motivation

We Indians usually never take our health seriously, then all of a sudden if something bad happens to us, it takes more effort and time to get fixed and fully recovered. We observed this and start researching about this. We discussed same with our head of department and few family doctors we know, after this we read some research papers and articles. After which we came to know that a person waits for an average 90 minutes just for its 10-20 minutes consultation with a doctor. More Indians Die Due to Poor Quality Healthcare and Late Diagnosis than Due to Lack of Access to Healthcare services. And this numbers were much higher in India. We observed that the current diagnosing mechanism were very pathetic and tricky to use. It also used to cost a lot and most of them are not at all possible to set up at home. Now imagine if we can have an application that can ease these things not fully but up to some extent and could save someone to get sick So, we decided to mix our ancient Indian Ayurveda practices with modern day technologies .and our project is one of the many roots that may one day help make those dreams of ours possible.

ARCHITECTURE AND DESIGN PHASES

The whole system designed in this project can be divided into multiple parts, which will be explained one by one below.

Dataset

The dataset for the system consists of multiple images taken from various sources. Variable data enables the system to maintain the spontaneity as we discussed earlier.

Theimages in the dataset contains a mixture of images taken from personal photos and public images taken during our visit to Sevadharam NGO and also the images available on the internet as shown in figure 3.1,3.2 & 3.3.

Figure 1. Yellow Color Nails of a person with Jaundice

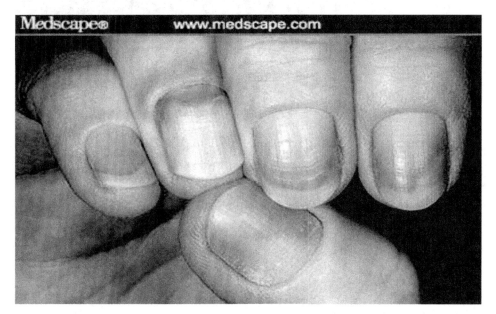

Figure 2. Spoon shaped Nail of a person with Iron deficiency and anemia

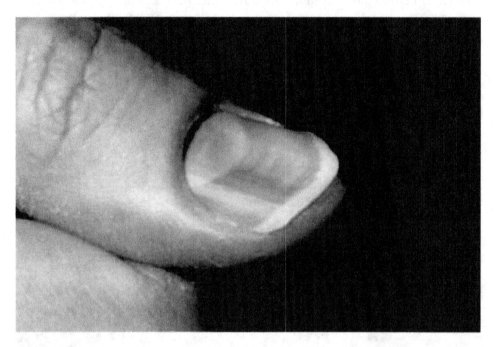

Figure 3. Nails of a Healthy Person

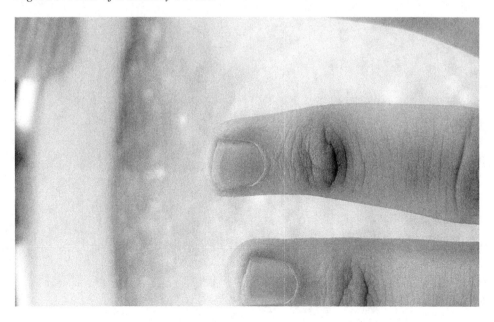

Figure 4. System Architecture

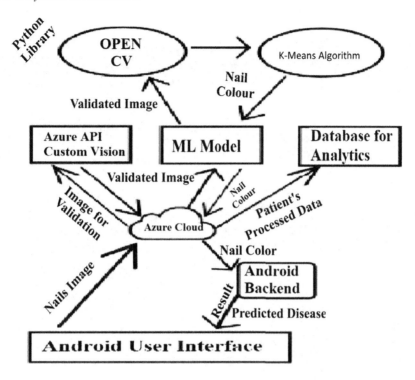

Initially a dedicated android application will allow users to click a picture of their nails, which will be sent to the virtual machine hosted in Microsoft Azure cloud as shown in figures 4 & 5. This picture will be validated through azure custom vision API. After successful validation the same image will be sent to the custom ML model for further detection of the nail color which will allow the application to predict the possible set of diseases. This diagnosis will alert the individual for the same. We have also done fieldwork at Sevadharam NGO in our locality for checking the accuracy of our application which gave us the desired result for diagnosis of jaundice.

Figure 5. Model Implementation

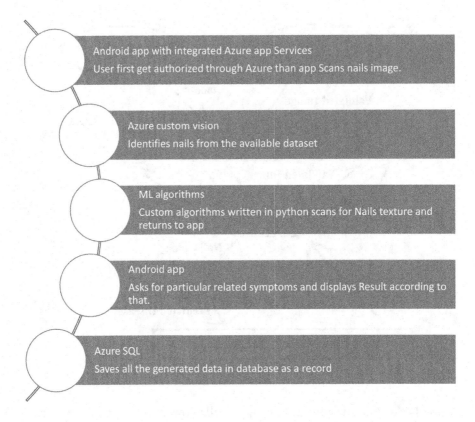

- **Phase 1:** Firstly we take Input Image from User (Expected they provide the nail Image) Through our Android App User Interface
- **Phase 2:** Then Our Input Image sent to the azure cloud Where our machine Learning Model Hosted.
- **Phase 3:** Then our input Image sent to the Azure Custom Vision API
- **Phase 4:** Azure Custom Vision Api is used to validate the Image which is an image recognition service.
- **Phase 5:** for next phase K means algorithm will be used to retrieve the nail color.
- **Phase 6:** we used Harcascade Classifier to train and test the Model. We uses 1000 images for training the model and 300 images to test the model
- **Phase 7**: After getting the Disease color from Ml model it will be sent to the Android app backend where color get assign to the respective Disease.
- **Phase 8**: Result will be Displayed at Android App User Interface.

The various objective functions used are listed below describe how Means works.

$$J = \sum_{i=1}^{m} \sum_{k=1}^{K} w_{ik} \|x^i - \mu_k\|^2$$

(1)

Where wik=1 for data point xi if it belongs to cluster k; otherwise, wik=0. Also, μk is the centroid of xi's cluster.

E-step can be calculated using equation given below:

$$\frac{\partial J}{\partial w_{ik}} = \sum_{i=1}^{m} \sum_{k=1}^{K} \|x^i - \mu_k\|^2$$

$$\Rightarrow w_{ik} = \begin{cases} 1 & \text{if } k = argmin_j \|x^i - \mu_j\|^2 \\ 0 & \text{otherwise.} \end{cases}$$

(2)

The data point xi is assigned to the closest cluster moderator by its sum of squared distance from cluster's centroid.

M-step is calculated using equation given below:

$$\frac{\partial J}{\partial \mu_k} = 2 \sum_{i=1}^{m} w_{ik}(x^i - \mu_k) = 0$$

$$\Rightarrow \mu_k = \frac{\sum_{i=1}^{m} w_{ik} x^i}{\sum_{i=1}^{m} w_{ik}}$$

(3)

$$\frac{1}{m_k} \sum_{i=1}^{m_k} \|x^i - \mu_{c^k}\|^2$$

(4)

different pictures, some of which are pigs and the rest could be pictures of anything (cats, dogs, etc).

IMPLEMENTATION AND RESULTS

After the successful implementation we went to sevadharam NGO society, Sector 15 Faridabad. To check the effectiveness of this application with real patients. At current stage our application was not able to detect all desired disease, but it was successfully able to detect small problems like low blood count, jaundice etc. Results are as follows in figure 10 and 11.

Figure 6. App camera taking image

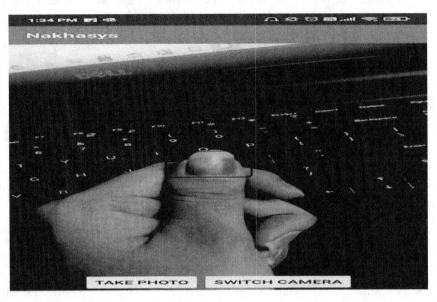

Figure 7. App displaying Result

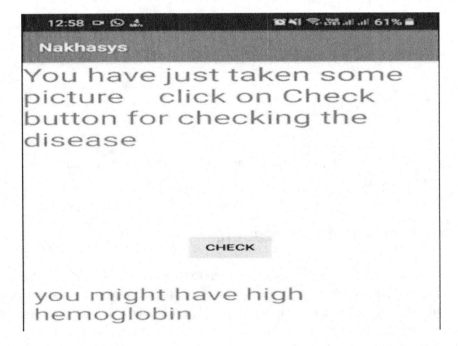

Advantages of Proposed Solution

- Reduces diagnosis time.
- Timely Diagnosis can lead to better treatment.
- Creates a healthy habit of Regular Health Checkups
- Data generated can be used for Research and Reference purposes.
- Best in field doctor can be accessed right from home.
- Including several Severe health issues prediction on an early stage.

CONCLUSION AND FUTURE WORK

Soon AIs will be much stronger than what we have today. Since the system is developed fully in python this can be imported as a module for any further development or integration to other complex programs. We think that in the future after accumulating huge datasets and increasing accuracy, we will be able to provide a very low-cost diagnosing platform to majority of the population. We will also try to upgrade our application accuracy by not just analyzing nail color but also, it's various segments like nails texture, shape, condition etc. Which could result in timely prediction of disease leading to proper timely medication? This would also result into generating habits of daily check-ups. As the world is getting more technical so we should also be updated with the time and create devices to help humankind and our application will help to reduce timings between check-ups and manage that in easier ways. Data generated by this application could help various authorities at top to make their strategy to deal with healthcare nationwide.

REFERENCES

Ananth. (2020). *Machine Learning – Intelligent Decisions based on Data*. Witanworld. Retrieved from https://witanworld.com/article/2020/08/09/machinelearning/

Fawcett, R. S., Linford, S., & Stulberg, D. L. (2004). Nail abnormalities: Clues to systemic disease. *American Family Physician*, 69(6), 1417–1424. PMID:15053406

Funde, A. G., & Thepade, S. D. (2016, June). Recognising Sign using fractional energy of cosine haar hybrid wavelet transform of American Sign images. In *2016 Conference on Advances in Signal Processing (CASP)* (pp. 290-294). IEEE. 10.1109/CASP.2016.7746182

Gandhat, S., Thakare, A. D., Avhad, S., Bajpai, N., & Alawadhi, R. (2016). Study and analysis of nail images of patients. *International Journal of Computers and Applications*, *143*(13), 38–41. doi:10.5120/ijca2016910055

Hardik, P., & Shah, D. M. (2012). The model for extracting a portion of a given image using color processing. *International Journal of Engineering Research & Technology (Ahmedabad)*, 181.

Indi, T. S., & Gunge, Y. A. (2016). Early stage disease diagnosis system using human nail image processing. *IJ Information Technology and Computer Science*, *7*(7), 30–35. doi:10.5815/ijitcs.2016.07.05

Kraus, M. A., & Drass, M. (2020). Artificial intelligence for structural glass engineering applications—Overview, case studies and future potentials. *Glass Structures & Engineering*, *5*(3), 247–285. doi:10.100740940-020-00132-8

Madaan, V., & Goyal, A. (2020). Predicting ayurveda-based constituent balancing in human body using machine learning methods. *IEEE Access : Practical Innovations, Open Solutions*, *8*, 65060–65070. doi:10.1109/ACCESS.2020.2985717

Mente, R., & Marulkar, S. V. (2017). A review: Fingernail images for disease detection. *Int. J. Eng. Comput. Sci*, *6*(11), 22830–22835. doi:10.18535/ijecs/v6i11.01

Pathak, K. M., Yadav, S., Jain, P., Tanwar, P., & Kumar, B. (2020, June). A facial expression recognition system to predict emotions. In *2020 International Conference on Intelligent Engineering and Management (ICIEM)* (pp. 414-419). IEEE. 10.1109/ICIEM48762.2020.9160229

Saranya, V., & Ranichitra, A. (2017). Image segmentation techniques to detect nail abnormalities. *Scholar, 2*(1).

Sharma, A., & Tanwar, P. (2020, June). Deep analysis of autism spectrum disorder detection techniques. In *2020 International conference on intelligent engineering and management (ICIEM)* (pp. 455-459). IEEE. 10.1109/ICIEM48762.2020.9160123

Sharma, A., & Tanwar, P. (2021). Machine learning techniques for autism spectrum disorder (ASD) detection. *International Journal of Forensic Engineering*, *5*(2), 111–125. doi:10.1504/IJFE.2021.118912

Sharma, A., & Tanwar, P. (2022). Deep Learning Techniques for Detection of Autism Spectrum Syndrome (ASS). In Proceedings of Data Analytics and Management: ICDAM 2021, Volume 2 (pp. 337-345). Springer Singapore.

Sharma, V., & Shrivastava, A. (2015). System for Disease detection by analyzing finger nails Color and Texture. *International Journal of Advanced Engineering Research and Science, 2*(10).

Singal, A., & Arora, R. (2015). Nail as a window of systemic diseases. *Indian Dermatology Online Journal, 6*(2), 67. doi:10.4103/2229-5178.153002 PMID:25821724

Thakare, A., Meshram, S., & Baradkar, H. M. (2017). An Automated Medical Support System For Detecting Human Health Conditions Based On Noval Bicluster Method. *IJCTA, 10*(8), 223–228.

ADDITIONAL READING

Tunc, S. E., Ertam, I., Pirildar, T., Turk, T., Ozturk, M., & Doganavsargil, E. (2007). Nail changes in connective tissue diseases: Do nail changes provide clues for the diagnosis? *Journal of the European Academy of Dermatology and Venereology, 21*(4), 497–503. doi:10.1111/j.1468-3083.2006.02012.x PMID:17373977

Chapter 7

IoT–Based Automatic Boom Barrier for Enhancing Surveillance Security in Public Places

Monika Mehta
NIFTJ, India

Shivani Mishra
HMR Institute of Technology and Management, India

Santosh Kumar
HMR Institute of Technology and Management, India

Muskaan Bansal
HMR Institute of Technology and Management, India

ABSTRACT

In order to reduce the unnecessary waste of the workforce, the proposed system has been developed. In this chapter, a secure environment from that future will secure and help increase motivation for intelligent things and productivity and enter newly grown markets, startups, and entrepreneurs. The significant contribution to knowledge was to improve the automatic boom barrier system, considering the low cost of the budget. This chapter is concerned with providing an automatic boom barrier, the gate operated by Raspberry Pi. Some of the features considered during this system's design were cost-effective and easy to use compared to existing systems. Security plays an essential role in making smart cities using the "automatic boom barrier system."

DOI: 10.4018/978-1-6684-5255-4.ch007

INTRODUCTION

A boom barrier, also known as a boom gate, is a bar or pole pivoted to allow the boom to block vehicular or pedestrian access through a controlled point. Typically, the tip of a boom gate rises in a vertical arc to a near-vertical position. Boom gates are often counterweighted, so the pole is easily tipped (Ata et al., 2019; Deshmukh & Joshi, 2019; Jain et al., 2017; Mishra et al., 2019). Boom gates have often paired either end to end or offset appropriately to block traffic in both directions. Some boom gates also have a second arm which hangs 300 to 400 mm below the upper arm when lowered to increase approach visibility, and which hangs on links, so it lies flat with the main boom as the barrier is raised. Some barriers also feature a pivot roughly halfway, whereas the barrier is raised, the outermost half remains horizontal, with the barrier resembling an upside-down *L* when raised.

In this system, Raspberry-Pi is the central controller. Also, the web camera, motor, and ultrasonic sensor are the crucial parts of this device. Firstly, Identify a car through KNN and Raspberry Pi. It will then automatically operate the Raspberry Pi if it is under the ultrasonic sensor range (for example – if any vehicle arrived, then the Raspberry Pi camera auto-capture number plate). After that, the Pi recognized the car photo. The car details are then stored in a known database like Plate number, date, time. After that, data comparison with the existing database will find the authorized car and then automatically operate (example-open the gate); otherwise, not perform any operation.

Figure 1. Automatic boom barrier architecture in the proposed environment

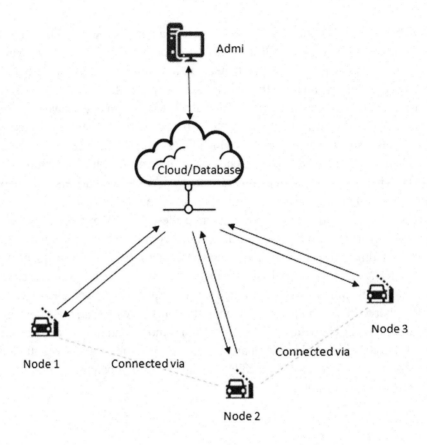

This paper contains five sections, including an introduction and conclusion. The next section, Related Work, tells us about the problem's concern with security challenges, market opportunities, and needs. The next section gives a detailed view of the system's configuration, the hardware involved, and the proposed system and its Implementation through the components used in our system. The database stores the information of the vehicle number plate for the authorized and unauthorized vehicle. Similarly, the web page will help a user interact easily with this device running on the local server to record vehicle details. In the next section, the results of the proposed work have been discussed. Finally, the work is summarized with future recommendations and application areas.

RELATED WORK

There was the same functionality in the previously existing system that used an RFID sensor as our system work. However, there is some problem like an installation problem and some workforce for controlling the system. To overcome these problems, we make a low-cost system, not a requirement for any installation, and manually entering use only for unknown vehicles, but it will work automatically for the known vehicle. We use IoT because it can use different APIs to combine more than one language to make technology behave like a weapon in the security matter (Gawade & Meeankshi, 2017; Persada et al., 2019; Pratama et al., 2020; Saleem et al., 2020; Sethuramalingam, 2019). With the help of IoT, we can make any powerful technology concerned with security reasons. Table 1 describes the existing technology used along with its limitation.

Table 1. Literature survey

Sr. No	Technology name	Description	Year	Limitation
1.	Automated gate	Using a local web/android app to open the gate.	2014	It required a web server or android. Not do any automatic function.
2.	Movement sensed an automatic gate	Using the ATMEL microcontroller and PIR sensor to detect the movement. It sends a signal to the microcontroller, which opens the door for a particular amount of time.	2015	Continue press and hold the Jog button
3.	Power Sliding doors	Using control from remote button pushing on or off.	2017	Use remote Button
4.	IOT Electronic door opener	Using an online GUI system for login. Give the command for any activity that is controlled by the local server	2018	Give the command for performing all activities
5.	Automatic Boom Barrier using Raspberry	A raspberry pi with a camera is the central part of this system. This system uses an ultrasonic sensor for the detection of a vehicle.	2019	Not working correctly at night (improve with night vision camera).

METHODOLOGY

To open the gate, we use a motor with the combination of an ultrasonic sensor and the camera module to recognize the vehicle number plate. We use an ANPR (automatic number plate recognition) system from (Satyanarayana et al., 2019; Shieh et al., 2019;

Swaraj et al., 2019). In terms of recognizing the number plate, we set the ultrasonic range to the desired distance to detect the vehicle coming in range to capture the image and process of recognition performed with the ANPR system. The proposed architecture consists of 3 LEDs, red, green, and yellow, respectively, indicating the boom barrier, red light status indicates the system is working, green shows the gate is open, and yellow indicates the vehicle is unknown. A database system has been added to record the authorized car's number plate in the proposed system, which compared it with the arrival car's number plate. In case the vehicle number plate is not authorized, then the gate will not open, and the yellow light will glow, and the number plate will store in the unknown vehicle database system; otherwise, the boom barrier will open, and the green light indicates. In case the authorized user or guard wants to add a new vehicle to the authorized vehicle database system, a GUI interface will help the user interact with the system quickly. The user can run it on any browser with the help of a domain name. Afterward, the user or guard can add a new vehicle inside the authorized vehicle database system, and the gate will open automatically. The system required MySql and Apache Server for record management and front-end monitoring, respectively (Al-Turjman & Malekloo, 2019; Diaz Ogás et al., 2020; Kasera & Acharjee, 2022; Kumar & Kushwaha, 2019; Padyab et al., 2019). Raspberry pi, a motor, ultrasonic sensor, LEDs, and camera module fulfill the need for hardware architecture.

Figure 2. Implementation of Automatic Boom barrier using these components

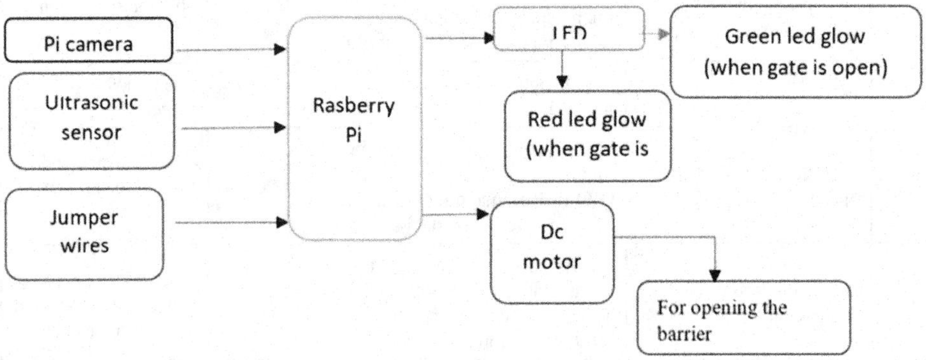

Proposed System and Implementation

To implement this system/device, below the block diagram is used. Figure 1 shows the pi camera, LEDs, Power supply, Raspberry pi, and jumper wire used to connect the devices. DC motor is used to open the boom in an anti-clock direction, and when the car passed, the motor rotates in the clockwise direction to shut down of boom barrier. Figure 2 shows how the system work and all the components interface with each other.

Figure 3. Ultrasonic sensor Connection

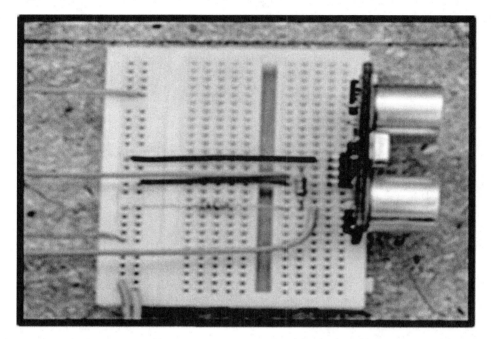

Components

In this system or device, the DC motor is used to fix the rotatory gear, and the boom barrier is used with a linear gear, which gives us the motion is circular to linear transfer motion and used for automatic turning the boom barrier for open or close. We use the reference of the ultrasonic sensor working from (Jain et al., 2017). Ultrasonic sensors are used to detect the range of a car by scraping the car number plate. In a realistic system, the sensors will use only in the user's desirable need for detection on the vehicle's arrival.

Figure 4. Methodology Flowchart

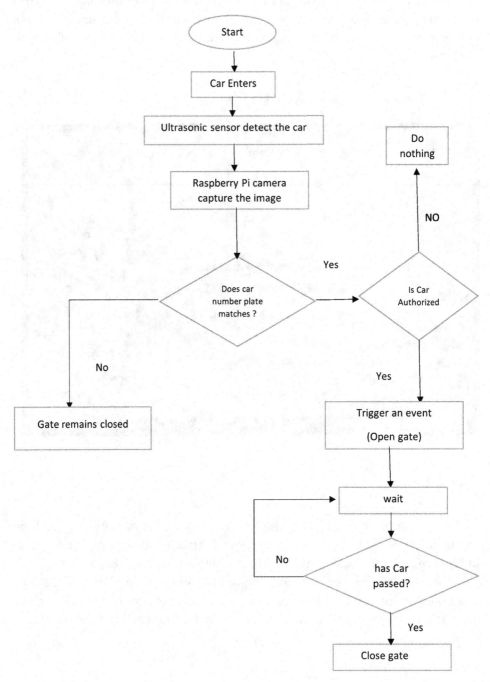

Database

An automatic boom barrier uses the database file system to store vehicle number plate information for the authorized and unauthorized vehicle. Two different databases used, which shown in below figure 5 name is given as vehicle for keep the record of knowing vehicle which data is matched from the existing database and unknown_vehicle for keeping the record of the unknown vehicle which data is not matched from the existing database which is described below:

Figure 5. Table names

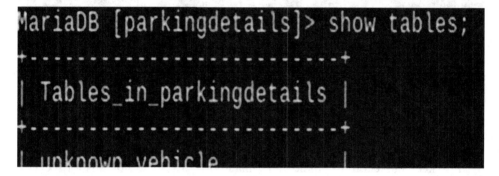

Register Vehicle

There are five attributes in the in-vehicle table: SR_No, Vehicle_Number, Entry_ Time, Exit_Time, and time and date. Vehicle_Number is as primary key and taking data as varchar, SR_ NO taking as an integer value, Entry_Time, Exit_Time and TimeAndDate taking database as DateTime.

Figure 6. Describe Vehicle Table

```
MariaDB [parkingdetails]> describe vehicle
    -> ;
+----------------+--------------+------+-----+---------+-------+
| Field          | Type         | Null | Key | Default | Extra |
+----------------+--------------+------+-----+---------+-------+
| SR_NO          | int(11)      | YES  |     | NULL    |       |
| Vehicle_Number | varchar(200) | NO   | PRI | NULL    |       |
| Entry_Time     | datetime     | YES  |     | NULL    |       |
```

Unknown_ vehicle

We also keep the record of unknown or unauthorized vehicle's details for security purposes that can use in the future in some abnormal cases.

Figure 7. Describe Unknown Vehicle Table

```
MariaDB [parkingdetails]> describe unknown_vehicle;
+----------------+--------------+------+-----+---------+-------+
| Field          | Type         | Null | Key | Default | Extra |
+----------------+--------------+------+-----+---------+-------+
| SR_NO          | int(11)      | YES  |     | NULL    |       |
| Vehicle_Number | varchar(200) | NO   | PRI | NULL    |       |
| Entry_Time     | datetime     | YES  |     | NULL    |       |
| Exit_Time      | datetime     | YES  |     | NULL    |       |
| TimeAndDate    | datetime     | YES  |     | NULL    |       |
```

Gate Control Layout

This paper aims to create a modern design of the boom barrier, which has a low cost, easy to implement, and automation technique, which will require the least human effort to open and close the automatic boom barrier. To enrich the result, an ultrasonic sensor and camera are used to detect the vehicle.

Distance Calculation

We use some expression to calculate the distance from the object(car) through the ultrasonic sensor. The product of distance denotes as v with time t is to be divided by two as the signal has traveled twice.

$$V = (340 \times t) \div 2$$

V= distance in meter

t = Time in seconds

Webpage

In order to store data, the MySQL server is used (Ata et al., 2019). After that, create a web page that will help users interact easily with this device running on a local server to record vehicle details. Create two webpages for showing new vehicle entry and show the details of authorized vehicles, respectively. These two pages shown below:

Authorized Vehicle Details

In the first record table name is **Authorized vehicle details Figure 8.** It contains the information of authorized or visitor vehicle's number plate already existing in the database with the previous tracking record's help. It helps to track a person on which time he/she arrived.

Figure 8. Authorized vehicle details

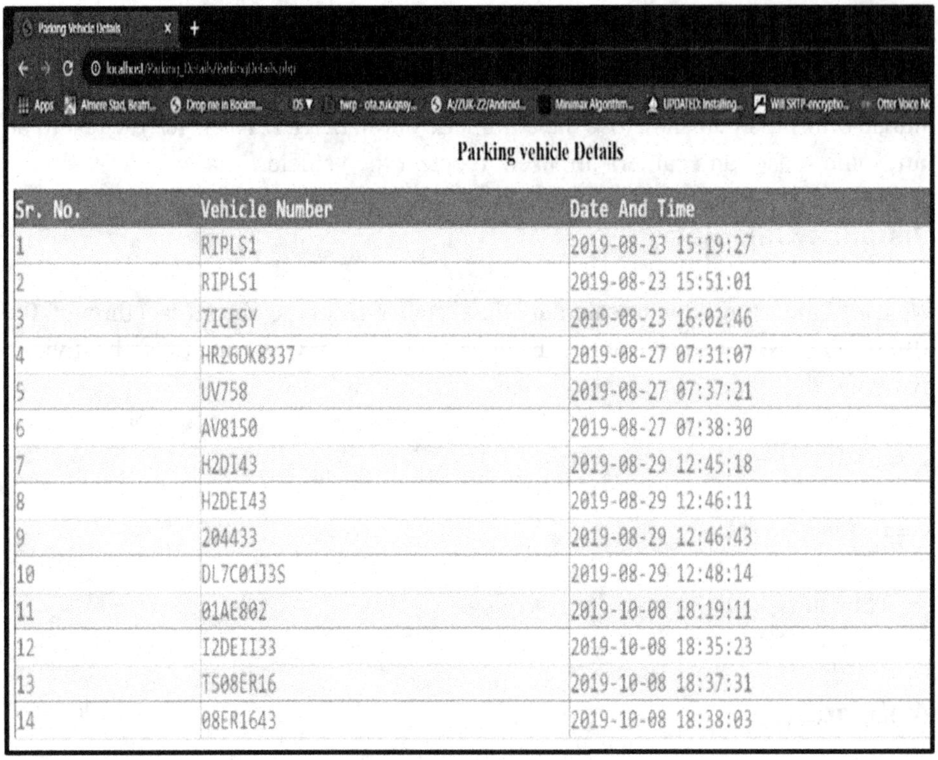

Parking vehicle Details

Sr. No.	Vehicle Number	Date And Time
1	RIPLS1	2019-08-23 15:19:27
2	RIPLS1	2019-08-23 15:51:01
3	7ICESY	2019-08-23 16:02:46
4	HR26DK8337	2019-08-27 07:31:07
5	UV758	2019-08-27 07:37:21
6	AV8150	2019-08-27 07:38:30
7	H2DI43	2019-08-29 12:45:18
8	H2DEI43	2019-08-29 12:46:11
9	204433	2019-08-29 12:46:43
10	DL7C01J3S	2019-08-29 12:48:14
11	01AE802	2019-10-08 18:19:11
12	I2DEII33	2019-10-08 18:35:23
13	TS08ER16	2019-10-08 18:37:31
14	08ER1643	2019-10-08 18:38:03

Authorization Access

Authorization access is the way of another security measure is often doubt with authentication. In authentication, we have received a signal of glowing led, and we need to be sure that the information is existing in the storage database. In access (or car authorization), we first check the visitors' number plate identity before access to the system is allowed.

For New Vehicle Details

For a new user who wants to become under authorized user, make a html form using php through Apache server connecting with the database. To authorize a new vehicle first, we have to register the vehicle through the database system's vehicle number. After the registration process, the record will be submitted through the authorized vehicle storage web page.

Figure 9. For new vehicle entry details

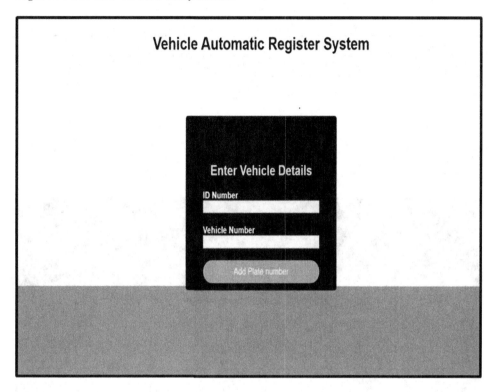

In the above, Figure 9 shows the webpage for taking New Entry with details: ID number and Vehicle number. In ID number one can give any numeric data for verification in the future, and vehicle number takes alphanumeric data of one's car number plate. ID number is a primary key in the database that cannot be null and must be unique. After that, click on the **Add plate number** button, the webpage redirected to the same webpage after clicking on the Add button, and the response will record successfully.

RESULT

The system was successfully implemented and able to detect the authorized vehicle, and as the output green light glowed as shown in Figure 11, and it can also recognize and store the unknown vehicle number plate into the unknown database system. This system can open the boom barrier. We tested it so many times and got 90% accuracy.

Table 2.

Test Case	Result
With Times Roman Font	ü
With Monotype Corsiva Font	û

The final result of automatic boom barrier:

Figure 10. Automatic boom barrier in case of no vehicle

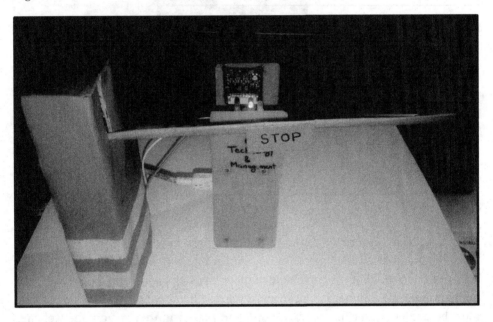

In Figure 10, the ultrasonic sensor senses the range of vehicles under the sensor range, and then the camera captures the image. The red light shows that there is some car for detecting, and the system is working.

Figure 11. Automatic boom barrier in case of a vehicle

Figure 11. shows that this vehicle number in our authorized database because the green light is glowing. Furthermore, it denotes that if the authorized car arrived, then the boom barrier will open automatically for some time. After that, the boom barrier will close automatically until the car has passed the boom barrier. If the orange light glow means the car is unauthorized, which record is not in the existing database stored in the unknown vehicle shown in Figure 11.

CONCLUSION

The automatic boom barrier helps to reach our goal of making smart cities with the additional security feature. The cities are turning dense by each day, and controlling the crime in day-to-day life by detecting the criminal vehicle, including GPS tracking system in online mode is needed. This device can be used for security purposes from a long-distance place that is based on a network.

Let us assume a single device that communicates the nodes (another device) to track and monitor a smart city security system's architecture. This system/device can track the vehicle on a highway as well as at any checkpoint. There is only one admin that can track and monitor at multiple places simultaneously with the help of data stored inside the cloud's database. All the nodes share their data to the cloud through an internet connection. This device can play a crucial role in vehicle theft, vehicle movement activity for security service providers and the government.

REFERENCES

Al-Turjman, F., & Malekloo, A. (2019). Smart Parking in Cloud-Based IoT. In *The Cloud in IoT-enabled Spaces* (pp. 103–155). CRC Press. doi:10.1201/9780429319181-5

Ata, K. M., Soh, A. C., Ishak, A. J., Jaafar, H., & Khairuddin, N. A. (2019). Smart Indoor Parking System Based on Dijkstra's Algorithm. *Int. J. Integr. Eng, 2*(1), 13–20.

Deshmukh, A., & Joshi, R. D. (2019). Understanding the architecture of internet of things using a case study of smart parking. *Asian Journal For Convergence in Technology.*

Diaz Ogás, M. G., Fabregat, R., & Aciar, S. (2020). Survey of smart parking systems. *Applied Sciences (Basel, Switzerland), 10*(11), 3872. doi:10.3390/app10113872

Gawade, P., & Meeankshi, A. (2017). IOT based smart public transport system. *International Journal of Scientific and Research Publications, 7*(7), 390–396.

Jain, I., Malik, S., & Agrawal, S. (2017). Automatic Railway Barrier System, Railway Tracking and Collision Avoidance using IOT. *International Journal of Computers and Applications, 975,* 8887.

Kasera, R. K., & Acharjee, T. (2022). A Smart Indoor Parking System. *SN Computer Science, 3*(1), 1–17. doi:10.100742979-021-00875-3 PMID:34723205

Kumar, T., & Kushwaha, D. S. (2019). An intelligent surveillance system based on IoT for internal security of a nation. *International Journal of Information Security and Privacy, 13*(3), 1–30. doi:10.4018/IJISP.201907010101

Mishra, A., Karmakar, A., Ghatak, A., Ghosh, S., Ojha, A., & Patra, K. (2019). Low cost parking system for smart cities: A vehicle occupancy sensing and resource optimization technique using IoT and Cloud PaaS. *Int J Sci Technol Res, 8*(9), 115–122.

Padyab, A., Habibipour, A., Rizk, A., & Ståhlbröst, A. (2019). Adoption barriers of IoT in large scale pilots. *Information (Basel), 11*(1), 23. doi:10.3390/info11010023

Persada, R. P., Aulia, S., Burhanuddin, D., & Sugondo, H. (2019). Automatic face and VLP's recognition for smart parking system. *Telkomnika, 17*(4), 1698–1705. doi:10.12928/telkomnika.v17i4.11746

Pratama, C., Aulia, S., Ramadan, D. N., & Hadiyoso, S. (2020). Vehicle License Plate Detection for Parking Offenders Using Automatic License-Plate Recognition. *Journal of Southwest Jiaotong University, 55*(4), 32. doi:10.35741/issn.0258-2724.55.4.32

Saleem, A. A., Siddiqui, H. U. R., Shafique, R., Haider, A., & Ali, M. (2020, January). A review on smart IOT based parking system. In *International Conference On Soft Computing And Data Mining* (pp. 264-273). Springer. 10.1007/978-3-030-36056-6_26

Satyanarayana, D., Dulla, M., Giduturi, A. A., Chandra, D. S., & Prathap, S. (2019). *Developing an advanced smart parking system using IoT*. Academic Press.

Sethuramalingam, D. (2019). *Security for smart vehicle in iot. In The IoT and the Next Revolutions Automating the World*. IGI Global.

Shieh, J.-Y., Huang, S.-X., & Su, Y.-X. (2019). Automatic Allocation System for Parking Lot Based on QR Code. *Journal of the Gujarat Research Society*, *21*(1), 10–12.

Swaraj, M., Munagala, M. K., Bharti, P., & Jayavarthini, C. (2019). smart parking system using facial recognition, optical character recognition and internet of things (IoT). *Int. Res. J. Eng. Technol*, *6*, 1278–1282.

Chapter 8
Health Monitoring of Polymer Matrix Composites Using Vibration Technique

Sreekanth T. G.
PSG College of Technology, India

Senthilkumar M.
https://orcid.org/0000-0002-3720-0941
PSG College of Technology, India

Manikanta Reddy S.
PSG College of Technology, India

ABSTRACT

Glass and carbon fiber-reinforced plastics have become increasingly popular in engineering applications as relatively new materials, and it is expected that this trend will continue. E-glass laminates have become more common in aviation components such as wings, fuselages, and stabilizers as stronger, more durable, and tougher resins such as epoxies have evolved. A sudden breakdown of an engineering component like aircraft usually results in a significant financial loss, as well as posing a risk to human life. Vibration-based detection is one type of global damage identification method. Changes in physical qualities like damping, mass, and stiffness bring noticeable changes in the modal parameters in vibration-based damage detection approaches. This chapter demonstrates how vibration-based analysis can be used to forecast the severity and position of delamination in composites. The position and area of delamination in composite beams are determined using a supervised feed-forward multilayer back-propagation artificial neural network (ANN) in the MATLAB neural network toolbox.

DOI: 10.4018/978-1-6684-5255-4.ch008

INTRODUCTION

Even though carbon and glass fibre reinforced composites were primarily made for the aerospace industry, their lightness, high damping factor, and environmental resistance make them appealing in other technical fields like as transportation, automotive, marine, and wind power. Glass fibre polymer is frequently employed in traditional engineering composite structures like automotive body panels, whereas carbon fibre polymer is widely used in the aerospace applications like manufacturing of wings and fuselages. E-glass laminates have become more common in aviation components such as wings, fuselages, and stabilisers as stronger, more durable, and tougher resins like epoxies have evolved (Mangalgiri, 1999). The invention of S-glass in the 1960s, which has better strength and rigidity than E-glass, led to the creation of a large variety of aircraft components and systems. Glass/epoxy panels are also employed in various current fighter aircraft elements, such as the B2 bomber's trailing edge.

The key issues concerning composites in aircraft applications is that damage to the composite cannot be identified by visual inspection prior to flight. However, composites may have internal damage because of a low-velocity impact that left no visible alterations on the surface. Another important source of concern is the composite's polymeric matrix component. Moisture collects in polymeric matrix ingredients, which slowly but steadily alters composite characteristics. It can also build up in matrix micro-cracks and delamination's between layers of composite laminates. This trapped moisture/water would expand and encourage subsequent micro-cracking or delamination's as the aeroplane flies at top altitudes where the heat may dip below freezing point. As time goes on, aircraft may experience more flight cycles, and this process of freezing and defrosting will cause micro-cracks to grow larger, eventually leading to delamination's (Irving & Soutis, 2019).

Metals used in aerospace, such as aluminium, are well-known for their fatigue properties. Composite fatigue behaviour is extremely complex and underappreciated. The fatigue behaviour of aircraft metals has been well understood now because of recent research in this area. The fatigue data for composites is not commonly recognised. In addition, the fatigue behaviour of a composite is affected by constituent fibres, matrix, and layup sequence; hence fatigue behaviour might differ from part to part. This statement illustrates why fatigue behaviour in aerospace composites is still a high-yielding research topic. To this point, the designers have relied on extensive certification exams and tasks to ensure that the composites they utilise have sufficient fatigue behaviour. These safety precautions were time-consuming and costly. As a result, the development of new dependable solutions is undoubtedly a significant research focus.

Polymer Matrix Composite (PMC) is consisting of a polymer resin matrix that is reinforced with glass, carbon, and aramid fibres. PMC has a good strength-to-weight ratio. It has a high fatigue resistance, as well as ease of manufacturing and low price. Polyethylene, polystyrene, and Nylon 66 are examples of thermoplastics, while epoxy, polyester, and phenol-formaldehyde are examples of thermoset polymers. This chapter discusses characteristics of delamination identification in laminated composites as revealed by a vibration measurement-based technique. The focus of this study is on Glass Fibre Reinforced Polymer (GFRP) composites with epoxy as the matrix. Manufacturing of composites with and without damages was done for experimentation. Vibration tests were performed on GFRP samples using LabVIEW software.

The presence of damages alters the vibration behaviour of composites, such as mode shapes, natural frequencies, and so on, and so this indicator can be used to locate and quantify delaminations. The inverse problem can be used to find out the location and area of delaminations using variations in vibration characteristics as inputs. Using natural frequency shifts as indicative vibration characteristics, an Artificial Neural Network (ANN) is used to establish the presence, location, and magnitude of delaminations in GFRP composites. The essential dataset for ANN is created using Finite Element Analysis.

COMPOSITE MATERIAL FAILURE MECHANISMS

Damage to laminate composites occurs on micro, meso, and macro scales, depending on the extent of the inspection. Fibre/matrix debonding, voids, and porosity are examples of molecular level damages that are described by micro-mechanics. The actual quality of a composite structure is largely unaffected by these types of damages. They may, however, be the primary cause of macro-level damage start, and hence have a major impact on the component's structural integrity. Interface delamination, fibre fractures, and matrix cracking are examples of prevalent macro-scale defects (Montesano & Sharifpour, 2020). The most common types of fault identified in Fibre Reinforced Polymers (FRPs) at the in-service stage is matrix cracking. The effect of matrix cracking is limited because the fibre bears the bulk of the external loads. Despite intense loading circumstances like as impact or explosion, fibre fracture does not occur frequently due to large fracture toughness of the fibres (Sreekanth et al 2021).

Delamination is another common and serious type of failure in FRPs, and it can be caused by a variety of factors. These factors could include a problem in the manufacturing, assembly, or in-service stages, or a combination of them. Material/structural discontinuities that cause interlaminar strains are the common cause of delaminations. Delaminations can also develop at stress-free edges due to mismatches in individual layer properties. It can also happen in areas where there is out-of-plane loading, such as when curved beams flex. It's also the important failure type in composites, because delamination diminishes the composite's strength (Latifi 2015). When static loading is applied, there is a risk of local buckling when compression loading is applied. When a structure is subjected to dynamic loading, delamination decreases stiffness, which might result in a larger deflection magnitude for the overall structure. Foreign object impact is the common cause of delamination in FRPs. When neighbouring layers debond internally, it is undetectable until the structure's performance deteriorates dramatically. This emphasises the importance of early detection and assessment of structural delaminations so that a plan can be devised to prevent additional delamination growth.

HEALTH MONITORING USING VIBRATION TECHNIQUE

Because of different factors such as incorrect design, working environmental circumstances, incidental events, operational fluctuations, and so on, all static and dynamic systems deteriorate with time. Visual inspection is by far the most basic, straightforward, and cost-effective way for detecting defects in structures. To detect faults in composites, various non-destructive and destructive approaches are employed in practise. Because it uses sensors, data gathering and transmission devices, and computational approaches with strong processing ability, Structural Health Monitoring (SHM) is a preferable non-destructive technique (Senthilkumar et al., 2021).

Even during service life of the product, both new and existing severe damages should be detected and tracked. SHM approaches can be used in this situation. It could also be used to calculate the impact of damage on the composites' remaining life (Farrar et al., 2007). SHM also helps to prevent sudden breakdown of the structure in use by reducing inspection downtime. The vibration methodology is a global method for detecting damages that recognises changes in modal variables based on changes in physical parameters such as damping, mass, and stiffness. In general, frequency-domain and time-domain techniques are the two sorts of evaluation methods (Fritzen & Claus Peter, 2005). Changes in modal parameters such as natural frequency, frequency response functions, damping, and mode shapes are used in the frequency-domain technique to identify and quantify damage (Sreekanth et al., 2021).

MANUFACTURE OF GFRP BEAMS

There are three sorts of PMC dependent on the reinforcement medium like glass, carbon and aramid (GFRP, CFRP & AFRP respectively). Comparisons of properties of them are revealed in Table 1.

Table 1. Material properties of different FRPs

Properties	AFRP	CFRP	GFRP
Tensile Strength (MPa)	2050-2350	600-3400	500-4500
Young's Modulus (GPa)	245 - 640	150 - 640	36-85
Elongation (%)	0.7 - 1.9	0.5 – 1.8	1.2 - 5

Glass fibre is strong and light weighted material which is used in many applications like manufacturing parts for aircrafts, boats, automobiles, bathtubs and water tanks, roofing, external door skins, etc. Raw materials for GFRP are much cheaper and it can be more easily moulded into required shapes (Senthilkumar et al., 2021, 2022a, 2022b). The most common types of glass fibre are E-glass and S-glass. Compared to E-glass, S-glass offers much higher tensile strength, elastic modulus and stiffness. E-Glass is a lightweight woven composites that is extensively utilised in marine, industrial, and aerospace applications, thus it is a good fit for this study.

There are different types of resin using in the composite industry; out of which, the majority of parts are made with either polyester, vinyl ester or epoxy. Epoxy resin prevents misalignment of fibres during processing and also has low shrink rates compared to other resins. The stacking sequence of $[0/45/90/-45]_{2S}$ which consists of 16 layers of composite laminates was selected for the work, because of its vast uses and application in the aerospace and in the blades of wind turbine applications. This stacking sequence is quasi-isotropic in nature so that it can take axial as well as inclined loads. Also, the quasi-isotropic composites have the smallest induced damage and the highest peak load. As shown in the Figure 1, the sequence of stacking has been selected, the samples have to be fabricated by hand layup according to the selected stacking sequence.

Figure 1. Stacking Sequence

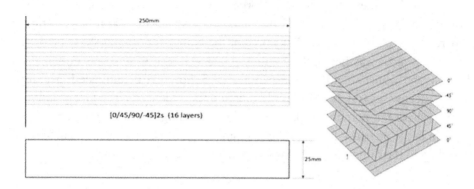

Dimension of the beam is decided based on ASTM -D3039. The beam has 250 mm length and 25 mm wide, and thickness relied on the number of plies. Fabrication of GFRP was done by using hand layup process and the resources used are E-Glass fibre, Epoxy Resin LY556 and Epoxy Hardener at (10:1 ratio). The 16 layers of the Glass fibre is cut from the woven for the dimensions of 400 mm x 200 mm. The initial layer is laid on a plastic sheet and the mixed resin is applied gently over the surface of the first layer using the brush and again the second layer is stacked upon the first layer, the second layer is pressed by using the rollers. For the remaining layers, the procedure is followed in the same way as shown in the Figure 2.

Figure 2. Fabricated PMC Plate

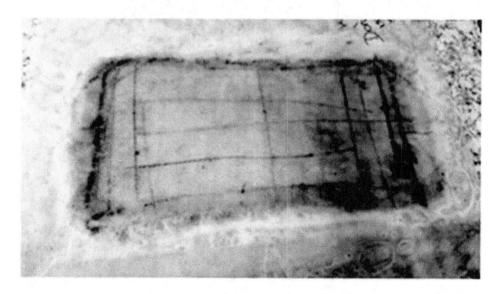

Waterjet cutting was preferred for cutting the composite plate without delamination according to the dimensions of ASTM D3039 standard for tensile testing of specimens with dimensions of 250 mm x 25 mm and specimens with 300 mm x 25 mm is prepared for vibration testing. Thickness of the composite was found to be 4 mm, where each layer was having 0.25 mm thickness. Extra 50 mm was provided for clamping the beam as cantilever beam. Figure 4.5 shows the delaminated specimens were fabricated separately and the delamination was created by using the parchment papers, where the parchment paper was cut according to the delaminations size and kept in the interface layers of the laminates and the delaminated specimens cut according to the dimensions of 300 mm x 25 mm are shown in the Figure 3.

Figure 3. Specimens with Delamination

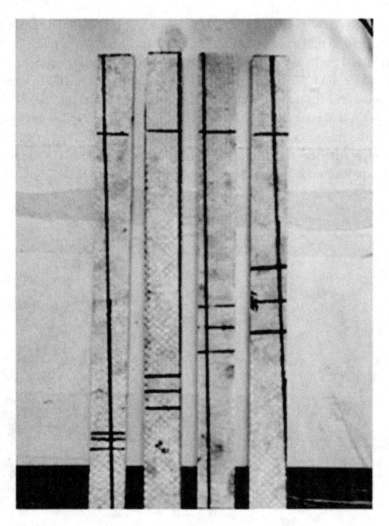

Delaminations were generated on beams at 5 different axial positions and layers with varying areas in each place for experimental verification of numerical and ANN results, as can be seen in Table 2. Specimen 1 has no delaminations, hence there are no details in Table 2.

Table 2. Areas and locations of delaminations

Sample	Area of Delamination (mm²)	Delamination layer	Delamination location measured from the Free End (mm)
2	250	1	50
3	625	5	60
4	250	8	85
5	1125	11	120
6	750	14	140

EXPERIMENTAL ANALYSIS

Vibration testing setup consists of Data acquisition system which transforms the analog wave forms into digital values for processing, Tri-axial accelerometer with 5 mV/g, impact hammer and LabVIEW software installed in the personal computer. Accelerometer (Model: 356A01, M/s PCB Piezotronics) is used to measure the vibration response of composite beams. The wax type adhesive is used to mount the accelerometer on the composite beam. The instrumental impact hammer, MEGGIT - Model 2302 is used for modal analysis. The data were recorded on the computer by means of data acquisition Analogue to Digital card as shown in Figure 4.

Figure 4. DAQ System used for the Experiment

The display unit used is a Personal Computer. All the data collected in the experiments are with the assist of the LabVIEW software installed in the PC. When the beam is getting excited, the signals transferred to the software through DAQ and presented in graphical form through the software. Mainly the data includes graphs of amplitude vs. frequency or time. Figure 5 shows snapshot of online data collection using LabVIEW software during the experiment.

Figure 5. Using LabVIEW for Obtaining Natural Frequencies

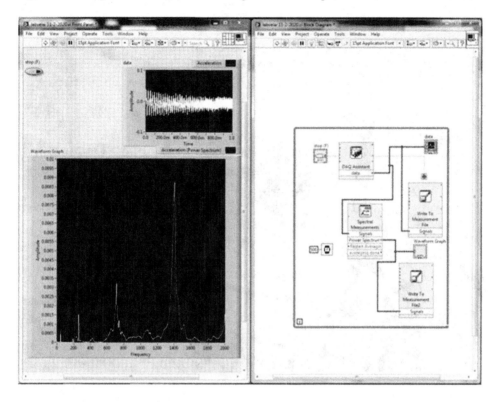

The connections were simple, and the fabricated specimen was fixed at the one end to act as a cantilever beam. The accelerometer was kept above the specimen and made sure that the accelerometer was held firmly along the top surface of the specimen and then DAQ was turned on, as shown in the Figure 6. The loop was created in the LabVIEW software for the proper working of the DAQ. Finally, the series of impact force was given in the beam by using the impact hammer. The software gives the graph of amplitude (y axis) vs frequency (x axis).

Figure 6 Experimental setup

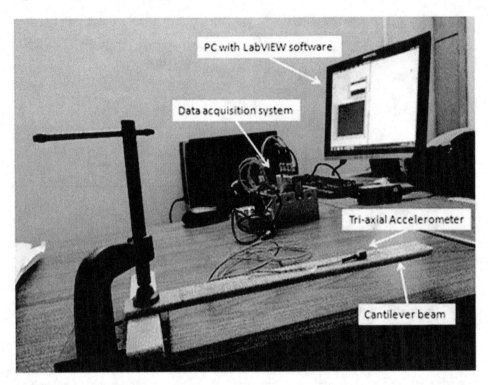

VIBRATION TESTING RESULTS

Specimen 1 (without delaminations) and specimen 2 (with 250 mm² delamination) are considered for experimentation. Objective of the experiment is to obtain first four frequencies for each of the specimen. Three beams with the specimen 1 and 2 dimensions were considered for the experiment, and the average values of frequencies from these three trials are obtained as in Table 3.

Table 3. Vibration testing results

Specimen 1 (without delamination)	Natural Frequency			
Modes	Trial 1 (Hz)	Trial 2 (Hz)	Trial 3 (Hz)	Average (Hz)
1	47.667	47.5	47.4	47.5
2	320.66	321.67	319.65	320.66
3	876.5	878.6	874.4	876.5
4	1694.1	1702.7	1710.8	1702.5
Specimen 2 (with 250 mm² delamination)	Natural Frequency			
Modes	Trial 1 (Hz)	Trial 2 (Hz)	Trial 3 (Hz)	Average (Hz)
1	41.33	41.5	41.5	41.44
2	256.666	255.66	257	256.44
3	709	712	718	713.00
4	1379	1378.66	1365.83	1374.49

Numerical Analysis

ANSYS Parametric Design Language (APDL) is a trustworthy scripting language that allows parameterizing your model and automating routine activities. If the excitation frequency is close to one of the model's inherent modes, it gives a sense of how the replica will behave to any excitation at any frequency. In a nutshell, modal analysis aids in determining natural frequencies (free vibration frequencies) and mode shapes. Because modelling composite beams falls under the category of three-dimensional modelling of solid structures, the type of element used to model the beams was layered Solid 185. The delaminated beams' first five frequencies are determined.

The composite material property is obtained through analytical method, rule of mixtures (Kaw 2005). The fibre volume fraction is obtained as 56% using the following equation. For calculation, the volume of each of the constituents is obtained from known weight and density.

$$V_f = v_f / v_c,$$

$$v_c = v_f + v_m + v_h$$

where, V_f= volume faction of fibre, v_c= volume of the composite, v_f = volume of the fibre, v_m= volume of the matrix, v_h= volume of hardener. The material constants for E-Glass and Epoxy composed in the volume ratio of 0.56:0.44 are calculated as follows:

Volume fraction of the matrix, V_m: V_m = 1- V_f = 0.44 Young's modulus along the fibre directions, E_1 & E_2:

$$E_1 = E_2 = E_f V_f + E_m V_m = 42.1 \text{ GPa}$$

where, E_f = 72 GPa and E_m = 3.81 GPa
Young's modulus in transverse direction E_3:

$$E_3 = E_f E_m / (V_f E_m + V_m E_f) = 7.39 \text{ GPa}$$

Shear modulus G:

$$G = G_f G_m / (V_f G_m + V_m G_f) = 2.4 \text{GPa}$$

where, G_f = 5.8 GPa and G_m = 1.31 GPa

Poisson's ratio = $V_f v_f + V_m v_m$ = 0.29

where, v_f = 0.23 and v_m = 0.37

Density, $\rho = \rho_f V_f + \rho_m V_m$ = 1764 kg/m^3

Where ρ_f = 2130 kg/m^3 and ρ_m = 1300 kg/m^3

COMPARISON OF NUMERICAL AND EXPERIMENTAL ANALYSIS RESULTS

The four frequencies were compared to the experimental data for all composites fabricated to validate the FEA results. When the percentage error for every case is considered, it is discovered that, in the vast majority of cases, FEA produces higher frequencies than that of the equivalent experimental results. A maximum error of 4.3 percent for beams without delaminations and a maximum error of 7.1 percent for beams with delaminations are achieved, as indicated in table 4.

Table 4. Experimental and FEA results comparison

Natural Frequency for undamaged composite (Hz)			
Mode	Experimental	FEA	Error (%)
1	47.51	49.65	-4.3%
2	320.62	310.73	3.19%
3	876.56	869.94	0.75%
4	1702.51	1706.2	-0.22%

Frequency for beam with delamination positioned 50 mm left from free end with 250 mm² delamination area (Hz)			
Mode	Experimental	FEA	Error (%)
1	41.4	44.28	-6.4%
2	256.44	276.1	-7.1%
3	713	767.94	-7.1%
4	1374.49	1452.3	-5.3%

The differences between numerical and experimental results can be due to fabrication error, experimental frequency measurement error, etc. The first two frequencies of the samples as indicated in table 4 are shown in figures 7- 10. The FE model, on the other hand, was capable of determining the first 4 frequencies with an inaccuracy of less than 8%, implying that FE modelling is enough for creating the dataset.

Figure 7. Bending Mode 1 - Without Delaminations

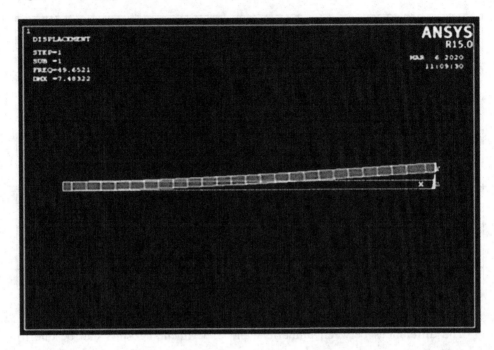

Figure 8. Bending mode 2 - Without Delaminations

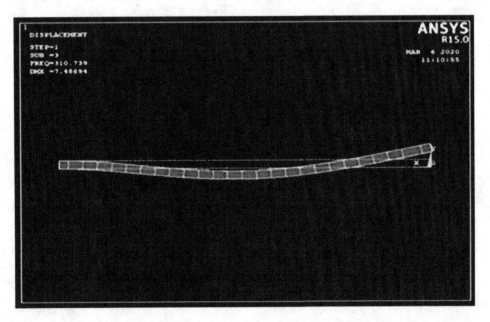

Figure 9. Bending mode 1 - With Delamination

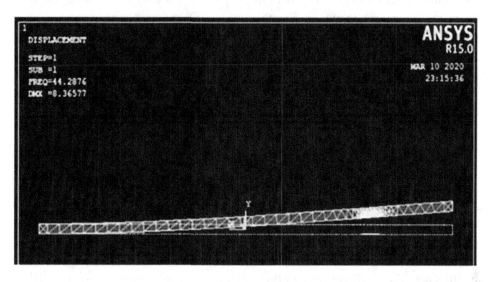

Figure 10. Bending mode 2 - With Delaminations

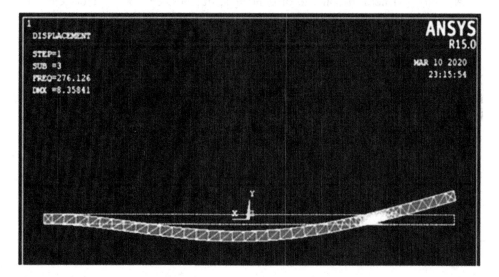

DATABASE GENERATION

A large number of composite samples with various sizes and positions of delaminations were subjected to FE simulation. The database size required to train ANN is important for accurately diagnosing delaminations (position and area) and also finds the time taken by algorithms to do so. For this study, 150 delamination scenarios were numerically produced by combining delaminations at various positions, 5 distinct layer interfaces, and 5 different sizes. For each delamination scenario, first 5 natural frequencies were acquired and utilised as input to ANN, while delamination position were ANN output. A total of 140 such datasets were supplied to the network for training, with the remainder being used for validation.

ANN FOR DAMAGE EVALUATION

The increased interest in problems linked to structural condition monitoring gives an opportunity for Artificial Intelligence (AI) to push its boundaries. AI is a branch of research that aims to replicate human intelligence in robots. It can also make faster decisions with fewer errors. More SHM studies are now relying on artificial intelligence (AI) to detect degradation in structural components (Yan et al 2017). For effective damage evaluation, non-destructive techniques such as thermography, vibration testing, acoustic emission, and ultrasonic testing can be utilised in conjunction with AI.

A biological neuron consists of dendrites, nucleus, cell body, axon, etc. The dendrites will get information from the neighbouring predecessor neurons, and it will pass this information to the neighbouring successor neurons through the axon. ANN is also similar to human brain, where artificial neuron receives information, weighted inputs and a bias and sends the total result to the transfer function for generating a nonlinear function. ANN is used in areas where an abundance of data is available for solving problem (Vallabhaneni & Maity, 2011).

Figure 11. ANN used for Delamination Prediction

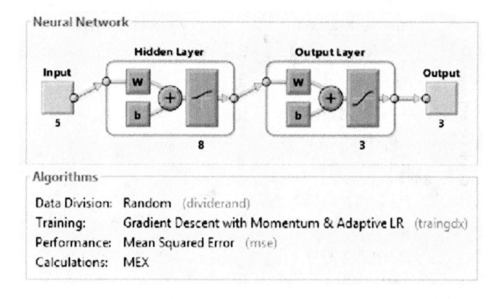

The goal of this study is to explore how well natural frequencies can be utilised to locate and forecast damage severity and size. Feed-forward multilayer back-propagation ANN with supervision (MATLAB Neural Network Toolbox) is used to identify the location and degree of the damage. The neural network size is critical since smaller networks cannot accurately represent the system, while bigger networks over-train it (Sreekanth et al 2022). As a solution, trial and error was used to optimise the size. The ANN is trained using a database generated. As illustrated in figure 11, ANN has five inputs (frequencies), three outputs (location, layer, and size of delamination), and one hidden layer. The linear regression investigation results is indicated in Figure 12. The Pearson's correlation coefficients (R-value) are 0.975, 0.970, 0.985 and 0.975 respectively for training, validating, testing and all data. This implies that the model developed using ANN is giving reasonably good fitting of the results. The R-value of the training data indicates good learning ability for the network as it approximates the actual values of results.

Figure 12. Regression Analyses of Data Predicted by the ANN Model

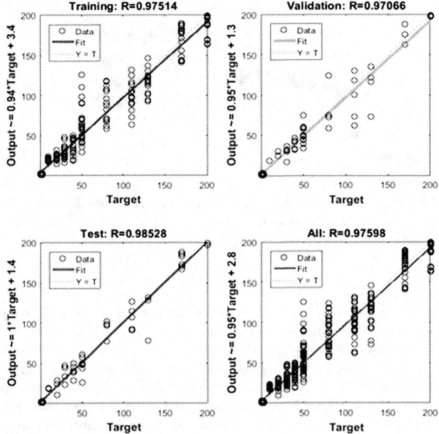

PREDICTION OF DELAMINATION LOCATION AND SEVERITY

FE models are created to verify the ANN approach in determining delamination parameters. Using FE model data, Table 5 compares real and anticipated delamination characteristics for cantilever composite beams. Using Experimental Validation Data, Table 6 compares real and anticipated delamination characteristics for the same.

Table 5. Real versus predicted delaminations parameters using FE model data

	Beam Number	Real	Predicted	Percentage Error
Layer of delamination	1	3	3	Not Applicable
	2	9	9	
	3	7	7	
	4	14	14	
Delamination location (mm)	1	75	73.9	-1.46
	2	95	94.2	-0.84
	3	135	136.2	0.88
	4	160	159.1	-0.56
Delamination Area (mm²)	1	1250	1243.1	-0.55
	2	750	745.9	-0.54
	3	375	379.3	1.1
	4	875	879.2	0.48

Table 6. Real versus predicted delamination parameters using Experimental data

	Beam Number	Real	Predicted	Percentage Error
Delaminated layer	1	5	4	Not Applicable
	2	8	8	
	3	11	9	
	4	14	15	
Delamination location (mm)	1	60	55.0	-8.3
	2	85	90.9	+7
	3	120	116.1	-3.3
	4	140	132.3	-5.6
Delamination Area (mm²)	1	625	575.1	-8
	2	250	299.8	+20
	3	1125	1025.0	-8.8
	4	750	824.9	+10

Prediction results using ANN for numerical and experimental validation data is shown in Figure 13 and 14, respectively, with the delamination locations and areas being scaled approximately to the beams dimensions. The rectangles with green solid edges designate the actual delaminations and those with red solid edges designate the predicted ones. The prediction accuracy of experimentally recorded natural frequencies is less than that of numerical data. This could be due to difficulties in correctly fabricating geometrical aspects of beams or problems in experimentally measuring natural frequencies.

Figure 13. Actual and ANN Predicted Delamination using Numerical Validation Data

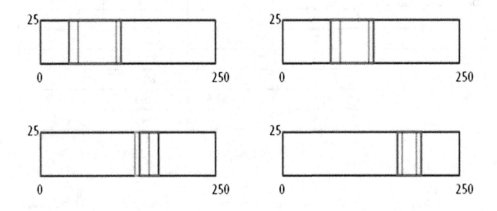

Figure 14. Actual and ANN Predicted Delamination using Experimental Validation Data

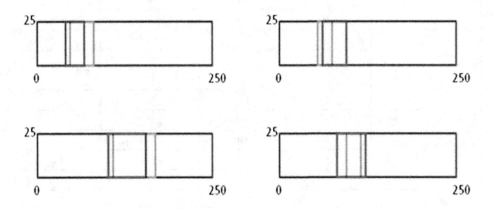

CONCLUSION

The area and position of the delaminations are predicted using vibration-based analysis on GFRP beams in this chapter. Natural frequencies in composite beams were found to be drastically lowered as a result of delamination. In comparison to the first 2 natural frequencies, the third, fourth, and fifth frequencies decrease dramatically with increasing delamination size. The first 5 frequencies are fed into the ANN, which then outputs delamination possibilities (locations and sizes). Both numerically simulated and physically recorded frequency data were utilized to scrutinize the ANN's prediction accuracy in location and severity analysis. The numerical validation accuracy is better than experimental, which may be attributable to dataset used for training the network is numerical based. The current study can be expanded in the future by enhancing the ANN's delamination detection performance and comparing it to other techniques.

REFERENCES

Farrar, C. R., & Worden, K. (2007). An introduction to structural health monitoring. *Philosophical Transactions of the Royal Society A: Mathematical, Physical and Engineering Sciences, 365*(1851), 303-315.

Fritzen, C. P. (2005). Vibration-based structural health monitoring–concepts and applications. *Key Engineering Materials*, *293*, 3–20.

Irving, P., & Soutis, C. (Eds.). (2019). *Polymer composites in the aerospace industry*. Woodhead Publishing.

Kaw, A. K. (2005). *Mechanics of composite materials*. CRC Press.

Latifi, M., Van Der Meer, F. P., & Sluys, L. J. (2015). A level set model for simulating fatigue-driven delamination in composites. *International Journal of Fatigue*, *80*, 434–442.

Mangalgiri, P. D. (1999). Composite materials for aerospace applications. *Bulletin of Materials Science*, *22*(3), 657–664. doi:10.1007/BF02749982

Montesano, J., & Sharifpour, F. (2021). Modelling damage evolution in multidirectional laminates: micro to macro. *Multi-Scale Continuum Mechanics Modelling of Fibre-Reinforced Polymer Composites*, 463-507.

Senthilkumar, M., Reddy, S. M., & Sreekanth, T. G. (2022a). Dynamic Study and Detection of Edge Crack in Composite Laminates Using Vibration Parameters. *Transactions of the Indian Institute of Metals*, *75*(2), 361–370.

Senthilkumar, M., Sreekanth, T. G., & Manikanta Reddy, S. (2021). Nondestructive health monitoring techniques for composite materials: A review. *Polymers & Polymer Composites*, *29*(5), 528–540.

Sreekanth, T. G., Senthilkumar, M., & Reddy, S. M. (2021). Fatigue Life Evaluation of Delaminated GFRP Laminates Using Artificial Neural Networks. *Transactions of the Indian Institute of Metals*, *74*(6), 1439–1445.

Sreekanth, T. G., Senthilkumar, M., & Reddy, S. M. (2021). Vibration-based delamination evaluation in GFRP composite beams using ANN. *Polymers and Polymer Composites, 29*(9), S317-S324.

Sreekanth, T. G., Senthilkumar, M., & Reddy, S. M. (2022b). Natural Frequency based delamination estimation in GFRP beams using RSM and ANN. *Frattura ed Integrità Strutturale, 16*(61), 487-495.

Vallabhaneni, V., & Maity, D. (2011). Application of radial basis neural network on damage assessment of structures. *Procedia Engineering*, *14*, 3104–3110.

Yan, R., Chen, X., & Mukhopadhyay, S. C. (2017). *Structural Health Monitoring*. Springer.

Chapter 9
Lung Cancer Detection Using Deep Learning Techniques

Manya Sangwan
J.C. Bose University of Science and Technology, India

Sapna Gambhir
ⓘ https://orcid.org/0000-0001-5020-8000
J.C. Bose University of Science and Technology, India

Sumita Gupta
Amity School of Engineering and Technology, Amity University, Noida, India

ABSTRACT

Early detection that can be done to detect lung cancer is through radiological examination. Chest X-Ray or chest radiography is one of the tools that can be used to analyze lung diseases including pneumonia, bronchitis, and lung cancer. The image from the radiography will show the shape of the lungs difference between normal and abnormal lungs. In abnormal lungs, it will show nodules in the lungs on the results radiography image, but on the other hand, in normal lungs, it does not show nodules in the lungs on the radiographic image. This study to detect lung cancer using radiographic images using deep learning techniques. Therefore, by carrying out early revealing of lung cancer, it is hoped that this scheme will provide suitable action and directions for lung cancer patients and decrease lung cancer transience.

DOI: 10.4018/978-1-6684-5255-4.ch009

INTRODUCTION

Cancer diagnosis and treatment have been one of the supreme challenges facing mankind in recent years. Early exposure to the tumor will make it easier to save mil-lions of lives around the world every year. In particular, lung cancer is one of the most common types of cancer. Lung cancer screening can be done using a CT scan, chest X-ray, and saliva cytology. However, CT scans can detect lung cancer tumors earlier and at a stage that is more likely to be treatable, than regular x-rays (Wender et al., 2013). Unlike traditional X-ray procedures, CT scans provide a more detailed and accurate picture that shows any abnormalities or irregularities. Trained radiologists are needed to accurately identify lung cancer on CT scan images. The costs required are relatively high, this causes the lower and middle-class people to be unable to reach the required costs. It obliquely leads to reduced exposure of early signs of lung cancer and thus makes curing this disease much more difficult. Therefore, it is necessary to do automation in detecting lung cancer along with the stage of cancer in CT scan images (de Koning et al., 2020; Tanoue et al., 2015).

The motivation for this study arises from a situation that is occurring in a large number of countries: the overload of work in many professions related to the field of radiologists and doctors, who are experts in interpreting the results obtained and making an appropriate diagnosis. This is a complicated task, requiring very high levels of concentration, and can take a great deal of time. Therefore, the experts who analyze the X-rays mustn't suffer from fatigue or other common problems that can impair their performance. However, this is not the norm. The long hours of work and the increase in people diagnosed with diseases such as lung cancer, who depend on the correct interpretation of X-rays for their early detection, place a huge workload for these specialists (Gabehart, 2003). Despite the difficulties involved in analyzing radiographs, the Radiologists indicate in one of its 5 fundamental principles that radiologists must be available to interpret high-risk cases 24 hours a day, every day of the week. The final objective of this study is the establishment of which application model is to support medical diagnosis and focus on the detection of lung cancer. An application capable of analyzing the entered radiographs will be created, generating the probabilities obtained by a model developed using Deep Learning techniques, and graphically showing the parts of the image that doctors should pay special attention to. To do this, we will carry out an initial analysis of the different Deep Learning frameworks and libraries available and select the most promising options.

LITERATURE REVIEW

Machine Learning in Medicine

Throughout the last decades, the field of medicine has been relying on the analysis of medical images (Litjens et al., 2017) from techniques such as radiographs (Shen et al., 2017), MRIs, ultrasound, or CT scans to detect, diagnose and find effective treatments for different diseases. Due to the enormous range of existing pathologies and the outsized number of factors that can lead humans to make a mistake in their diagnosis (Bruno et al., 2018), such as fatigue at work or a simple error in judgment, doctors and researchers are beginning to rely more and more on new technologies, capable of greatly facilitating their work. Throughout this document, we will focus on making the most of existing technologies to help specialists with tasks related to the analysis of medical images. To do this, we must introduce the main technologies and basic concepts that we will use.

Deep Learning

ML is a field of AI that aims to create systems that can learn and improve from earlier knowledge, lacking the necessitate to be unambiguously programmed. This knowledge procedure is based on the scrutiny of a huge quantity of data, instructions, or previous experiences so that patterns and similarities can be located that can be used in future cases (Brownlee, 2019). D L is a subfield of ML focused on the organization and functioning of the brain. According to Andrew Ng., A member of the Google Brain team (a Google research team focused on the field of artificial intelligence), defines Deep Learning as the use of brain simulations to (Brownlee, 2019):

- Make learning algorithms easier to use.
- Achieve breakthroughs in the field of AI.
- Bring computer equipment closer to human rationality.

This technique benefits enormously from advances in computational capacity and obtaining an extensive amount of data, which allow the training of increasingly complex systems. Unlike previous systems, Deep Learning manages to obtain the main characteristics from the data entered (Brownlee, 2019; Wang et al., 2017), without the need for their extraction by experts in the field. This feature, known as "Automatic feature extraction", allows teams not experts in the subject studied to carry out their tests and investigations. This field is intensely encouraged by the architecture of the human brain. In it, there are around 1011 neurons, each of which has about 100,000 synapses, that is, connections with other neurons that have an associated weight. Utilizing this weight, the importance of the information transmitted by each neuron is measured, obtaining a final output impulse (Hartung, 2016). Current Deep Learning systems are based on artificial neurons that mimic this behavior. These neurons process the information received and produce an output. As can be seen in Figure 1, first of all, a weighted sum of the received values is performed. After this, the result of the sum is passed through a non-linear function known as the activation function to obtain the output value of the neuron.

Figure 1. Basic structure of an artificial neuron with Softmax Activation

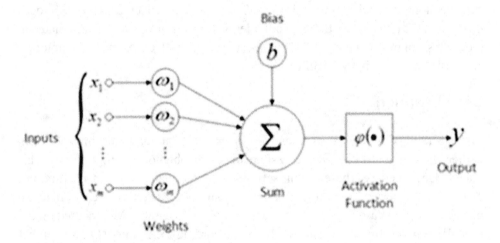

These neurons are combined into hierarchical structures made up of layers, known as ANN (Gu et al., 2015). These structures are collected as a set of neurons, communicating with each other, to transform the input information gradually in anticipation of acquiring progressively more abstract depictions that allow us to attain the purpose of the sys-tem (in our case, to detect if there are findings of diseases in medical imaging). Next, we will focus on explaining the operation of these systems based on two technologies:

- Multilayer perceptrons, popularized in the late 1980s and widely used until the discovery of technologies that offer better results.
- Convolutional networks, widely used to solve problems today.

Multilayer Perceptron (MLP)

The multilayer perceptron is a structure consisting of an input layer (Razzak et al., 2017), followed by one or more hidden layers in charge of transforming the initial data. The results obtained in these layers are connected to an output layer, which produces the final output of the system. The flow of information always travels the network from left to right. The multilayer perceptron training process consists of the following steps:

1. Weights are randomly initialized
2. The entrance is propagated forward
3. The error made is calculated and reversed
4. The initial weights are adapted
5. Go back to step 2 until the desired values are obtained

The main problem with these systems is that multilayer perceptrons are not able to extrapolate correctly. That is, if the network is not properly trained or the number of iterations (epochs) is not enough, inaccurate outputs can be obtained. Furthermore, these networks depend on a large number of layers to achieve sufficient power. A large number of hidden layers will imply that the first layers of the system will have a much less impact because the propagation algorithms will reduce the error obtained on its way to the beginning of the network. However, not all are disadvantages in these systems. MLPs have a large number of pros. Among them, they are fault-tolerant systems, easily extensible, and capable of approximating any function with the desired degree of precision (universal approximation) are advantages that will be exploited by later technologies, such as convolutional networks deep or CNNs.

Deep Convolutional Networks

Unlike MLPs, convolutional networks will be intelligently trained, choosing initial weights and activation functions carefully to get the best results, and not randomly as in the past. The architecture of these networks is the same as that used in MLPs, however, the operation varies considerably. In convolutional networks (Freidman, 2017; Mallat, 2016) it is about extracting characteristics or "features" from the initial images, taking into ac-count the spatial structure of the image (systems used to process images).

This means that it does not matter where a characteristic pattern is recognized in the initial image. If a structure is detected, the network will learn to detect that structure elsewhere in the initial image (and other images). This characteristic is based on the principle of spatial permanence.

Figure 2. Spatial permanence and local dependence

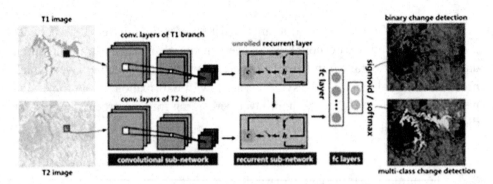

In addition, these systems will be able to extract the relevant information, being able to recognize patterns through changes in lighting, rotations, increases or decreases in size, and other basic transformations. To achieve this goal, convolutional networks use a structure formed by the com-bination of convolutional layers followed by pooling layers. Finally, the architecture with dense layers as in previous systems (output layers).

Convolutional Layers

This type of layer gets its name from the operation known as convolution (González-Muñiz & Díaz Blanco, 2020; Rossi et al., 2021). In this operation, the input image in matrix form (a matrix in case of black and white images or three matrices representing each color in the case of RGB) is filtered using a mask known as a convolutional filter. This mask is accompanied by a square weight matrix known as a "kernel", typically much smaller in size than the input image. Using the kernel weights, the input image is traversed, performing mathematical operations (scalar products) to generate a new output matrix. The kernel movement is performed from left to right, from top to bottom until all possible positions are processed. In current systems, a large number of convolutional filters are used, capable of detecting elements of the image such as edges, corners, or detecting movement in the case of image processing.

Figure 3. Behavior of a Convolutional Operation

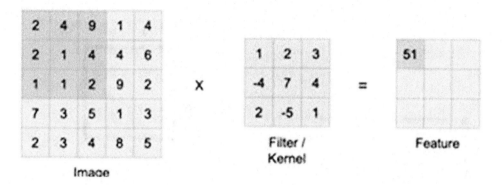

Sub-Sampling

Due to the large number of operations performed, convolutional layers consider-ably increase the number of neurons. In a 32x32 black and white image, if we decided to use 16 convolutional filters, we would get 16,384 output neurons after performing the operations described above.

Therefore, if we decided to introduce a new convolutional layer from the output of our previous layer, the number of neurons would increase dramatically, forcing our system to have an immense processing capacity. To avoid this, a process is known as subsampling (Saha, 2018) from the resulting departures. This process aims to reduce the size of our filtered images without eliminating any of the most important characteristics detected by each of the convolutional filters used.

There are several types of subsampling. In this document, we will focus on the type most used in current networks (used in all our architectures), known as "Pooling" layers. The pooling type layers have the objective of reducing the dimensionality of the outputs of the convolutional layers, known as "Convolved features", without eliminating the characteristics main obtained. These characteristics must be invariable, allowing the system to detect the entity they represent through changes in position, rotation, lighting, and other modifications. To maintain these characteristics, there are two different options. In Figure 4, we can see the results that would be obtained using 2x2 size Max-pooling and Average-pooling layers on a 5x5 size image. The Max-Pooling layers take the highest value found in the set of cells (2x2 in size in this case).

Figure 4. Results obtained using Max and Average pooling layers of size 2x2

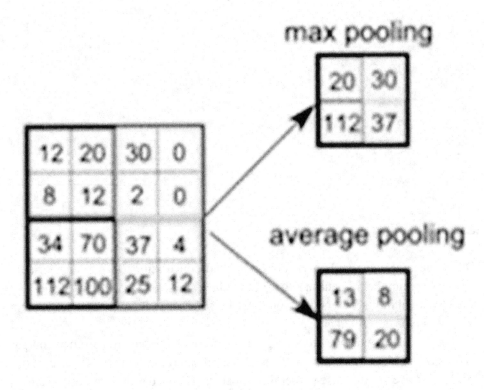

On the other hand, Average-Pooling layers calculate the average value of all cells that are taken into account at all times. Like convolutional layers, layers of type pooling runs through the initial arrays from left to right and from top to bottom.

Reduction of Over-Adjustment

Overfitting (Goodfellow et al., 2016) is an undesirable feature in any Deep system. Learning. It can be said that when a system has a high level of overfitting, the characteristics you are learning are strongly correlated with the data introduced. The greater the overfitting, the less capacity our model will have to generalize, it is that is, to be able to make predictions using completely new data from the characteristics extracted from the data from which you have learned. Fortunately, there is a multitude of methods capable of reducing overfitting in our models. In this section, we will focus on Dropout, Batch Normalization layers as methods to reduce overfitting.

Figure 5. Overfitting, underfitting, and desired situation for the predictions of a system

Underfitting   Desired   **Overfitting**

Dropout Layers

Dropout layers (Srivastava et al., 2014) try to reduce the overfitting of a neural network by incapacitating multiple neurons, randomly selected. In a cape Dropout with a coefficient of 0.5, 50% of the neurons will "freeze", preventing contribution by propagating values to the following layers, and preventing the update of the weights in them.

This operation makes sense thanks to a well-known characteristic of neural networks as a specialization. As the system learns, groups of neurons emerge whose weights tend to stabilize, specializing in the detection of a certain set of features. Ad-jacent neurons may become completely dependent on this specialization, which may result in a model that conforms too much to the data of training. When a large number of neurons associated with a specific task are frozen, others neurons must compensate for this workload, resulting in the learning of multiple feature sets. This causes the network is not so sensitive to the weights of certain sets of neurons, causing it to generalize better and reduce over-fitting.

Figure 6. Visualization of the behavior of the Dropout layers

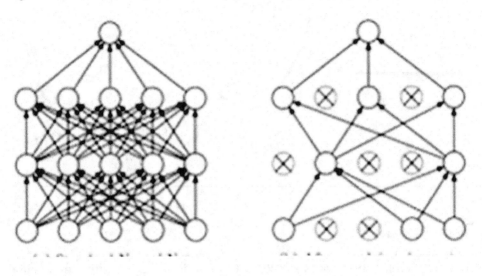

Typical Structure of a Convolutional Network

LeNet

The LeNet network architecture created by Le Cun in the year 1998, is one of the classic ones used for convolutional neural networks. Re-searchers LeCun, Bottou, Bengio, and Haffner proposed this type of network architecture in 1998, originally designed to recognize handwritten and typewritten characters. An overview of this network and its characteristics can be found in the article made by (Liew et al., 2016). The structure of the LeNet-5 network consists of two convolutional layers and layers of Average pooling. The difference between Maxpooling and Average pooling is that, When the image patches are passed, the Maxpooling takes the largest value of the matrix, while the Average pooling adds all the elements of the matrix and divides them by their total number. At the end of the network, there is a layer of Softmax. It is also important to mention that all layers have an activation function tanh or hyperbolic tangent.

AlexNet

In 2010, the large-scale image recognition competition of ImageNet5. The objective of this competition is to detect objects, animals, and other structures that can be observed with the naked eye in the real world. Just two years after the appearance of this large-scale database, it is made public the article "ImageNet Classification with Deep Convolutional Neural Networks" (Krizhevsky et al., 2012). In it, a known deep convolutional network architecture is proposed later as AlexNet as shown in Figure 7, due to the name of its creator. This architecture represented a gigantic step in the field of Deep Learning, achieving exceed the average precision obtained by a human when faced with this problem of classification. AlexNet's accuracy was 84.7%, much higher than those offered by the existing systems at that time. The system closest to AlexNet had been able to obtain an accuracy of only 73.8%.

Figure 7. AlexNet Architecture

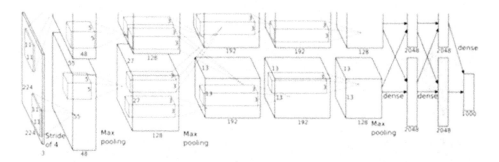

AlexNet used a much larger architecture than previous CNN-based systems. This architecture, consisting of 5 convolutional layers, followed by subsampling lay-ers, and, finally, three dense layers used to classify the 1000 existing classes in the set from ImageNet, used about 60 million parameters and 650,000 neurons. The System training was performed in just over five days, using two of the cards' most powerful graphics of the moment (GTX 580).

Today, systems have been developed capable of producing much better results than AlexNet, based on new types of architecture such as Residual or Inception blocks. However, the study and optimization of architectures to improve convolutional networks deep-seated companies is still in full growth, focusing mainly on improving results and the use of growing computing capacity.

VGGNet

VGGNet, created by (Simonyan & Zisserman, 2014), represented in Figure 8 is an abbreviation for the group that invented it, Visual Geometry Group from the University of Oxford. In the classification task, he improved significantly the results of the AlexNet network and the ZFNet (winner of the year 2013). This type of network has different versions, the most outstanding in the field of knowledge of images the VGG-16 and the VGG-19. A more detailed description of this neural network architecture can be found in the article made by (Tsung, 2018). The VGG neural network is characterized by its simplicity, since, unlike the AlexNet, this network uses a more compact 3x3 layer convolutional architecture. placed on top of each other, thereby adding a greater level of depth to the network. Two of these layers, fully connected, are followed by a classifier-type softmax.

Figure 8. Architecture used for the convoluted neural network structure of VGG

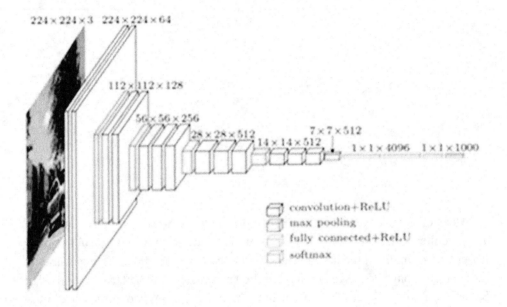

It is one of the most used networks in the community due to its ability to extract relevant characteristics of the images, however, this network consists of more than 140 million parameters, so it may be a bit difficult to handle. Among the works that were carried out within this network distribution neuronal was that of experimentation in terms of the number of layers used in architecture, such as the one carried out by (Tsung, 2018) demonstrating that the VGG-16 improves performance and error rate by adding layers to the VGG-11 architecture, while the VGG-19 architecture worsens its results by doing the same, for which the authors stopped adding layers.

GoogLeNet

GoogLeNet, created by (Ioffe & Szegedy, 2015) and represented in Figure 9 was the winner of the contest ImageNet of the year 2014, reaching an error level of 6.67%, which years later was able to improve and lower it to 5.1%. Its accuracy It got quite close to that of a human being. This network was inspired by the LeNet-5 architecture but added some elements coughs that increased the depth level of the net. He used the normalization of patches and the RMSProp optimizer. It also drastically reduced the number of parameters used thanks to its architecture that is based on small convolutions ñas. Compared to the AlexNet and its 60 million parameters, GoogleNet has 4 million. Another difference of networks such as VGGNet, ZDNet, and AlexNet, is that the Global average pooling at the end of the network instead of using patch layers traditional end. What characterizes this network concerning others is the creation of its called module Inception module which bases its operation on having different types and sizes of convolutions for the same input and saves their different output values as part of the training, a more detailed description of This network architecture can be consulted with the author (Tsung, 2018).

Figure 9. Architecture used for the convoluted neural network structure GoogleNet

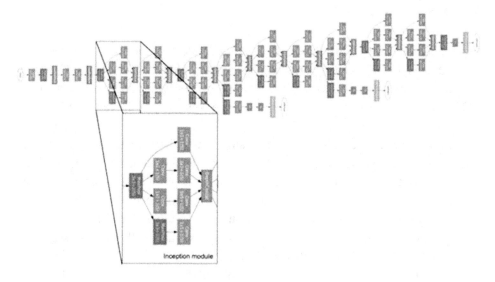

ResNet

ResNet was created by (He et al., 2015) represented in Figure 10 its English name of Residual Neural Network performed by researcher Kaiming. He proposed a new architecture based on passing more powerful connections and features to normalize the size of images. The connecting pass can be described as closed units or closed recurring units that have been recently applied in the network's Recurrent neurons. Thanks to this new network architecture, it was possible to train a neural network with 152 layers, and still have less computational complexity than the VGG network. He had a 3.57% error rate, which he managed to beat the level of performance of a human being for the first time in a tool of image processing and recognition.

Figure 10. Architecture used for the convoluted neural network structure ResNet

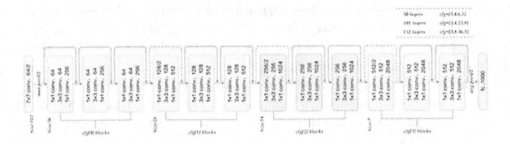

Related References

Research conducted by (Chatchaiwatkul et al., 2021) identifies normal lung conditions, lungs affected by tuberculosis, and lungs affected by pleural effusion by COVID-19 as feature extraction using the CNN method for classifying lung conditions using VGG-16. The accuracy obtained is 93% for the condition of the lungs affected by COVID-19.

Research conducted by (Bohr & Memarzadeh, 2020) which made the system detect the location of a tu-mor or breast cancer obtained an accuracy rate of 91%. The data used for this detection process uses a mammogram image with a combined data processing method of MLP algorithms and a multilevel threshold. Medical images were obtained from the segmentation results, namely the gray image which was used as input in the extraction process using CNN and RGB images used in the process of determining the location of a tumor or cancer.

Research conducted by (Russakovsky et al., 2015) works under the architecture of dense CNN also recognized as DenseNet-169. The authors determined that the ideal feature extraction architecture to support the loss of gradient is DenseNet-169, as your pre-trained network consists of 169 layers of equal sizes directly to each other. In the last phase, the classification, different techniques were used such as SVM, Random Forest, Naive Bayes, K- nearest, among others. Research determined the combination of the DenseNet-169 architecture as a feature extractor and SVM as the classifier.

Research conducted by (Acharya et al., 2018) proposed a model for the classification of cases of schizophrenia through electroencephalography (EEG) signal analysis with the use of deep learning methods. Using other studies carried out for the same type of disease using trait classifiers such as Random Forest, they realized that the information obtained from the characteristics of EGG signals are of high dimensionality, variability, and multichannel, for which they proposed to apply the technique of Pearson's correlation coefficient (PCC), thereby reducing this type of characteristics and bring them to a heat matrix that could serve as input for a neural network convolutional. Finally, the results that his study shows are based on metrics of precision, specificity, and sensitivity. The ultimate goal is to establish a prediction model with techniques such as PCC for precision in the diagnosis and classification of different mental illnesses that use EGG signals.

Research conducted by (Khosravi et al., 2018) chooses CNN as the basis for their classification models, obtaining good results. With the SPP-model net, it was possible to eliminate the restriction that the input image had a fixed size, which was a great advance and improved the precision of all types of architectures based on CNNs. Another characteristic that made the networks better was increasing their depth, as seen with GoogLeNet, although the latter models are more susceptible to overfitting and to underfitting in the case of having little training data or little time, problems whose solution is still being sought. Still, everything points to using the technique of Deep-Image, which allows, on the one hand, to use images of different sizes and, on the other, to increase the amount of data.

State of Art

This section compiles the research carried out on the state of the art for computational diagnostic and detection tools in the medical area. Are few investigations found that focus more on the initial classification on which this study is focused, the focus of most being a diagnosis of the anomaly already located.

Table 1. Summary of the Various Works that uses Deep Learning Models

Ref.No	Database Used	Techniques Used	Model Used	Results
(Kumar et al., 2016)	ImageCLEF	Use 90% of the database for set training, 10% for the validation set.	Transfer Learning , SVM, and fine-tuning of existing neural networks like AlexNet, GoogLeNet.	TL+SVM:96%, Fine tuning+Softmax:94%, Fine tuning+SVM:96%.
(Rawat & Wang, 2017)	Varied (Color Images, Black and White, Scriptures, High definition)	Researchers make a study of neural networks with simple architectures.	Canonical View	DCNN: with 7 Layers, Accuracy:96%. DeepFace: with 8 layers, Accuracy:97%. DeepID: with 7 layers, Accuracy:97%. FaceNet: with 22 layers, Accuracy:99%
(Becker et al., 2017)	BCDR Approximately1143patients diagnosed with breast cancer, giving a total of 286 cases study.	Authors investigated with ANN, separating your results with a different type of breast tissue density.	Deep learning Artificial Neural Networks (DANN)	The accuracy achieved: 82%
(Huynh et al., 2016)	Database: Own and not public. Obtained from the Medical Center of the University of Chicago, approved under Institutional Review. 219 mammograms with lesions confirmed by experts.	Researchers used three methods: 1. CNN and Pre-Trained SVM, 2. Analytical Extraction of Features with SVM, 3. Assembly Classifier.	CNN/SVM	Accuracy: CNN and Pre-Trained SVM:81%, Analytical Extraction of Features with SVM:81%, and Assembled Classifier:86%.
(Rastegari et al., 2016)	ImageNet	It is performed by a classification tool of normal images (challenge Imagenet) combined- do network architectures, with binary networks and Xnor-Network	DCNN	ResNet18 has an accuracy of 69.3% and 89.2% respectively, and GoogLeNet 71.3% and 90% in the two combinations.
(Singh et al., 2018)	Different format images were taken from the joint NIH database (National Institute of Health).	Classifier transfer learning what orders images by the type it represents, being these MRI, CT, X-ray, Ultrasound, etc.	CNN	Accuracy: VGG16=62%,VGG19=98.18%, ResNet50=90%, InceptionV3=99.45%, Xception=98.36%, MobileNet=98.73%, Inception ResNetv2=98.18%.
(Ahn et al., 2019)	ImageCLEF	Researchers used the methodology in which they place a convoluted layer over a pre-trained network of a different domain. The selected network is that of AlexNet.	CNN	AlexNet inculcated with GoogLeNet=82.48% and GoogLeNet inculcated with ResNet=83.14%
(Ayyachamy et al., 2019)	Images are collected from different databases PRO-MISE, LITS, BRATS, Neck & Head Dataset, Database from Cornell University, and a repository thorium TCIA	The network is used ResNet-18 pre-trained to classify a multimodal database, classifying each of the images by region.	CNN	The accuracy achieved: On average with all of the regions, a classification of the 92%. This tool is available to help the training of radiologists for the diagnosis of medical imaging.
(Clancy et al., 2019)	ChestX-Ray, ImageNet, DDMS, and Breast Density.	Different methods for training a network convolutional neuronal. 7 models are made different, in which the databases vary, and training parameters change also between two pre-trained networks.	CNN	Accuracy achieved: AlexNet and ResNet-10. Models: Firts Model (A):75%, Second Model (B):75%, Third Model (C):80%, Fourth Model(D):66%, Fifth Model(E):67%, Sixith Model(F):67%, Seventh Model(G):66%.

Continued on following page

Table 1. Continued

Ref.No	Database Used	Techniques Used	Model Used	Results
(Yang et al., 2019)	breast & CBIS-DDSM.	This article will despise images classified on the level 0 BI-RADS, since they are considered as benign malias, to train a more narrow network It specifies in BI-RADS zones such as 3 and 4, which are those that present malignant anomalies.	Deep Learning Models	The accuracy achieved: It is compared against human experts in the BI-RADS classification level 3 and 4. Experts:54.1%, Tool 75.7%.

OBSERVATIONS

After having briefly reviewed the applications in computer vision, the reader should already be aware of the potential that Deep Learning techniques have. At this point, we want to talk about how these algorithms can be applied, and how they are being applied, to analyze medical images, thus making you aware of the many advantages they provide are depicted as under:-

Classification

Image classification is one of the medical tasks to which Deep Learning has contributed the most so far, if not the most. For this reason, there are many works in images of different modalities (CT, MRI, US) and for all types of body parts (i.e., brain, lungs, breasts, retina, etc.) (Litjens et al., 2017). The usual image classification scheme begins by having as input a set of many images, which would be an examination performed on a patient, and as output a single diagnostic variable, for example, saying whether a certain disease is present or not. It is worth noting the fact that the set of images is taken as a single sample, which makes the data set enormously smaller compared to those formed by non-medical natural images.

Next, different techniques are applied to this approach that are usually based on Transfer Learning, by means of pre-trained networks in sets of natural images for the extraction of characteristics, or by adjusting these same pre-trained networks to their own medical data that you have. In any case, it is advantageous in that it avoids the network training step.

The architectures that are typically used to carry out this task are SAEs, RBMs, both trained in an unsupervised manner, and CNNs, the latter type of network being the most used in recent years (76.6% of the articles published between 2015 and 2017 confirm it (Litjens et al., 2017)). Furthermore, the use of CNNs has been shown to perform very well, challenging the precision of human experts.

Classification of Objects (Injuries)

Another type of classification is that carried out on a single image, and not on a set, with the aim of classifying small parts of said image into two or more classes. For this, the parts to be classified must already be identified, either by a previous stage of the network or manually. As parts of the image or objects, reference is made to all kinds of anatomical structures, injuries, tumors, etc. For this task to be carried out successfully, it is of great importance to have both local information about the object itself to be classified and information about the global context, of what surrounds said injury. You can understand this need by making a comparison with a doctor, who if he only sees a piece of an image, he will not be able to make an accurate diagnosis. However, having both types of information is somewhat difficult when working with Deep Learning architectures, and for this reason it is proposed as a solution to combine architectures, usually a CNN with another CNN or a CNN with an RNN, so that they can be process large amounts of information, large images.

Another handicap when classifying injuries is incorporating the 3D information from the images. Many of the networks that exist so far have been developed specifically for computer vision problems, and therefore for 2D images, and cannot directly handle 3D information. Integrating 3D information is interesting because it has been shown to greatly improve the classification task, and can be done using pre-trained RBMs, SAEs, and CSAEs in an unsupervised way with dispersed autocoders, and also with CNNs trained end-to-end extreme (End-to-end).

Detection

When it comes to classifying objects, it has been mentioned that these objects already have to be previously identified and located. Thus, it can be seen that the detection of a certain anatomical structure is a very important step in medical image analysis, and if it is not carried out correctly, it will cause problems such as an incorrect segmentation of the structure of interest or how to hinder the clinical flow of a therapy or an intervention.

Locating structures in medical images usually involves analyzing the volumes in 3D, for which three different lines are followed: interpreting the volume in 3D as a series of orthogonal 2D planes composed of each other; identify the ROI, which will be the anatomical region of interest, by means of pre-trained CNNs and RBMs, and by classification; and modify the learning process so that the network directly predicts the location of the structure of interest. Therefore, these processes, whereas locating the structures of interest in 2D, treating the task as if it were a classification process, is the most used, while the last of them is the most complicated, but which is expected in the future. get to have better localization results.

To conclude, also comment on the application of Deep Learning methods to work with medical videos, which shows the high potential of RNNs to locate structures in a temporal domain.

Object Detection (Injuries)

The detection of the regions of interest, of the lesions, is one of the key points in any medical diagnosis, as well as being one of the tasks that gives more work to specialists. The most common is that in an image there is more than one small lesion, and consequently in the detection task each and every one of them must be located and identified. For this task we have what are known as Detection Assistance Systems or CADe, in which we constantly work to improve their precision in detection, reduce the time of reading the images, and ultimately advise the experts and help them in their daily work.

The typical way in which these systems work is the following: first a classification of all the pixels of the image is made using a CNN, and then some type of pre-processing is applied to obtain all the candidate objects. The architecture of these CNNs and the methodology that they follow is analogous to that used in the classifi-cation of objects, since they are comparable tasks. In the same way as in the classifi-cation, in this other it is also useful to incorporate context information, for which CNNs are being used multi-stream.

Even having many aspects in common, obviously there are many others in which the detection of objects differs from their classification, such as the fact that, in the detection task, all the pixels are classified as either candidates or As non-candidates, there will always be many more pixels corresponding to the non-candidate class, which are also usually pixels that are very easy to discriminate (they share more similar characteristics). If this relative ease of classification is added to the great difference in proportion of one over the other, it turns out that the algorithm ends up focusing more on classifying those pixels that are not of interest than those that are, since the pixels of the lesion in particular end up being a challenge.

Segmentation

Segmentation of Organs and Substructures

Technically, segmentation is usually defined as identifying the group of pixels that make up the outline or interior of the object of interest. In medical imaging, the segmentation of organs and other substructures is essential to be able to make a quantitative analysis of clinical parameters in relation to the shape and volume of the same structures (i.e., for brain or cardiac analyzes). In addition, segmentation is a first step in computer detection systems, gaining even greater importance. Due to this importance of correctly segmentation of the structures of interest, there are many models that propose different approaches to address the problem, from specific CNN architectures to RNNs. The specific CNNs it is worth mentioning U-Net, published in 2015 (Ronneberger, 2017; Ronneberger et al., 2015a; Ronneberger et al., 2015b).

Its main novelties are the combination, in equal amounts, of layers of up sampling and layers of down sampling, and the presence of connections between opposite convolution and deconvolution layers, which allow characteristics of these layers to be concatenated. With these two improvements, and from a training perspective, this means that the images can be processed by the network in a single forward step, resulting in the segmentation map directly. Furthermore, thanks to this structure, the U-net takes into account the global context of the image, something that as has been discussed continuously is a great advantage compared to standard CNNs. From the model of this U-Net other authors have implemented other architectures that provide certain improvements.

On the other hand, to avoid, or at least reduce, the redundant computation caused by the use of sliding windows to classify pixels, there are authors who propose using FCNNs. The performance of these networks is very satisfactory since they can be applied to multiple targets at the same time (ie with the same trained FCNN, both the brain in MRIs, the pectoral muscle in MRIs and the coronary arteries in CTAs are segmented from different images.) (Moeskops et al., 2016). Finally, the main challenge facing segmentation techniques today is to reduce the rate of incorrectly classified pixels, for which recently it has been proposed to combine FCNNs with Graphic Models and with Conditional Random Fields (CRFs), which manage to refine the output of the classification task.

Injury Segmentation

Lesion segmentation combines both the challenges of object detection and segmentation of organs and substructures. With the detection of objects they share the characteristics of the imbalance between classes, and that it is necessary to have both local information and the global context so that the location of the injury is precise, and for the latter, networks of the type U-net and its derivatives.

Thus, lesion segmentation combines the approaches of object detection with those of organ segmentation, and any progress made in these two fields is likely to spill over into lesion segmentation.

Registration

The registration of medical images, also known as the spatial alignment of im-ages, consists of giving an initial image, applying a coordinate transformation, obtaining a final image. Often a specific type of transformation is assumed (ie nonparametric) and a predetermined metric is used. Even though deep networks are not so widely used for this task, they can bring many benefits when it comes to obtaining the best possible record. For this, two strategies are used; use the networks to estimate a measure of similarity between two given images, and from this apply an iterative optimization strategy; or directly predict the transformation parameters using deep regression networks. There are not many research articles on the subject yet and the few that do have a distinctly different approach, so claiming that one method is more promising than another would not be the most appropriate for now.

CONCLUSION

Trained radiologists are needed to accurately identify lung cancer on CT scan images. The costs required are relatively high, this causes the lower and middle-class people to be unable to reach the required costs. It indirectly leads to reduced detection of early signs of lung cancer and thus makes curing this disease much more difficult. Therefore, it is necessary to do automation in detecting lung cancer along with the stage of cancer in CT scan images. Developing computer-assisted methods for the accurate detection of cancer malignancies can reduce costs so that the treatment and recovery process is more successful. One approach that has been successfully used is to use an Artificial Neural Network (ANN) which is inspired by neural networks in humans. The concept was then further developed in Deep Neural Networks (DNN). The DNN method which until now has the most significant results in image recognition is the Convolutional Neural Network (CNN). CNN was first introduced by LeCun et al. (1998) CNN allows extracting features in a hierarchical manner using multiple convolution layers and max-pooling. However, CNN, like other Deep Learning methods, has the ability, namely the long model training process for mammoth datasets or voluminous images. In this study, it is evaluated that the CNN model can be effectively applied in classifying the level of malignancy of cancer on CT scan images of the lungs to get appropriate results with specificity with accuracy.

REFERENCES

Acharya, U. R., Oh, S. L., Hagiwara, Y., Tan, J. H., & Adeli, H. (2018). Deep convolutional neural network for the automated detection and diagnosis of seizure using EEG signals. *Computers in Biology and Medicine*, *100*, 270–278. doi:10.1016/j. compbiomed.2017.09.017 PMID:28974302

Ahn, E., Kumar, A., Feng, D., Fulham, M., & Kim, J. (2019, April). Unsupervised deep transfer feature learning for medical image classification. In *2019 IEEE 16th International Symposium on Biomedical Imaging (ISBI 2019)* (pp. 1915-1918). IEEE. 10.1109/ISBI.2019.8759275

Ayyachamy, S., Alex, V., Khened, M., & Krishnamurthi, G. (2019, March). Medical image retrieval using Resnet-18. In *Medical imaging 2019: imaging informatics for healthcare, research, and applications* (Vol. 10954, pp. 233–241). SPIE.

Becker, A. S., Marcon, M., Ghafoor, S., Wurnig, M. C., Frauenfelder, T., & Boss, A. (2017). Deep learning in mammography: Diagnostic accuracy of a multipurpose image analysis software in the detection of breast cancer. *Investigative Radiology*, *52*(7), 434–440. doi:10.1097/RLI.0000000000000358 PMID:28212138

Bohr, A., & Memarzadeh, K. (2020). The rise of artificial intelligence in healthcare applications. *Artificial Intelligence in Healthcare*, 25–60. doi:10.1016/B978-0-12-818438-7.00002-2

Brownlee, J. (2019). *Deep Learning & Artificial Neural Networks*. https://machinelearningmastery.com/what-is-deep-learning/

Bruno, M. A., Duncan, J. R., Bierhals, A. J., & Tappouni, R. (2018). Overnight resident versus 24-hour attending radiologist coverage in academic medical centers. *Radiology*, *289*(3), 809–813. doi:10.1148/radiol.2018180690 PMID:30277849

Chatchaiwatkul, A., Phonsuphee, P., Mangalmurti, Y., & Wattanapongsakorn, N. (2021, June). Lung Disease Detection and Classification with Deep Learning Approach. In *2021 36th International Technical Conference on Circuits/Systems, Computers and Communications (ITC-CSCC)* (pp. 1-4). IEEE. 10.1109/ITC-CSCC52171.2021.9501445

Clancy, K., Zhang, L., Mohamed, A., Aboutalib, S., Berg, W., & Wu, S. (2019, March). Deep learning for identifying breast cancer malignancy and false recalls: a robustness study on training strategy. In Medical Imaging 2019: Computer-Aided Diagnosis (Vol. 10950, pp. 20-25). SPIE. doi:10.1117/12.2512942 de Koning, H. J., van der Aalst, C. M., de Jong, P. A., Scholten, E. T., Nackaerts, K., Heuvelmans, M. A., Lammers, J.-W. J., Weenink, C., Yousaf-Khan, U., Horeweg, N., van 't Westeinde, S., Prokop, M., Mali, W. P., Mohamed Hoesein, F. A. A., van Ooijen, P. M. A., Aerts, J. G. J. V., den Bakker, M. A., Thunnissen, E., Verschakelen, J., ... Oudkerk, M. (2020). Reduced lung-cancer mortality with volume CT screening in a randomized trial. *The New England Journal of Medicine, 382*(6), 503–513. doi:10.1056/NEJMoa1911793 PMID:31995683

Freidman, L. (2017). *Lecture 3: Convolutional Neural Networks.* MIT 6.S191. https://www.youtube.com/watch?v=v5JvvbP0d44

Gabehart, R. A. (2003). *Overwork and Stress: The Need for Policy on Working Hours in the Healthcare Professions.* UCHC Graduate School Masters Theses 2003 - 2010. https://opencommons.uconn.edu/uchcgs_masters/41

González-Muñiz, A., & Díaz Blanco, I. (2020). *Convolutional layers with Keras.* doi:10.13140/RG.2.2.14621.13288/1

Goodfellow, I., Bengio, Y., & Courville, A. (2016). *Deep learning.* MIT Press.

Gu, J., Wang, Z., Kuen, J., Ma, L., Shahroudy, A., Shuai, B., Liu, T., Wang, X., Wang, G., Cai, J., & Chen, T. (2015). Recent Advances in Convolutional Neural Networks. *Pattern Recognition, 77,* 354–377. Advance online publication. doi:10.1016/j.patcog.2017.10.013

HartungR. (2016). *Membrane Potentials for beginners.* https://www.youtube.com/watch?v=VOh3pj0RsI0&t=499s

He, K., Zhang, X., Ren, S., & Sun, J. (2015). *Deep residual learning for image recognition cite.* arXiv preprint arxiv:1512.03385.

Huynh, B. Q., Li, H., & Giger, M. L. (2016). Digital mammographic tumor classification using transfer learning from deep convolutional neural networks. *Journal of Medical Imaging (Bellingham, Wash.), 3*(3), 034501. doi:10.1117/1.JMI.3.3.034501 PMID:27610399

Ioffe, S., & Szegedy, C. (2015). *Batch normalization: Accelerating deep network training by reducing internal covariate shift.* arXiv preprint arXiv:1502.03167.

Khosravi, P., Kazemi, E., Imielinski, M., Elemento, O., & Hajirasouliha, I. (2018). Deep Convolutional Neural Networks Enable Discrimination of Heterogeneous Digital Pathology Images. *EBioMedicine, 27,* 317–328. doi:10.1016/j.ebiom.2017.12.026 PMID:29292031

Krizhevsky, A., Sutskever, I. E., & Hinton, G. (2012). ImageNet Classification with Deep Convolutional Neural Networks. *Neural Information Processing Systems, 25.* Advance online publication. doi:10.1145/3065386

Kumar, A., Kim, J., Lyndon, D., Fulham, M., & Feng, D. (2016). An ensemble of fine-tuned convolutional neural networks for medical image classification. *IEEE Journal of Biomedical and Health Informatics, 21*(1), 31–40. doi:10.1109/JBHI.2016.2635663 PMID:28114041

Liew, S. S., Hani, M. K., Radzi, S. A., & Bakhteri, R. (2016). Gender classification: A convolutional neural network approach. *Turkish Journal of Electrical Engineering and Computer Sciences, 24*(3), 1248–1264. doi:10.3906/elk-1311-58

Litjens, G., Kooi, T., Bejnordi, B. E., Setio, A. A. A., Ciompi, F., Ghafoorian, M., van der Laak, J. A. W. M., van Ginneken, B., & Sánchez, C. I. (2017). A survey on deep learning in medical image analysis. *Medical Image Analysis, 42,* 60–88. doi:10.1016/j.media.2017.07.005 PMID:28778026

Mallat, S. (2016). Understanding Deep Convolutional Networks. *Philosophical Transactions - Royal Society. Mathematical, Physical, and Engineering Sciences, 374*(2065), 20150203. Advance online publication. doi:10.1098/rsta.2015.0203 PMID:26953183

Moeskops, P., Wolterink, J. M., Van Der Velden, B. H., Gilhuijs, K. G., Leiner, T., Viergever, M. A., & Išgum, I. (2016). Deep learning for multi-task medical image segmentation in multiple modalities. In *Medical Image Computing and Computer-Assisted Intervention–MICCAI 2016: 19th International Conference, Athens, Greece, October 17-21, 2016, Proceedings, Part II 19* (pp. 478-486). Springer International Publishing.

Rastegari, M., Ordonez, V., Redmon, J., & Farhadi, A. (2016). Xnor-net: imagenet classification using binary convolutional neural networks. *Proceedings of the European Conference on Computer Vision.*

Rawat, W., & Wang, Z. (2017). Deep convolutional neural networks for image classification: A comprehensive review. *Neural Computation, 29*(9), 2352–2449. doi:10.1162/neco_a_00990 PMID:28599112

Razzak, M., Naz, S., & Zaib, A. (2017). *Deep Learning for Medical Image Processing: Overview.* Challenges and Future.

Ronneberger, O. (2017). Invited talk: U-net convolutional networks for biomedical image segmentation. In Bildverarbeitung für die Medizin 2017-Algorithmen-Systeme-Anwendungen. Proceedings des Workshops vom 12. bis 14. März: 2017 in Heidelberg (p. 3). Academic Press.

Ronneberger, O., Fischer, P., & Brox, T. (2015a). Lecture Notes in Computer Science: Vol. 9351. U-Net: Convolutional Networks for Biomedical Image Segmentation. MICCAI 2015.

Ronneberger, O., Fischer, P., & Brox, T. (2015b). U-net: Convolutional networks for biomedical image segmentation. *Medical Image Computing and Computer-Assisted Intervention–MICCAI 2015: 18th International Conference, Munich, Germany, October 5-9, 2015 Proceedings*, *18*(3), 234–241.

Rossi, A., Hagenbuchner, M., Scarselli, F., & Tsoi, A. (2021). A Study on the effects of recursive convolutional layers in convolutional neural networks. *Neurocomputing*, *460*, 59–70. Advance online publication. doi:10.1016/j.neucom.2021.07.021

Russakovsky, O., Deng, J., Su, H., Krause, J., Satheesh, S., Ma, S., Huang, Z., Karpathy, A., Khosla, A., Bernstein, M., Berg, A. C., & Fei-Fei, L. (2015). Imagenet large scale visual recognition challenge. *International Journal of Computer Vision*, *115*(3), 211–252. doi:10.100711263-015-0816-y

Saha, S. (2018). *A Comprehensive Guide to Convolutional Neural Networks*. Academic Press.

Shen, D., Wu, G., & Suk, H. I. (2017). Deep learning in medical image analysis. *Annual Review of Biomedical Engineering*, *19*(1), 221–248. doi:10.1146/annurev-bioeng-071516-044442 PMID:28301734

Simonyan, K., & Zisserman, A. (2014). *Very deep convolutional networks for large-scale image recognition.* arXiv preprint arXiv:1409.1556.

Singh, S., Ho-Shon, K., Karimi, S., & Hamey, L. (2018, November). Modality classification and concept detection in medical images using deep transfer learning. In *2018 International conference on image and vision computing New Zealand (IVCNZ)* (pp. 1-9). IEEE. 10.1109/IVCNZ.2018.8634803

Srivastava, N., Hinton, G., Krizhevsky, A., Sutskever, I., & Salakhutdinov, R. (2014). Dropout: A Simple Way to Prevent Neural Networks from Overfitting. *Journal of Machine Learning Research*, *15*, 1929–1958.

Tanoue, L. T., Tanner, N. T., Gould, M. K., & Silvestri, G. A. (2015). Lung cancer screening. *American Journal of Respiratory and Critical Care Medicine, 191*(1), 19–33. doi:10.1164/rccm.201410-1777CI PMID:25369325

Tsung. (2018). *Review: Googlenet (inception v1)- winner of ilsvrc 2014 (image classification).* Available at: https://medium.com/coinmonks/

Wang, X., Peng, Y., Lu, L., Lu, Z., Bagheri, M., & Summers, R. M. (2017). ChestX-Ray8: Hospital-Scale Chest X-Ray Database and Benchmarks on Weakly-Supervised Classification and Localization of Common Thorax Diseases. *2017 IEEE Conference on Computer Vision and Pattern Recognition (CVPR)*, 3462-3471. 10.1109/CVPR.2017.369

Wender, R., Fontham, E. T., Barrera, E. Jr, Colditz, G. A., Church, T. R., Ettinger, D. S., & Smith, R. A. (2013). American Cancer Society lung cancer screening guidelines. *CA: a Cancer Journal for Clinicians, 63*(2), 106–117. doi:10.3322/caac.21172 PMID:23315954

Yang, W. T., Su, T. Y., Cheng, T. C., He, Y. F., & Fang, Y. H. (2019, March). Deep learning for breast cancer classification with mammography. In *International forum on medical imaging in Asia 2019* (Vol. 11050, pp. 190-195). SPIE. 10.1117/12.2519603

Chapter 10
Mechanism for Crawling, Filtering, and Presenting Opinionated Content on Online Products to the Customers

Rosy Madaan
CSE Department, FET, Manav Rachna International Institute of Research and Studies, India

ABSTRACT

There is a large amount of data available on the web in form of opinions, which need to be accessed for mining opinions. This is an ever-growing field that brings together the reviews, blogs, discussions on forums, Twitter, microblogs, and social networks. A user may be looking for opinions on some commodity or product for making decision regarding purchase for which there is the need of a system based on question answering. This gives rise to a question answering (QA) system. This system works on all the aspects of question answering along with the mining of opinions. The chapter discusses all the modules of the question answering system along with how the opinions are mined. The details of implementation along with the performance analysis of the proposed system are given in the chapter. On performance evaluation, a high value of opinion accuracy has been found that shows that the system performs well.

DOI: 10.4018/978-1-6684-5255-4.ch010

INTRODUCTION

The information present in form of text on the WWW can be classified broadly into two major categories namely facts and opinions (Sasikal and Mary, 2020). Facts are statements written about events and the entities existing in the world in an objective form. Opinions are the statements written in an objective form that reflect sentiments (Hu and Liu, 2004) or perceptions of people about the real world events and entities. Much of the existing research on processing the textual information present on the WWW has been focussed on how factual information can be mined and retrieved. The related areas are information retrieval, Web search, natural language processing and text mining (Boiy and Moens, 2008). This is the era of huge digital content on the web in form of opinions and a little work has been done in the direction of processing the opinions. However, opinions are so important that whenever a person needs to make a decision about purchase of any item, he/she discusses with other customers (Popescu and Etzioni, 2007) and collect their opinions. This is applicable for both the individuals and the organizations.

In order to gather opinions about its products, a company needs to conduct surveys, organize focused groups and to employ external consultants. Also, the companies need to collect opinions of its competitors. The task of finding opinion sources and monitoring them on the Web is actually a formidable task because there exist a big number of diverse sources existing on the WWW and a huge volume of information is present on each source. Classifying an opinion is a very important aspect of opinion mining which has been studied widely in the NLP community. Opinion classification is defined as "determining whether an opinion on an object is positive, negative or neutral". For example, the system classifies the reviews gathered on movies into three type's i.e. positive, negative or neutral reviews. This type of problem is clearly a classification learning problem. In opinion classification, the words which are related to the topic are not important. Instead, the words that indicate polarity of an opinion (Bhatia, Sarma, and Bhatia, 2015) as positive, negative or neutral are important. The words excellent, great, amazing, worst, horrible, bad, worst, etc. can be used to decide the polarity. Most of the techniques for opinion classification apply some forms of machine learning techniques. The whole task of presenting opinions (Bhatia, Sarma, and Bhatia, 2018) to the user involves finding relevant sources, extract sentences comprising of opinions, summarizing them and organizing them into usable forms. This calls for the need of an automated system that takes a user's question as input and presents opinion(s) as answer(s). Such a system is termed as Question Answering (QA) system.

The paper has been organized in the following manner: section 2 discusses recent research carried out in this area; section 3 presents the proposed system for question answering; the analysis of the proposed work is given in section 4 and last section provides conclusion.

RELATED WORK

Liu (2008) focuses on methods in the direction of addressing the new challenges that arise by sentiment aware applications, as compared to those that are already present in more traditional fact-based analysis (Sadegh, Ibrahim, and Othman, 2012). The paper presented the work done on how evaluative text can be summarized. Also, it discussed issues in broader terms regarding privacy, economic impact and manipulation that arise due to the development of information-access services which are opinion-oriented.

O'Leary (2015) presented that review summarization, review classification, extraction of synonyms and antonyms, tracking of opinions in online discussions etc. are some applications of sentiment classification in information systems. Yu, Zha, and Chua (2012) worked on the sentiment classification problem at different levels i.e. at word-level, document-level, sentence-level and aspect-level. Also, some techniques for solution of these problems have been introduced.

Kumar, Desai, and Majumdar (2016) exploits the hierarchical organization of consumer reviews and proposed how to generate answers appropriate for the questions that demand for the opinions about products.

Sadegh, Ibrahim, and Othman (2012) presented the design and implemented the Opinion crawler. The proposed crawler downloads the opinions from several sites. The crawler is also responsible for detecting the web pages that undergo updation very frequently by computing the timestamp for deciding when the revisit is to be done in order to gather relevant opinions. Precison and recall have been used as the quality parameters for evaluating performance of the designed crawler. For justification of this, real data sets have been taken into consideration.

Khan et al. (2014) presented a flowchart in which show the overall picture of classification of twitter data (Sharma and Chitre, 2014). This has been illustrated from a popular micro blogging service, Twitter and other sites where users share their opinions. Results of trend analysis are evaluated in terms of basic information retrieval search strategies i.e. Precision and Recall.

An opinion-mining module has been developed that consisted of creating a dataset in which emotions are tagged with opinions. In this module, the sentences are processed, their polarity is predicted or recognized in terms of positive/negative, their emotion type is identified whether bored, frustrated, excited, neutral and engagement. The corpus has been evaluated along with evaluating the accuracy of text polarity and emotion recognition (Kumar, Desai, and Majumdar, 2016).

Wang et al. (2019) concentrates on automatic extraction and mining of the reviews that have been collected from various websites like Amazon. The algorithms such as Naïve Bayes classifier, SentiWordNet and Logistic Regression are used for classification of the review as positive and negative.

With the dominance of social media and online forum, field of opinion mining, targeting at analyzing and discerning the latent opinion in reviews generated by the user on the Internet, has risen as a sizzling research topic. This survey emphasizes on two important subtasks in this field. At first, the general framework of opinion mining is presented and the evaluation metrics would be described. Then, the methodologies for stance detection on diverse bases, such as online forum and social media are deliberated. After that, methods for product aspect mining are broken into three key groups which are corpus level aspect, corpus level aspect extraction and opinion mining.

A survey has been conducted in that focuses on two important subtasks in this field i.e. stance detection and mining product aspects. This paper is concerned with the introduction to the general framework for mining of opinions. Then, the paper discusses the methodologies for detection of stance on different sources like social media and online forums are discussed. The approaches for product aspect mining are classified into three main categories:

- corpus level aspect extraction,
- corpus level aspect and opinion mining, and
- document level aspect and opinion mining on the basis of the processing units and tasks. Also, various challenges and possible solutions to them are discussed.

OPINIONS AND THEIR CLASSIFICATION

There are three main components an opinion (as shown in Figure 1) is comprised of:

- Opinion holder: This section comprises the name and other identity of a person or an organization which holds a particular opinion related to object of interest. o
- Object: The product on which person(s) expresses their opinion.
- Opinion: This statement given by an opinion holder which may be in form of a view, attitude, or appraisal.

Figure 1. Components of an Opinion

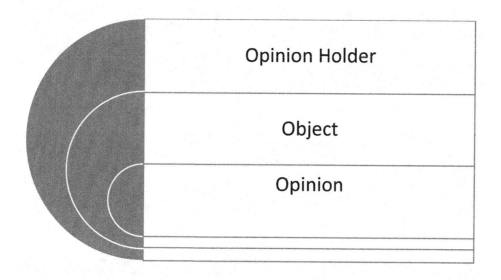

More specifically, an object O is defined as an entity which can be a person, product, commodity, topic, event, or organization. It is represented as

- An organization of components, sub-components, in form of a hierarchy.
- A component is represented by a node and is associated with a set of attributes.
  - The root node given by O (which also has a set of attributes)

There are three tasks (as shown in Figure 2) involved in this type of classification:

1. Identification and extraction of product's features from the reviews that the reviewers have expressed their opinions on like "the sound quality of this phone is just mind blowing". In this, "sound quality" is the product feature.
2. Classification of the opinion on the features into three major categories: positive opinion, negative opinion or neutral opinion.
3. Generation of summary about the opinions.

Figure 2. Tasks involved in this type of classification

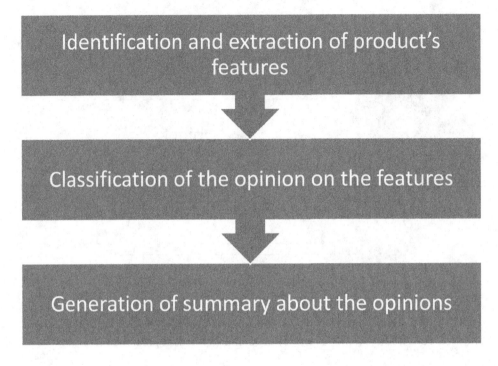

There are several kinds of questions that may come up like with an objective to:

1. To find opinions on a specific product (or some features of the product), e.g.,
    o list opinions of an opinion holder on a iphone, what are opinions of public on a child-labour?
2. Find how opinions on a product vary over time.
    a. How two products A and B be compared?
    b. How is iPhone better than Android?

PROPOSED APPROACH

The architecture of QA system for mining opinions has been proposed that returns answer(s) to the questions of the user in form of opinions, which are further classified into some specific categories.

The proposed system comprises of following five functional modules as shown in Fig.3:

1. crawl & extract opinions
2. filter opinions
3. ONTOLOGY based product feature extraction
4. opinion indexer
5. Detecting opinion/answer
6. Precise opinion lookup
7. Exact opinion lookup
8. Similarity measures of sentiment in questions & texts

Figure 3. Design of QA system for mining opinions (proposed system)

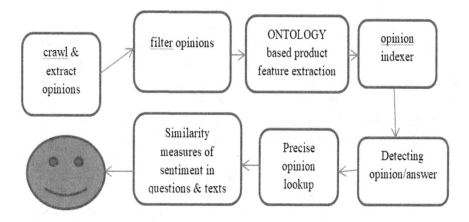

Each of the functional components along with required data structures is described as follows.

- **Crawl opinions and extracts opinions:** A fully automated opinion crawler downloads the web pages and twitters/comments on Facebook to extract opinions from them which are maintained in the opinion repository.
- **Filters opinions**: The objective of this module is to filter m opinions out of the set of n opinions such that the extracted opinions are the higher quality opinions and retain most of the information. All the opinions stored in the opinion repository are processed for analysis of their quality. The higher quality opinions are selected and are stored in quality opinion repository. This is used to discard those opinions which are not at all related to the product. For this, a bag of words approach can be used such that those opinions are extracted that having terms matching with the product. Moreover, the opinions having more number of matching terms are picked up and those with lower

number of terms are ignored. Filtered opinions are stored in *Filtered Opinion Repository*.

- **ONTOLOGY based product feature extraction:** Amarouche, Benbrahim, and Karsou (2015) using the existing domain based Ontologies product features are extracted and indexed corresponding to the types of product such that an index is maintained in which searching is performed to output opinions for the products searched by the user. Consider the Ontology for Digital camera. Using the above Ontology, an index is maintained as shown in Table 2. Like, for the product *Digital camera;* features extracted using the Ontology (shown in Fig.4) are *ImageRatio, SensorSize and SensorType*.

Ali et al. (2020) Online customer reviews provide new potential customers with relevant information about a product or service. It has been empirically shown that the type of reviews (positive or negative) a product receives significantly impacts its future sales. In this paper, the online customers' reviews analysis for the identification of key product attributes to be used in the conceptual design phase of a product is outlined. Our goal is to bring a value-added link between the Middle of Life phase to the Beginning of Life phase in the closed-loop product lifecycle management (PLM) by developing an ontology-based reasoning system to provide information that represents the customers' opinions for the product's conceptual design. The main contributions of the proposed approach are the integration between the ontology and the Natural Language Processing system in extracting the customers' reviews data in the overall framework. The utility of the proposed approach is shown through the application on the digital camera product review dataset from Amazon.

- **Opinion indexer:** The filtered opinions are indexed by the opinion indexer in such a way that the opinions corresponding to the user's question are searched and are provided in response as answer(s) to his question. There are two types of index maintained by *Opinion indexer- Product list* and *Product feature based opinion index* (as shown in Table 1 and Table 2 respectively).

Table 1. Product list

Type	Product
Iphone	
Samsung	Phone
Oppo	
Vivo	
Whirlpool	
LG	
Samsung	Washing machine
Onida	
IFB	

Table 2. Product feature based opinion index

Product	Type	Feature	Opinion(s)
Phone	Iphone	Battery	The iPhone 6's battery life is solid but we can't help but feel that we would happily give up a millimetre of thickness for a few more hours of use.
		Camera	Apple has lavished the iPhone 6S with a serious front camera upgrade this time around.
		Call quality	Even without VoLTE the iPhone 6 has good call quality.
		Screen	3D Touch is, without question, the defining feature of the iPhone 6S' screen.
		Price	As of 5th July 2019, Apple iPhone 6s price in India starts at Rs. 27,999
	Samsung	Battery	Coming to the highlight of the Samsung smartphone along with its design is the
Phone			5,000mAh battery. Long story cut short, the massive 5,000mAh battery of Samsung seems to run forever even in the most taxing of situations.
		Camera	The Samsung Galaxy M30 comes with a vertically aligned three camera setup on the back. According to the specifications, the primary camera comes with a 13-megapixel camera sensor with an f/1.9 aperture and PDAF autofocus, the second camera comes with a 5-megapixel sensor for depth mapping and the third camera comes with a 5-megapixel sensor and an ultra-wide lens.
		Memory	Last month, Samsung released its largest capacity EVO Plus microSD card at 512GB memory capacity, twice the previous max capacity.
		Price	The Samsung Galaxy M40 is priced at Rs. 19,990 in India. The Samsung Galaxy A70 sports an in-display fingerprint sensor — a key selling point, and also a feature that is quickly becoming common in this price segment.
	Oppo	.....	.....
	Vivo	.....	.....

Detecting opinion module will search for the user's question in the *Feature based opinion index* maintained by the *Opinion indexer* and provides answer(s) in return.

For extracting precise opinions, focus is on the extraction using sentiment information contained in the sentence. On the other hand, exact opinions are presented as answer(s) to the user.

Similarity measures of sentiment in questions and texts can be measured by named entities extraction in questions and then linking the named entities with sentiment values which is expressed around their contexts. Likewise, correct answers could be extracted from the text with the use of similarity measures of sentiment both in questions and texts.

IMPLEMENTATION AND PERFORMANCE EVALUATION

The proposed system is implemented using C#.net as the front-end and SQL as the backend. To evaluate the performance of the proposed system, feedback was taken by five users. In total 20 questions were given to each user. Every user entered each question one by one on the system's interface and analyzed the answer(s) returned by the system. Opinion accuracy was taken as a performance metric to analyze the proposed system. Snapshot of the implementation of the proposed system is shown in Figure 4.

Figure 4. Screenshot of implementation of the system

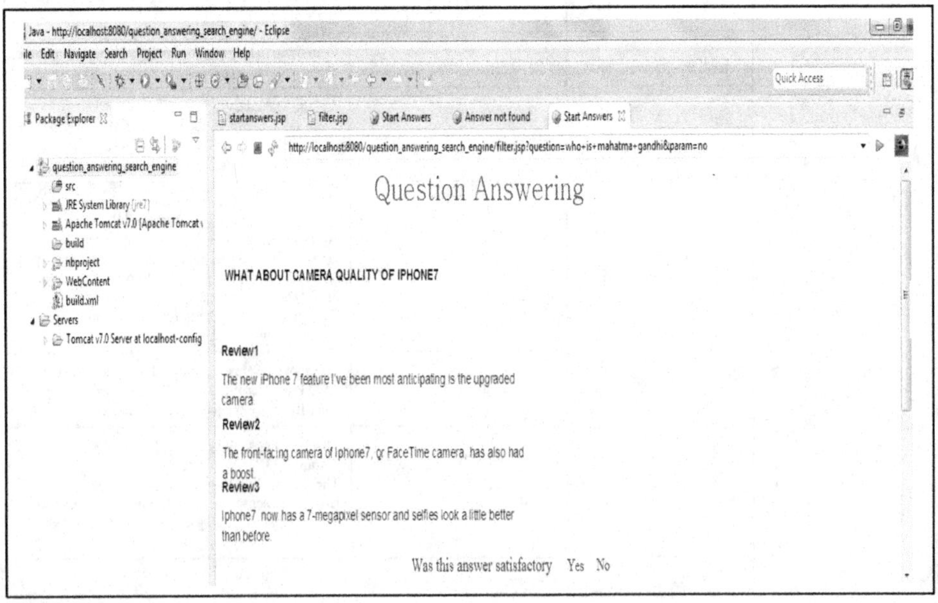

Figure 5. Performance analysis of the proposed system

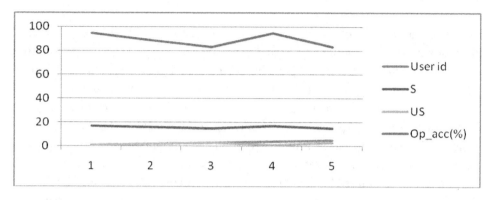

Opinion accuracy is defined as the fraction of number of opinion(s) found satisfactory over the total number of opinion(s) returned by the system i.e., Op_acc=S/(S+NS), where S is the number of opinion(s) found satisfactory and NS is the number of opinion(s) found unsatisfactory. The results of the analysis are shown in Table 3. Consider the following data obtained after analysis:

Table 3. Analysis in terms of Op_acc

User id	S	US	Op_acc(%)
1	17	1	94.4
2	16	2	88.8
3	15	3	83.3
4	17	1	94.4
5	15	3	83.3

It can easily be analyzed from the Table 3 that the Opinion accuracy is above 80% which shows that the proposed system performs well.

The performance analysis of the proposed system is shown graphically in Fig.5. It shows that the system performs well and the users are about 80% satisfied with the opinions fetched corresponding to the product about which the questions are asked.

CONCLUSION

The information available in form of opinions over the WWW, in form of tweets, Facebook comments and reviews available on the shopping sites is really a useful source of information for the people who are interested in buying some product(s). Also, the polarity of the opinions plays a crucial role in the decision making process of the customer. The customer may enter his question and expects to have opinions in form of answers in response. In this work, a Question Answering system has been designed that takes a question as input and provides opinion(s) in response. Opinion lookup module will search for the user's question in the Product Feature based opinion index maintained by the Opinion indexer and provides answer(s) in return. On analyzing the performance of the proposed system, the system's accuracy has been found to be more than 80% which show the consistent behaviour of the system.

REFERENCES

Amarouche, K., Benbrahim, H., & Kassou, I. (2015). Product opinion mining for competitive intelligence. *Procedia Computer Science, 73*, 358–365.

Bhatia, S., Sharma, M., & Bhatia, K. K. (2015). Sentiment knowledge discovery using machine learning algorithms. *Journal of Network Communications and Emerging Technologies, 5*(2), 8–12.

Bhatia, S., Sharma, M., & Bhatia, K. K. (2018). Sentiment Analysis and Mining of Opinions. In Internet of Things and Big Data Analytics Towards Next-Generation Intelligence (pp. 503-523). Springer.

Boiy, E., & Moens, M.F. (2008). *A machine learning approach to sentiment analysis in multilingual Web texts*. Academic Press.

Hu, M., & Liu, B. (2004). Mining and Summarizing Customer Reviews. *Proc. of ACM SIGKDD Intl. Conf. on Knowledge Discovery and Data Mining (KDD'04)*, 168–177. 10.1145/1014052.1014073

Jeyapriya, A., & Selvi, C. K. (2015). Extracting aspects and mining opinions in product reviews using supervised learning algorithm. In *Electronics and communication systems (ICECS), 2015 2nd International conference on 2015 February 26* (pp. 548–552). New York: IEEE.

Khan, F. H., Bashir, S., & Qamar, U. (2014). TOM: Twitter opinion mining framework using hybrid classification scheme. *Decision Support Systems, 31*(57), 245–257.

Khan, K., Baharudin, B., Khan, A., & Ullah, A. (2014). Mining opinion components from unstructured reviews: A review. *Journal of King Saud University-Computer and Information Sciences*, *26*(3), 258–275.

Liu, B. (2008). *Opinion mining and summarization.* In *Tutorial at the World Wide Web Conference (WWW)*, Beijing, China.

O'Leary, D. E. (2015). Twitter mining for discovery, prediction and causality: Applications and methodologies. *Intelligent Systems in Accounting, Finance & Management*, *22*(3), 227–247.

Pang, B., & Lee, L. (2008). Opinion mining and sentiment analysis. *Foundations and Trends® in Information Retrieval, 2*(1–2).

Popescu, A. M., & Etzioni, O. (2007). Extracting product features and opinions from reviews. In *Natural language processing and text mining* (pp. 9–28). Springer. doi:10.1007/978-1-84628-754-1_2

Sadegh, M., Ibrahim, R., & Othman, Z. A. (2012). Opinion mining and sentiment analysis: A survey. *International Journal of Computers and Technology*, *2*(3), 171–178.

Sasikal, P., & Mary, L. (2020). Sentiment analysis of online product reviews using DLMNN and future prediction of online product using IANFIS. *Journal of Big Data, 7*.

Sharma, N. R., & Chitre, V. D. (2014). Opinion mining, analysis and its challenges. *International Journal of Innovations & Advancement in Computer Science*, *3*(1), 59–65.

Yu, J., Zha, Z. J., & Chua, T. S. (2012). Answering opinion questions on products by exploiting hierarchical organization of consumer reviews. In *Proceedings of the 2012 joint conference on empirical methods in natural language processing and computational natural language learning* (pp. 391–401). Association for Computational Linguistics. https://people.cs.kuleuven.be/~bettina.berendt/WebMining10/L3.pdf

ADDITIONAL READING

Ali, M. M., Doumbouya, M. B., Louge, T., Rai, R., & Karray, M. H. (2020). Ontology-based approach to extract product's design features from online customers' reviews. *Computers in Industry*, *116*, 103175.

Amas Bustillos, R., Zatarain Cabada, R., Barrón Estrada, M. L., & Hernández Pérez, Y. (2019). Opinion mining and emotion recognition in an intelligent learning environment. *Computer Applications in Engineering Education*, *27*(1), 90–101. doi:10.1002/cae.22059

Kumar, K. S., Desai, J., & Majumdar, J. (2016, December). Opinion mining and sentiment analysis on online customer review. In *2016 IEEE International Conference on Computational Intelligence and Computing Research (ICCIC)* (pp. 1-4). IEEE. 10.1109/ICCIC.2016.7919584

Meduru, M., Mahimkar, A., Subramanian, K., Padiya, P. Y., & Gunjgur, P. N. (2017). Opinion Mining Using Twitter Feeds for Political Analysis. *International Journal of Computer*, *25*(1), 116–123.

Padmaja, S., & Fatima, S. S. (2013). Opinion mining and sentiment analysis-an assessment of peoples' belief: A survey. *International Journal of Ad hoc Sensor & Ubiquitous Computing*, *4*(1), 21. doi:10.5121/ijasuc.2013.4102

Wang, R., Zhou, D., Jiang, M., Si, J., & Yang, Y. (2019). A Survey on Opinion Mining: From Stance to Product Aspect. *IEEE Access : Practical Innovations, Open Solutions*, *7*, 41101–41124. doi:10.1109/ACCESS.2019.2906754

Compilation of References

Aamodt, A., & Plaza, E. (1994). Case-based reasoning: Foundational issues, methodological variations, and system approaches. *AI Communications, 7*(1), 39–59.

Acharya, C., Coop, A., & Polli, J., & MacKerell, A. (2011). Recent Advances in Ligand-Based Drug Design: Relevance and Utility of the Conformationally Sampled Pharmacophore Approach. *Current Computer-aided Drug Design, 7*(1), 10–22.

Acharya, U. R., Oh, S. L., Hagiwara, Y., Tan, J. H., & Adeli, H. (2018). Deep convolutional neural network for the automated detection and diagnosis of seizure using EEG signals. *Computers in Biology and Medicine, 100*, 270–278. doi:10.1016/j.compbiomed.2017.09.017 PMID:28974302

Agrawal, P. (2018). Artificial Intelligence in drug discovery and development. *Journal of Pharmacovigilance, 6*(2). https://doi.org/10.4172/2329-6887.1000e173

Aha, D. W., Molineaux, M., & Ponsen, M. (2005). Learning to win: Case-based plan selection in a real-time strategy game. *Case-Based Reasoning Research and Development: 6th International Conference on Case-Based Reasoning, ICCBR 2005, Chicago, IL, USA, August 23-26, 2005 Proceedings, 6*, 5–20.

Ahn, E., Kumar, A., Feng, D., Fulham, M., & Kim, J. (2019, April). Unsupervised deep transfer feature learning for medical image classification. In *2019 IEEE 16th International Symposium on Biomedical Imaging (ISBI 2019)* (pp. 1915-1918). IEEE. 10.1109/ISBI.2019.8759275

Al-Turjman, F., & Malekloo, A. (2019). Smart Parking in Cloud-Based IoT. In *The Cloud in IoT-enabled Spaces* (pp. 103–155). CRC Press. doi:10.1201/9780429319181-5

Amarouche, K., Benbrahim, H., & Kassou, I. (2015). Product opinion mining for competitive intelligence. *Procedia Computer Science, 73*, 358–365.

Ananth. (2020). *Machine Learning – Intelligent Decisions based on Data*. Witanworld. Retrieved from https://witanworld.com/article/2020/08/09/machinelearning/

Antoniadis, I., Kontsas, S., & Spinthiropoulos, K. (2019). Blockchain and brand loyalty programs: A short review of applications and challenges. In *International Conference on Economic Sciences and Business Administration* (Vol. 5, No. 1, pp. 8-16). Spiru Haret University.

Anwar, T., Kumar, P., & Khan, A. (2021). *Modern Tools and Techniques in Computer-Aided Drug Design*. Molecular Docking for Computer-Aided Drug Design.

Aparoy, P., Kumar Reddy, K., & Reddanna, P. (2012). Structure and Ligand Based Drug Design Strategies in the Development of Novel 5-LOX Inhibitors. *Current Medicinal Chemistry, 19*(22), 3763–3778.

Arabi, A. A. (2021). Artificial Intelligence in Drug Design: Algorithms, applications, challenges and Ethics. *Future Drug Discovery, 3*(2). doi:10.4155/fdd-2020-0028

Arya, H., & Coumar, M. (2021). Lead identification and optimization. The Design & Development of Novel Drugs and Vaccines, 31-63.

Ata, K. M., Soh, A. C., Ishak, A. J., Jaafar, H., & Khairuddin, N. A. (2019). Smart Indoor Parking System Based on Dijkstra's Algorithm. *Int. J. Integr. Eng, 2*(1), 13–20.

Ayers, M., Jayatunga, M., Goldader, J., & Meier, C. (2022). *Adopting AI in Drug Discovery*. https://www.bcg.com/en-in/publications/2022/adopting-ai-in-pharmaceutical-discovery

Ayyachamy, S., Alex, V., Khened, M., & Krishnamurthi, G. (2019, March). Medical image retrieval using Resnet-18. In *Medical imaging 2019: imaging informatics for healthcare, research, and applications* (Vol. 10954, pp. 233–241). SPIE.

Bala, M. (2022). *4 Application Areas of Artificial Intelligence in Drug Discovery*. https://www.wipro.com/holmes/4-application-areas-of-artificial-intelligence-in-drug-discovery/

Becker, A. S., Marcon, M., Ghafoor, S., Wurnig, M. C., Frauenfelder, T., & Boss, A. (2017). Deep learning in mammography: Diagnostic accuracy of a multipurpose image analysis software in the detection of breast cancer. *Investigative Radiology, 52*(7), 434–440. doi:10.1097/RLI.0000000000000358 PMID:28212138

Berger Leighton, B., Daniels, N., & Yu, Y. (2022). *Computational biology in the 21st century*. https://dspace.mit.edu/handle/1721.1/116419

Bhatia, S., Sharma, M., & Bhatia, K. K. (2018). Sentiment Analysis and Mining of Opinions. In Internet of Things and Big Data Analytics Towards Next-Generation Intelligence (pp. 503-523). Springer.

Bhatia, S., Sharma, M., & Bhatia, K. K. (2015). Sentiment knowledge discovery using machine learning algorithms. *Journal of Network Communications and Emerging Technologies, 5*(2), 8–12.

Blaschke, T., Arús-Pous, J., Chen, H., Margreitter, C., Tyrchan, C., Engkvist, O., Papadopoulos, K., & Patronov, A. (2020). REINVENT 2.0: An AI Tool for De Novo Drug Design. *Journal of Chemical Information and Modeling, 60*(12), 5918–5922.

Bohr, A., & Memarzadeh, K. (2020). The rise of artificial intelligence in healthcare applications. *Artificial Intelligence in Healthcare*, 25–60. doi:10.1016/B978-0-12-818438-7.00002-2

Boiy, E., & Moens, M.F. (2008). *A machine learning approach to sentiment analysis in multilingual Web texts*. Academic Press.

Bourg, D. M., & Seemann, G. (2004). *AI for game developers*. O'Reilly Media, Inc.

Brownlee, J. (2019). *Deep Learning & Artificial Neural Networks*. https://machinelearningmastery.com/what-is-deep-learning/

Bruno, M. A., Duncan, J. R., Bierhals, A. J., & Tappouni, R. (2018). Overnight resident versus 24-hour attending radiologist coverage in academic medical centers. *Radiology*, *289*(3), 809–813. doi:10.1148/radiol.2018180690 PMID:30277849

Casino, F., Dasaklis, T. K., & Patsakis, C. (2019). A systematic literature review of blockchain-based applications: Current status, classification and open issues. *Telematics and Informatics*, *36*, 55–81.

Cavasotto, C., & Orry, W., A. (2007). Ligand Docking and Structure-based Virtual Screening in Drug Discovery. *Current Topics in Medicinal Chemistry*, *7*(10), 1006–1014.

Chatchaiwatkul, A., Phonsuphee, P., Mangalmurti, Y., & Wattanapongsakorn, N. (2021, June). Lung Disease Detection and Classification with Deep Learning Approach. In *2021 36th International Technical Conference on Circuits/Systems, Computers and Communications (ITC-CSCC)* (pp. 1-4). IEEE. 10.1109/ITC-CSCC52171.2021.9501445

Chen, W., Xu, Z., Shi, S., Zhao, Y., & Zhao, J. (2018, December). A survey of blockchain applications in different domains. In *Proceedings of the 2018 International Conference on Blockchain Technology and Application* (pp. 17-21). Academic Press.

Chen, W., Xu, Z., Shi, S., Zhao, Y., & Zhao, J. (2018, December). A survey of blockchain applications in different domains. In *Proceedings of the 2018 International Conference on Blockchain Technology and Application* (pp. 17-21). 10.1145/3301403.3301407

Clancy, K., Zhang, L., Mohamed, A., Aboutalib, S., Berg, W., & Wu, S. (2019, March). Deep learning for identifying breast cancer malignancy and false recalls: a robustness study on training strategy. In Medical Imaging 2019: Computer-Aided Diagnosis (Vol. 10950, pp. 20-25). SPIE. doi:10.1117/12.2512942

Danani, A. (2019). *Artificial Intelligence and Computer Aided Drug Design*. https://www.mdpi.com/journal/ijms/special_issues/computer_aided_drug_design

de Koning, H. J., van der Aalst, C. M., de Jong, P. A., Scholten, E. T., Nackaerts, K., Heuvelmans, M. A., Lammers, J.-W. J., Weenink, C., Yousaf-Khan, U., Horeweg, N., van 't Westeinde, S., Prokop, M., Mali, W. P., Mohamed Hoesein, F. A. A., van Ooijen, P. M. A., Aerts, J. G. J. V., den Bakker, M. A., Thunnissen, E., Verschakelen, J., ... Oudkerk, M. (2020). Reduced lung-cancer mortality with volume CT screening in a randomized trial. *The New England Journal of Medicine*, *382*(6), 503–513. doi:10.1056/NEJMoa1911793 PMID:31995683

Deshmukh, A., & Joshi, R. D. (2019). Understanding the architecture of internet of things using a case study of smart parking. *Asian Journal For Convergence in Technology.*

Diaz Ogás, M. G., Fabregat, R., & Aciar, S. (2020). Survey of smart parking systems. *Applied Sciences (Basel, Switzerland), 10*(11), 3872. doi:10.3390/app10113872

Dutta, S., & Bose, K. (2021). Remodelling structure-based drug design using machine learning. *Emerging Topics in Life Sciences, 5*(1), 13–27.

Ermagun, A., Chatterjee, S., & Levinson, D. (2017). Using temporal detrending to observe the spatial correlation of traffic. *PLoS One, 12*(5), e0176853. doi:10.1371/journal.pone.0176853 PMID:28472093

Ermagun, A., & Levinson, D. M. (2019). Development and application of the network weight matrix to predict traffic flow for congested and uncongested conditions. *Environment and Planning. B, Urban Analytics and City Science, 46*(9), 1684–1705. doi:10.1177/2399808318763368

Farrar, C. R., & Worden, K. (2007). An introduction to structural health monitoring. *Philosophical Transactions of the Royal Society A: Mathematical, Physical and Engineering Sciences, 365*(1851), 303-315.

Fawcett, R. S., Linford, S., & Stulberg, D. L. (2004). Nail abnormalities: Clues to systemic disease. *American Family Physician, 69*(6), 1417–1424. PMID:15053406

Ferreira, L., dos Santos, R., Oliva, G., & Andricopulo, A. (2015). Molecular Docking and Structure-Based Drug Design Strategies. *Molecules (Basel, Switzerland), 20*(7), 13384–13421.

Floresta, G., Zagni, C., Gentile, D., Patamia, V., & Rescifina, A. (2022). Artificial Intelligence Technologies for COVID-19 De Novo Drug Design. *International Journal of Molecular Sciences, 23*(6), 3261.

Freidman, L. (2017). *Lecture 3: Convolutional Neural Networks.* MIT 6.S191. https://www.youtube.com/watch?v=v5JvvbP0d44

Fritzen, C. P. (2005). Vibration-based structural health monitoring–concepts and applications. *Key Engineering Materials, 293*, 3–20.

Funde, A. G., & Thepade, S. D. (2016, June). Recognising Sign using fractional energy of cosine haar hybrid wavelet transform of American Sign images. In *2016 Conference on Advances in Signal Processing (CASP)* (pp. 290-294). IEEE. 10.1109/CASP.2016.7746182

Gabehart, R. A. (2003). *Overwork and Stress: The Need for Policy on Working Hours in the Healthcare Professions.* UCHC Graduate School Masters Theses 2003 - 2010. https://opencommons.uconn.edu/uchcgs_masters/41

Gandhat, S., Thakare, A. D., Avhad, S., Bajpai, N., & Alawadhi, R. (2016). Study and analysis of nail images of patients. *International Journal of Computers and Applications, 143*(13), 38–41. doi:10.5120/ijca2016910055

Gao, W., Mahajan, S., Sulam, J., & Gray, J. (2020). Deep Learning in Protein Structural Modeling and Design. *Patterns*, *1*(9), 100142.

Gawade, P., & Meeankshi, A. (2017). IOT based smart public transport system. *International Journal of Scientific and Research Publications*, *7*(7), 390–396.

Gentile, F., Yaacoub, J. C., Gleave, J., Fernandez, M., Ton, A.-T., Ban, F., Stern, A., & Cherkasov, A. (2022). Artificial Intelligence–enabled virtual screening of ultra-large chemical libraries with deep docking. *Nature Protocols*, *17*(3), 672–697. https://doi.org/10.1038/s41596-021-00659-2

González-Muñiz, A., & Díaz Blanco, I. (2020). *Convolutional layers with Keras*. doi:10.13140/RG.2.2.14621.13288/1

Goodfellow, I., Bengio, Y., & Courville, A. (2016). *Deep learning*. MIT Press.

Gu, J., Wang, Z., Kuen, J., Ma, L., Shahroudy, A., Shuai, B., Liu, T., Wang, X., Wang, G., Cai, J., & Chen, T. (2015). Recent Advances in Convolutional Neural Networks. *Pattern Recognition*, *77*, 354–377. Advance online publication. doi:10.1016/j.patcog.2017.10.013

Hammond, K. J. (1990). Case-based planning: A framework for planning from experience. *Cognitive Science*, *14*(3), 385–443.

Hardik, P., & Shah, D. M. (2012). The model for extracting a portion of a given image using color processing. *International Journal of Engineering Research & Technology (Ahmedabad)*, ●●●, 181.

HartungR. (2016). *Membrane Potentials for beginners*. https://www.youtube.com/watch?v=VOh3pj0RsI0&t=499s

He, K., Zhang, X., Ren, S., & Sun, J. (2015). *Deep residual learning for image recognition cite*. arXiv preprint arxiv:1512.03385.

Hu, M., & Liu, B. (2004). Mining and Summarizing Customer Reviews. *Proc. of ACM SIGKDD Intl. Conf. on Knowledge Discovery and Data Mining (KDD'04)*, 168–177. 10.1145/1014052.1014073

Hunter, W. (2009). Structure-based Ligand Design and the Promise Held for Antiprotozoan Drug Discovery. *The Journal of Biological Chemistry*, *284*(18), 11749–11753.

Huynh, B. Q., Li, H., & Giger, M. L. (2016). Digital mammographic tumor classification using transfer learning from deep convolutional neural networks. *Journal of Medical Imaging (Bellingham, Wash.)*, *3*(3), 034501. doi:10.1117/1.JMI.3.3.034501 PMID:27610399

Indi, T. S., & Gunge, Y. A. (2016). Early stage disease diagnosis system using human nail image processing. *IJ Information Technology and Computer Science*, *7*(7), 30–35. doi:10.5815/ijitcs.2016.07.05

Ioffe, S., & Szegedy, C. (2015). *Batch normalization: Accelerating deep network training by reducing internal covariate shift*. arXiv preprint arXiv:1502.03167.

Irving, P., & Soutis, C. (Eds.). (2019). *Polymer composites in the aerospace industry*. Woodhead Publishing.

Jain, I., Malik, S., & Agrawal, S. (2017). Automatic Railway Barrier System, Railway Tracking and Collision Avoidance using IOT. *International Journal of Computers and Applications*, *975*, 8887.

Jayanthi, G., & Jothilakshmi, P. (under review). Deep learner for traffic flow assessment on highways based on spatial - temporal traffic sequences. *IETE Journal of Research*.

Jayanthi, G. (2023). Multi Criteria Decision Making Analysis for sustainable Transport. In F. P. García Márquez & B. Lev (Eds.), *Sustainability: Cases and Studies in Using Operations Research and Management Science Methods* (pp. 1–8). Springer International Publishing.

Jayanthi, G., & García Márquez, F. P. (2021a). Travel time based traffic rerouting by augmenting traffic flow network with temporal and spatial relations for congestion management. In *Proceedings of the Fifteenth International Conference on Management Science and Engineering Management: Volume 1 15* (pp. 554-565). Springer International Publishing.

Jayanthi, G., & García Márquez, F. P. (2021b). Data mining and information technology in transportation—a review. In *Proceedings of the Fifteenth International Conference on Management Science and Engineering Management: Volume 2 15* (pp. 849-855). Springer International Publishing.

Jayanthi, G., García Márquez, F. P., & Ragavendra Prasad, M. (2022, May). Routing Vehicles on Highways by Augmenting Traffic Flow Network: A Review on Speed Up Techniques. *International Conference on Intelligent Emerging Methods of Artificial Intelligence & Cloud Computing Proceedings of IEMAICLOUD*, *2021*, 96–105.

Jayanthi, G., & Jothilakshmi, P. (2019). Prediction of traffic volume by mining traffic sequences using travel time based PrefixSpan. *IET Intelligent Transport Systems*, *13*(7), 1199–1210. doi:10.1049/iet-its.2018.5165

Jayanthi, G., & Jothilakshmi, P. (2021). Traffic time series forecasting on highways-a contemporary survey of models, methods and techniques. *International Journal of Logistics Systems and Management*, *39*(1), 77–110. doi:10.1504/IJLSM.2021.115068

Jeyapriya, A., & Selvi, C. K. (2015). Extracting aspects and mining opinions in product reviews using supervised learning algorithm. In *Electronics and communication systems (ICECS), 2015 2nd International conference on 2015 February 26* (pp. 548–552). New York: IEEE.

Jing, Y., Bian, Y., Hu, Z., Wang, L., & Xie, X. (2018). Deep Learning for Drug Design: An Artificial Intelligence Paradigm for Drug Discovery in the Big Data Era. *The AAPS Journal*, *20*(3).

Jubilant Biosys. (2022). *Ligand-based Drug Discovery*. https://www.jubilantbiosys.com/services/ligand-based-drug-discovery/#:~:text=Ligand%2Dbased%20drug%20discovery%20(LBDD,known%20to%20modulate%20the%20target

Kasera, R. K., & Acharjee, T. (2022). A Smart Indoor Parking System. *SN Computer Science*, *3*(1), 1–17. doi:10.100742979-021-00875-3 PMID:34723205

Kaw, A. K. (2005). *Mechanics of composite materials*. CRC Press.

Keshavarzi Arshadi, A., Webb, J., Salem, M., Cruz, E., Calad-Thomson, S., Ghadirian, N., Collins, J., Diez-Cecilia, E., Kelly, B., Goodarzi, H., & Yuan, J. (2020). Artificial Intelligence for COVID-19 Drug Discovery and Vaccine Development. *Frontiers in Artificial Intelligence*, 3.

Khan, F. H., Bashir, S., & Qamar, U. (2014). TOM: Twitter opinion mining framework using hybrid classification scheme. *Decision Support Systems*, *31*(57), 245–257.

Khan, K., Baharudin, B., Khan, A., & Ullah, A. (2014). Mining opinion components from unstructured reviews: A review. *Journal of King Saud University-Computer and Information Sciences*, *26*(3), 258–275.

Khorram, B., & Yazdi, M. (2018). A new optimized thresholding method using ant colony algorithm for Mr Brain Image Segmentation. *Journal of Digital Imaging*, *32*(1), 162–174. https://doi.org/10.1007/s10278-018-0111-x

Khosravi, P., Kazemi, E., Imielinski, M., Elemento, O., & Hajirasouliha, I. (2018). Deep Convolutional Neural Networks Enable Discrimination of Heterogeneous Digital Pathology Images. *EBioMedicine*, *27*, 317–328. doi:10.1016/j.ebiom.2017.12.026 PMID:29292031

Kinnings, S., & Jackson, R. (2011). ReverseScreen3D: A Structure-Based Ligand Matching Method To Identify Protein Targets. *Journal of Chemical Information and Modeling*, *51*(3), 624–634.

Kraus, M. A., & Drass, M. (2020). Artificial intelligence for structural glass engineering applications—Overview, case studies and future potentials. *Glass Structures & Engineering*, *5*(3), 247–285. doi:10.100740940-020-00132-8

Krizhevsky, A., Sutskever, I. E., & Hinton, G. (2012). ImageNet Classification with Deep Convolutional Neural Networks. *Neural Information Processing Systems*, *25*. Advance online publication. doi:10.1145/3065386

Kumar, A., Kim, J., Lyndon, D., Fulham, M., & Feng, D. (2016). An ensemble of fine-tuned convolutional neural networks for medical image classification. *IEEE Journal of Biomedical and Health Informatics*, *21*(1), 31–40. doi:10.1109/JBHI.2016.2635663 PMID:28114041

Kumar, T., & Kushwaha, D. S. (2019). An intelligent surveillance system based on IoT for internal security of a nation. *International Journal of Information Security and Privacy*, *13*(3), 1–30. doi:10.4018/IJISP.201907010101

Latifi, M., Van Der Meer, F. P., & Sluys, L. J. (2015). A level set model for simulating fatigue-driven delamination in composites. *International Journal of Fatigue*, *80*, 434–442.

Laurie, A., & Jackson, R. (2006). Methods for the Prediction of Protein-Ligand Binding Sites for Structure-Based Drug Design and Virtual Ligand Screening. *Current Protein & Peptide Science*, *7*(5), 395–406.

Liew, S. S., Hani, M. K., Radzi, S. A., & Bakhteri, R. (2016). Gender classification: A convolutional neural network approach. *Turkish Journal of Electrical Engineering and Computer Sciences*, *24*(3), 1248–1264. doi:10.3906/elk-1311-58

Litjens, G., Kooi, T., Bejnordi, B. E., Setio, A. A. A., Ciompi, F., Ghafoorian, M., van der Laak, J. A. W. M., van Ginneken, B., & Sánchez, C. I. (2017). A survey on deep learning in medical image analysis. *Medical Image Analysis*, *42*, 60–88. doi:10.1016/j.media.2017.07.005 PMID:28778026

Liu, B. (2008). *Opinion mining and summarization*. In *Tutorial at the World Wide Web Conference (WWW)*, Beijing, China.

Logout Page. (n.d.). Epic Games. https://www.unrealengine.com/id/logout?redirectUrl=https%3A%2F%2Fwww.unrealeng ine.com%2Fen-US%2F

Luo, J., Hu, J., Fu, L., Liu, C., & Jin, X. (2011). Use of Artificial Neural Network for a QSAR Study on Neurotrophic Activities of N-p-Tolyl/phenylsulfonyl L-Amino Acid Thiolester Derivatives. *Procedia Engineering*, *15*, 5158–5163.

Madaan, V., & Goyal, A. (2020). Predicting ayurveda-based constituent balancing in human body using machine learning methods. *IEEE Access : Practical Innovations, Open Solutions*, *8*, 65060–65070. doi:10.1109/ACCESS.2020.2985717

Makridakis, S., & Christodoulou, K. (2019). Blockchain: Current challenges and future prospects/applications. *Future Internet*, *11*(12), 258. doi:10.3390/fi11120258

Mallat, S. (2016). Understanding Deep Convolutional Networks. *Philosophical Transactions - Royal Society. Mathematical, Physical, and Engineering Sciences*, *374*(2065), 20150203. Advance online publication. doi:10.1098/rsta.2015.0203 PMID:26953183

Mangalgiri, P. D. (1999). Composite materials for aerospace applications. *Bulletin of Materials Science*, *22*(3), 657–664. doi:10.1007/BF02749982

Mente, R., & Marulkar, S. V. (2017). A review: Fingernail images for disease detection. *Int. J. Eng. Comput. Sci*, *6*(11), 22830–22835. doi:10.18535/ijecs/v6i11.01

Michael, J., Cohn, A., & Butcher, J. R. (2018). Blockchain technology. *The Journal*, *1*(7), 1–11.

Mishra, A., Karmakar, A., Ghatak, A., Ghosh, S., Ojha, A., & Patra, K. (2019). Low cost parking system for smart cities: A vehicle occupancy sensing and resource optimization technique using IoT and Cloud PaaS. *Int J Sci Technol Res*, *8*(9), 115–122.

Moeskops, P., Wolterink, J. M., Van Der Velden, B. H., Gilhuijs, K. G., Leiner, T., Viergever, M. A., & Išgum, I. (2016). Deep learning for multi-task medical image segmentation in multiple modalities. In *Medical Image Computing and Computer-Assisted Intervention–MICCAI 2016: 19th International Conference, Athens, Greece, October 17-21, 2016, Proceedings, Part II 19* (pp. 478-486). Springer International Publishing.

Mohanta, B. K., Jena, D., Panda, S. S., & Sobhanayak, S. (2019). Blockchain technology: A survey on applications and security privacy challenges. *Internet of Things*, *8*, 100107.

Mohanty, S., Harun, A. I., Rashid, M., Mridul, M., Mohanty, C., & Swayamsiddha, S. (2020). Application of Artificial Intelligence in COVID-19 drug repurposing. *Diabetes & Metabolic Syndrome: Clinical Research & Reviews*, *14*(5), 1027–1031.

Mohanty, S., Rashid, M., Mohanty, C., & Swayamsiddha, S. (2021). Modern computational intelligence based drug repurposing for diabetes epidemic. *Diabetes & Metabolic Syndrome: Clinical Research & Reviews, 15*(4), 102180.

Montañez-Godínez, N., Martínez-Olguín, A., Deeb, O., Garduño-Juárez, R., & Ramírez-Galicia, G. (2014). QSAR/QSPR as an Application of Artificial Neural Networks. *Methods in Molecular Biology (Clifton, N.J.)*, 319–333.

Montesano, J., & Sharifpour, F. (2021). Modelling damage evolution in multidirectional laminates: micro to macro. *Multi-Scale Continuum Mechanics Modelling of Fibre-Reinforced Polymer Composites*, 463-507.

Mouchlis, V., Afantitis, A., Serra, A., Fratello, M., Papadiamantis, A., Aidinis, V., Lynch, I., Greco, D., & Melagraki, G. (2021). Advances in De Novo Drug Design: From Conventional to Machine Learning Methods. *International Journal of Molecular Sciences, 22*(4), 1676.

Nakamoto, S. (2009). *Bitcoin: A peer-to-peer electronic cash system Bitcoin: A Peer-to-Peer Electronic Cash System.* https://bitcoin. org/en/bitcoin-paper

Narayanan, H., Dingfelder, F., Butté, A., Lorenzen, N., Sokolov, M., & Arosio, P. (2021). Machine Learning for Biologics: Opportunities for Protein Engineering, Developability, and Formulation. *Trends in Pharmacological Sciences, 42*(3), 151–165.

Nature.com. (2022). *Artificial intelligence turns to antibody selection.* https://www.nature.com/articles/d42473-019-00331-0

Newton, P. L., & Feng, J. (2016). *Unreal Engine 4 AI Programming Essentials.* Packt Publishing Ltd.

NorthEast BioLab. (2022). *Phases of Drug Development Process, Drug Discovery Process.* https://www.nebiolab.com/drug-discovery-and-development-process

O'Leary, D. E. (2015). Twitter mining for discovery, prediction and causality: Applications and methodologies. *Intelligent Systems in Accounting, Finance & Management, 22*(3), 227–247.

Oliveira, L., Zavolokina, L., Bauer, I., & Schwabe, G. (2018, December). *To token or not to token: Tools for understanding blockchain tokens.* ICIS.

Ow, G., Tang, Z., & Kuznetsov, V. (2016). Big data and computational biology strategy for personalized prognosis. *Oncotarget, 7*(26), 40200–40220. doi:10.18632/oncotarget.9571 PMID:27229533

Padyab, A., Habibipour, A., Rizk, A., & Ståhlbröst, A. (2019). Adoption barriers of IoT in large scale pilots. *Information (Basel), 11*(1), 23. doi:10.3390/info11010023

Pang, B., & Lee, L. (2008). Opinion mining and sentiment analysis. *Foundations and Trends® in Information Retrieval, 2*(1–2).

Pathak, K. M., Yadav, S., Jain, P., Tanwar, P., & Kumar, B. (2020, June). A facial expression recognition system to predict emotions. In *2020 International Conference on Intelligent Engineering and Management (ICIEM)* (pp. 414-419). IEEE. 10.1109/ICIEM48762.2020.9160229

Perkin Elmer. (2022). *Target Selection*. https://www. perkinelmer.com/category/target-selection?utm_so urce=Google&utm_medium=cpc&utm_campaign=LSC-DDS-2022-EMEAI-P aidSearch-SCH-EGM-ZZ&sfdc_id=7014V000002EBvr&LS=PPC&adgroup= 135555101655&ad=591153414423&keyword=target%20discovery%20an d%20validation&gclid=CjwKCAjwv-GUBhAzEiwASUMm4oFRT6A0G1e76cp 6QlVOeJlwTsxVwTUQTzcCXOsmN-DLFml4swI2EBoC7JoQAvD_BwE

Persada, R. P., Aulia, S., Burhanuddin, D., & Sugondo, H. (2019). Automatic face and VLP's recognition for smart parking system. *Telkomnika*, *17*(4), 1698–1705. doi:10.12928/telkomnika. v17i4.11746

Peter, S., Dhanjal, J., Malik, V., Radhakrishnan, N., Jayakanthan, M., & Sundar, D. (2019). Quantitative Structure-Activity Relationship (QSAR): Modeling Approaches to Biological Applications. Encyclopedia of Bioinformatics and Computational Biology, 661-676.

Popescu, A. M., & Etzioni, O. (2007). Extracting product features and opinions from reviews. In *Natural language processing and text mining* (pp. 9–28). Springer. doi:10.1007/978-1-84628-754-1_2

Pratama, C., Aulia, S., Ramadan, D. N., & Hadiyoso, S. (2020). Vehicle License Plate Detection for Parking Offenders Using Automatic License-Plate Recognition. *Journal of Southwest Jiaotong University*, *55*(4), 32. doi:10.35741/issn.0258-2724.55.4.32

Pushpakom, S., Iorio, F., Eyers, P., Escott, K., Hopper, S., Wells, A., Doig, A., Guilliams, T., Latimer, J., McNamee, C., Norris, A., Sanseau, P., Cavalla, D., & Pirmohamed, M. (2018). Drug repurposing: Progress, challenges and recommendations. *Nature Reviews. Drug Discovery*, *18*(1), 41–58.

Rastegari, M., Ordonez, V., Redmon, J., & Farhadi, A. (2016). Xnor-net: imagenet classification using binary convolutional neural networks. *Proceedings of the European Conference on Computer Vision.*

Rawat, W., & Wang, Z. (2017). Deep convolutional neural networks for image classification: A comprehensive review. *Neural Computation*, *29*(9), 2352–2449. doi:10.1162/neco_a_00990 PMID:28599112

Razzak, M., Naz, S., & Zaib, A. (2017). *Deep Learning for Medical Image Processing: Overview*. Challenges and Future.

Ronneberger, O. (2017). Invited talk: U-net convolutional networks for biomedical image segmentation. In Bildverarbeitung für die Medizin 2017-Algorithmen-Systeme-Anwendungen. Proceedings des Workshops vom 12. bis 14. März: 2017 in Heidelberg (p. 3). Academic Press.

Ronneberger, O., Fischer, P., & Brox, T. (2015a). Lecture Notes in Computer Science: Vol. 9351. U-Net: Convolutional Networks for Biomedical Image Segmentation. MICCAI 2015.

Ronneberger, O., Fischer, P., & Brox, T. (2015b). U-net: Convolutional networks for biomedical image segmentation. *Medical Image Computing and Computer-Assisted Intervention–MICCAI 2015: 18th International Conference, Munich, Germany, October 5-9, 2015 Proceedings, 18*(3), 234–241.

Rosenberg, N., & Frischtak, C. R. (1984). Technological innovation and long waves. *Cambridge Journal of Economics, 8*(1), 7–24.

Rossi, A., Hagenbuchner, M., Scarselli, F., & Tsoi, A. (2021). A Study on the effects of recursive convolutional layers in convolutional neural networks. *Neurocomputing, 460,* 59–70. Advance online publication. doi:10.1016/j.neucom.2021.07.021

Russakovsky, O., Deng, J., Su, H., Krause, J., Satheesh, S., Ma, S., Huang, Z., Karpathy, A., Khosla, A., Bernstein, M., Berg, A. C., & Fei-Fei, L. (2015). Imagenet large scale visual recognition challenge. *International Journal of Computer Vision, 115*(3), 211–252. doi:10.100711263-015-0816-y

Sadegh, M., Ibrahim, R., & Othman, Z. A. (2012). Opinion mining and sentiment analysis: A survey. *International Journal of Computers and Technology, 2*(3), 171–178.

Saha, S. (2018). *A Comprehensive Guide to Convolutional Neural Networks.* Academic Press.

Saleem, A. A., Siddiqui, H. U. R., Shafique, R., Haider, A., & Ali, M. (2020, January). A review on smart IOT based parking system. In *International Conference On Soft Computing And Data Mining* (pp. 264-273). Springer. 10.1007/978-3-030-36056-6_26

Saranya, V., & Ranichitra, A. (2017). Image segmentation techniques to detect nail abnormalities. *Scholar, 2*(1).

Sasikal, P., & Mary, L. (2020). Sentiment analysis of online product reviews using DLMNN and future prediction of online product using IANFIS. *Journal of Big Data, 7.*

Satyanarayana, D., Dulla, M., Giduturi, A. A., Chandra, D. S., & Prathap, S. (2019). *Developing an advanced smart parking system using IoT.* Academic Press.

Schumpeter, J. A. (1976). II. Capitalism. *Socialism and Democracy,* 1942.

Senthilkumar, M., Reddy, S. M., & Sreekanth, T. G. (2022a). Dynamic Study and Detection of Edge Crack in Composite Laminates Using Vibration Parameters. *Transactions of the Indian Institute of Metals, 75*(2), 361–370.

Senthilkumar, M., Sreekanth, T. G., & Manikanta Reddy, S. (2021). Nondestructive health monitoring techniques for composite materials: A review. *Polymers & Polymer Composites, 29*(5), 528–540.

Sethuramalingam, D. (2019). *Security for smart vehicle in iot. In The IoT and the Next Revolutions Automating the World.* IGI Global.

Sharma, A., & Tanwar, P. (2022). Deep Learning Techniques for Detection of Autism Spectrum Syndrome (ASS). In Proceedings of Data Analytics and Management: ICDAM 2021, Volume 2 (pp. 337-345). Springer Singapore.

Sharma, A., & Tanwar, P. (2020, June). Deep analysis of autism spectrum disorder detection techniques. In *2020 International conference on intelligent engineering and management (ICIEM)* (pp. 455-459). IEEE. 10.1109/ICIEM48762.2020.9160123

Sharma, A., & Tanwar, P. (2021). Machine learning techniques for autism spectrum disorder (ASD) detection. *International Journal of Forensic Engineering, 5*(2), 111–125. doi:10.1504/IJFE.2021.118912

Sharma, N. R., & Chitre, V. D. (2014). Opinion mining, analysis and its challenges. *International Journal of Innovations & Advancement in Computer Science, 3*(1), 59–65.

Sharma, P., Jindal, R., & Borah, M. D. (2022). A review of blockchain-based applications and challenges. *Wireless Personal Communications,* 1-43.

Sharma, V., & Shrivastava, A. (2015). System for Disease detection by analyzing finger nails Color and Texture. *International Journal of Advanced Engineering Research and Science, 2*(10).

Shen, D., Wu, G., & Suk, H. I. (2017). Deep learning in medical image analysis. *Annual Review of Biomedical Engineering, 19*(1), 221–248. doi:10.1146/annurev-bioeng-071516-044442 PMID:28301734

Shieh, J.-Y., Huang, S.-X., & Su, Y.-X. (2019). Automatic Allocation System for Parking Lot Based on QR Code. *Journal of the Gujarat Research Society, 21*(1), 10–12.

Sign in Page. (n.d.). Epic Games. Retrieved from https://www.unrealengine.com/id/login?client_id=17ce2d286483 4898ab71847859286c81&response_type=code

Simonyan, K., & Zisserman, A. (2014). *Very deep convolutional networks for large-scale image recognition.* arXiv preprint arXiv:1409.1556.

Singal, A., & Arora, R. (2015). Nail as a window of systemic diseases. *Indian Dermatology Online Journal, 6*(2), 67. doi:10.4103/2229-5178.153002 PMID:25821724

Singh, S., Ho-Shon, K., Karimi, S., & Hamey, L. (2018, November). Modality classification and concept detection in medical images using deep transfer learning. In *2018 International conference on image and vision computing New Zealand (IVCNZ)* (pp. 1-9). IEEE. 10.1109/IVCNZ.2018.8634803

Śledź, P., & Caflisch, A. (2018). Protein structure-based drug design: From docking to molecular dynamics. *Current Opinion in Structural Biology, 48,* 93–102.

Sreekanth, T. G., Senthilkumar, M., & Reddy, S. M. (2021). Vibration-based delamination evaluation in GFRP composite beams using ANN. *Polymers and Polymer Composites, 29*(9), S317-S324.

Sreekanth, T. G., Senthilkumar, M., & Reddy, S. M. (2022b). Natural Frequency based delamination estimation in GFRP beams using RSM and ANN. *Frattura ed Integrità Strutturale, 16*(61), 487-495.

Sreekanth, T. G., Senthilkumar, M., & Reddy, S. M. (2021). Fatigue Life Evaluation of Delaminated GFRP Laminates Using Artificial Neural Networks. *Transactions of the Indian Institute of Metals, 74*(6), 1439–1445.

Srivastava, N., Hinton, G., Krizhevsky, A., Sutskever, I., & Salakhutdinov, R. (2014). Dropout: A Simple Way to Prevent Neural Networks from Overfitting. *Journal of Machine Learning Research, 15*, 1929–1958.

Surabhi, S., & Singh, B. (2018). Computer aided drug design: An overview. *Journal of Drug Delivery and Therapeutics, 8*(5), 504–509.

Swaraj, M., Munagala, M. K., Bharti, P., & Jayavarthini, C. (2019). smart parking system using facial recognition, optical character recognition and internet of things (IoT). *Int. Res. J. Eng. Technol, 6*, 1278–1282.

Tanoue, L. T., Tanner, N. T., Gould, M. K., & Silvestri, G. A. (2015). Lung cancer screening. *American Journal of Respiratory and Critical Care Medicine, 191*(1), 19–33. doi:10.1164/rccm.201410-1777CI PMID:25369325

Thakare, A., Meshram, S., & Baradkar, H. M. (2017). An Automated Medical Support System For Detecting Human Health Conditions Based On Noval Bicluster Method. *IJCTA, 10*(8), 223–228.

Thompson, S. (2017). The preservation of digital signatures on the blockchain. *See Also,* (3).

Tsung. (2018). *Review: Googlenet (inception v1)- winner of ilsvrc 2014 (image classification).* Available at: https://medium.com/coinmonks/

Vallabhaneni, V., & Maity, D. (2011). Application of radial basis neural network on damage assessment of structures. *Procedia Engineering, 14*, 3104–3110.

Van Saberhagen, N. (2013). *CryptoNote v 2.0.* Academic Press.

Vyas, V., Bhati, S., Patel, S., & Ghate, M. (2021). Structure- and ligand-based drug design methods for the modeling of antimalarial agents: A review of updates from 2012 onwards. *Journal of Biomolecular Structure & Dynamics,* 1–26.

Wang, X., Peng, Y., Lu, L., Lu, Z., Bagheri, M., & Summers, R. M. (2017). ChestX-Ray8: Hospital-Scale Chest X-Ray Database and Benchmarks on Weakly-Supervised Classification and Localization of Common Thorax Diseases. *2017 IEEE Conference on Computer Vision and Pattern Recognition (CVPR),* 3462-3471. 10.1109/CVPR.2017.369

Wei, W., Wu, H., & Ma, H. (2019). An autoencoder and LSTM-based traffic flow prediction method. *Sensors (Basel), 19*(13), 2946. doi:10.339019132946 PMID:31277390

Wender, R., Fontham, E. T., Barrera, E. Jr, Colditz, G. A., Church, T. R., Ettinger, D. S., & Smith, R. A. (2013). American Cancer Society lung cancer screening guidelines. *CA: a Cancer Journal for Clinicians*, *63*(2), 106–117. doi:10.3322/caac.21172 PMID:23315954

Yaga, D., Mell, P., Roby, N., & Scarfone, K. (2019). Blockchain technology overview. *arXiv preprint arXiv:1906.11078*.

Yang, W. T., Su, T. Y., Cheng, T. C., He, Y. F., & Fang, Y. H. (2019, March). Deep learning for breast cancer classification with mammography. In *International forum on medical imaging in Asia 2019* (Vol. 11050, pp. 190-195). SPIE. 10.1117/12.2519603

Yan, R., Chen, X., & Mukhopadhyay, S. C. (2017). *Structural Health Monitoring*. Springer.

Yuan, C., Xu, M. X., & Si, X. M. (2017). Research on a new signature scheme on blockchain. *Security and Communication Networks*.

Yu, J., Zha, Z. J., & Chua, T. S. (2012). Answering opinion questions on products by exploiting hierarchical organization of consumer reviews. In *Proceedings of the 2012 joint conference on empirical methods in natural language processing and computational natural language learning* (pp. 391–401). Association for Computational Linguistics. https://people.cs.kuleuven.be/~bettina.berendt/WebMining10/L3.pdf

Yu, K., Beam, A., & Kohane, I. (2018). Artificial intelligence in healthcare. *Nature Biomedical Engineering*, *2*(10), 719–731. doi:10.103841551-018-0305-z PMID:31015651

Yu, W., & Chen, Z. (2021). Computer aided drug design based on Artificial Intelligence algorithm. *Journal of Physics: Conference Series*, *2066*(1), 012012. https://doi.org/10.1088/1742-6596/2066/1/012012

Zang, P., Mehta, M., Mateas, M., & Ram, A. (2007, January). Towards Runtime Behavior Adaptation for Embodied Characters. *IJCAI*, *7*, 1557–1562.

Zhai, S., Yang, Y., Li, J., Qiu, C., & Zhao, J. (2019, February). Research on the Application of Cryptography on the Blockchain. *Journal of Physics: Conference Series*, *1168*(3), 032077.

Zhavoronkov, A. (2018). Artificial Intelligence for drug discovery, Biomarker Development, and generation of novel chemistry. *Molecular Pharmaceutics*, *15*(10), 4311–4313. https://doi.org/10.1021/acs.molpharmaceut.8b00930

Zhou, Y., Wang, F., Tang, J., Nussinov, R., & Cheng, F. (2020). Artificial intelligence in COVID-19 drug repurposing. *The Lancet Digital Health*, *2*(12), e667–e676.

Related References

To continue our tradition of advancing information science and technology research, we have compiled a list of recommended IGI Global readings. These references will provide additional information and guidance to further enrich your knowledge and assist you with your own research and future publications.

Aasi, P., Rusu, L., & Vieru, D. (2017). The Role of Culture in IT Governance Five Focus Areas: A Literature Review. *International Journal of IT/Business Alignment and Governance, 8*(2), 42-61. https://doi.org/ doi:10.4018/IJITBAG.2017070103

Abdrabo, A. A. (2018). Egypt's Knowledge-Based Development: Opportunities, Challenges, and Future Possibilities. In A. Alraouf (Ed.), *Knowledge-Based Urban Development in the Middle East* (pp. 80–101). Hershey, PA: IGI Global. doi:10.4018/978-1-5225-3734-2.ch005

Abu Doush, I., & Alhami, I. (2018). Evaluating the Accessibility of Computer Laboratories, Libraries, and Websites in Jordanian Universities and Colleges. *International Journal of Information Systems and Social Change, 9*(2), 44–60. doi:10.4018/IJISSC.2018040104

Adegbore, A. M., Quadri, M. O., & Oyewo, O. R. (2018). A Theoretical Approach to the Adoption of Electronic Resource Management Systems (ERMS) in Nigerian University Libraries. In A. Tella & T. Kwanya (Eds.), *Handbook of Research on Managing Intellectual Property in Digital Libraries* (pp. 292–311). Hershey, PA: IGI Global. doi:10.4018/978-1-5225-3093-0.ch015

Afolabi, O. A. (2018). Myths and Challenges of Building an Effective Digital Library in Developing Nations: An African Perspective. In A. Tella & T. Kwanya (Eds.), *Handbook of Research on Managing Intellectual Property in Digital Libraries* (pp. 51–79). Hershey, PA: IGI Global. doi:10.4018/978-1-5225-3093-0.ch004

Agarwal, P., Kurian, R., & Gupta, R. K. (2022). Additive Manufacturing Feature Taxonomy and Placement of Parts in AM Enclosure. In S. Salunkhe, H. Hussein, & J. Davim (Eds.), *Applications of Artificial Intelligence in Additive Manufacturing* (pp. 138–176). IGI Global. https://doi.org/10.4018/978-1-7998-8516-0.ch007

Al-Alawi, A. I., Al-Hammam, A. H., Al-Alawi, S. S., & AlAlawi, E. I. (2021). The Adoption of E-Wallets: Current Trends and Future Outlook. In Y. Albastaki, A. Razzaque, & A. Sarea (Eds.), *Innovative Strategies for Implementing FinTech in Banking* (pp. 242–262). IGI Global. https://doi.org/10.4018/978-1-7998-3257-7. ch015

Alsharo, M. (2017). Attitudes Towards Cloud Computing Adoption in Emerging Economies. *International Journal of Cloud Applications and Computing, 7*(3), 44–58. doi:10.4018/IJCAC.2017070102

Amer, T. S., & Johnson, T. L. (2017). Information Technology Progress Indicators: Research Employing Psychological Frameworks. In A. Mesquita (Ed.), *Research Paradigms and Contemporary Perspectives on Human-Technology Interaction* (pp. 168–186). Hershey, PA: IGI Global. doi:10.4018/978-1-5225-1868-6.ch008

Andreeva, A., & Yolova, G. (2021). Liability in Labor Legislation: New Challenges Related to the Use of Artificial Intelligence. In B. Vassileva & M. Zwilling (Eds.), *Responsible AI and Ethical Issues for Businesses and Governments* (pp. 214–232). IGI Global. https://doi.org/10.4018/978-1-7998-4285-9.ch012

Anohah, E. (2017). Paradigm and Architecture of Computing Augmented Learning Management System for Computer Science Education. *International Journal of Online Pedagogy and Course Design, 7*(2), 60–70. doi:10.4018/IJOPCD.2017040105

Anohah, E., & Suhonen, J. (2017). Trends of Mobile Learning in Computing Education from 2006 to 2014: A Systematic Review of Research Publications. *International Journal of Mobile and Blended Learning, 9*(1), 16–33. doi:10.4018/ IJMBL.2017010102

Arbaiza, C. S., Huerta, H. V., & Rodriguez, C. R. (2021). Contributions to the Technological Adoption Model for the Peruvian Agro-Export Sector. *International Journal of E-Adoption, 13*(1), 1–17. https://doi.org/10.4018/IJEA.2021010101

Bailey, E. K. (2017). Applying Learning Theories to Computer Technology Supported Instruction. In M. Grassetti & S. Brookby (Eds.), *Advancing Next-Generation Teacher Education through Digital Tools and Applications* (pp. 61–81). Hershey, PA: IGI Global. doi:10.4018/978-1-5225-0965-3.ch004

Baker, J. D. (2021). Introduction to Machine Learning as a New Methodological Framework for Performance Assessment. In M. Bocarnea, B. Winston, & D. Dean (Eds.), *Handbook of Research on Advancements in Organizational Data Collection and Measurements: Strategies for Addressing Attitudes, Beliefs, and Behaviors* (pp. 326–342). IGI Global. https://doi.org/10.4018/978-1-7998-7665-6.ch021

Banerjee, S., Sing, T. Y., Chowdhury, A. R., & Anwar, H. (2018). Let's Go Green: Towards a Taxonomy of Green Computing Enablers for Business Sustainability. In M. Khosrow-Pour (Ed.), *Green Computing Strategies for Competitive Advantage and Business Sustainability* (pp. 89–109). Hershey, PA: IGI Global. doi:10.4018/978-1-5225-5017-4.ch005

Basham, R. (2018). Information Science and Technology in Crisis Response and Management. In M. Khosrow-Pour, D.B.A. (Ed.), Encyclopedia of Information Science and Technology, Fourth Edition (pp. 1407-1418). Hershey, PA: IGI Global. doi:10.4018/978-1-5225-2255-3.ch121

Batyashe, T., & Iyamu, T. (2018). Architectural Framework for the Implementation of Information Technology Governance in Organisations. In M. Khosrow-Pour, D.B.A. (Ed.), Encyclopedia of Information Science and Technology, Fourth Edition (pp. 810-819). Hershey, PA: IGI Global. doi:10.4018/978-1-5225-2255-3.ch070

Bekleyen, N., & Çelik, S. (2017). Attitudes of Adult EFL Learners towards Preparing for a Language Test via CALL. In D. Tafazoli & M. Romero (Eds.), *Multiculturalism and Technology-Enhanced Language Learning* (pp. 214–229). Hershey, PA: IGI Global. doi:10.4018/978-1-5225-1882-2.ch013

Bergeron, F., Croteau, A., Uwizeyemungu, S., & Raymond, L. (2017). A Framework for Research on Information Technology Governance in SMEs. In S. De Haes & W. Van Grembergen (Eds.), *Strategic IT Governance and Alignment in Business Settings* (pp. 53–81). Hershey, PA: IGI Global. doi:10.4018/978-1-5225-0861-8.ch003

Bhardwaj, M., Shukla, N., & Sharma, A. (2021). Improvement and Reduction of Clustering Overhead in Mobile Ad Hoc Network With Optimum Stable Bunching Algorithm. In S. Kumar, M. Trivedi, P. Ranjan, & A. Punhani (Eds.), *Evolution of Software-Defined Networking Foundations for IoT and 5G Mobile Networks* (pp. 139–158). IGI Global. https://doi.org/10.4018/978-1-7998-4685-7.ch008

Bhatt, G. D., Wang, Z., & Rodger, J. A. (2017). Information Systems Capabilities and Their Effects on Competitive Advantages: A Study of Chinese Companies. *Information Resources Management Journal, 30*(3), 41–57. doi:10.4018/IRMJ.2017070103

Bhattacharya, A. (2021). Blockchain, Cybersecurity, and Industry 4.0. In A. Tyagi, G. Rekha, & N. Sreenath (Eds.), *Opportunities and Challenges for Blockchain Technology in Autonomous Vehicles* (pp. 210–244). IGI Global. https://doi.org/10.4018/978-1-7998-3295-9.ch013

Bhyan, P., Shrivastava, B., & Kumar, N. (2022). Requisite Sustainable Development Contemplating Buildings: Economic and Environmental Sustainability. In A. Hussain, K. Tiwari, & A. Gupta (Eds.), *Addressing Environmental Challenges Through Spatial Planning* (pp. 269–288). IGI Global. https://doi.org/10.4018/978-1-7998-8331-9.ch014

Boido, C., Davico, P., & Spallone, R. (2021). Digital Tools Aimed to Represent Urban Survey. In M. Khosrow-Pour D.B.A. (Ed.), *Encyclopedia of Information Science and Technology, Fifth Edition* (pp. 1181-1195). IGI Global. https://doi.org/10.4018/978-1-7998-3479-3.ch082

Borkar, P. S., Chanana, P. U., Atwal, S. K., Londe, T. G., & Dalal, Y. D. (2021). The Replacement of HMI (Human-Machine Interface) in Industry Using Single Interface Through IoT. In R. Raut & A. Mihovska (Eds.), *Examining the Impact of Deep Learning and IoT on Multi-Industry Applications* (pp. 195–208). IGI Global. https://doi.org/10.4018/978-1-7998-7511-6.ch011

Brahmane, A. V., & Krishna, C. B. (2021). Rider Chaotic Biography Optimization-driven Deep Stacked Auto-encoder for Big Data Classification Using Spark Architecture: Rider Chaotic Biography Optimization. *International Journal of Web Services Research*, *18*(3), 42–62. https://doi.org/10.4018/ijwsr.2021070103

Burcoff, A., & Shamir, L. (2017). Computer Analysis of Pablo Picasso's Artistic Style. *International Journal of Art, Culture and Design Technologies*, *6*(1), 1–18. doi:10.4018/IJACDT.2017010101

Byker, E. J. (2017). I Play I Learn: Introducing Technological Play Theory. In C. Martin & D. Polly (Eds.), *Handbook of Research on Teacher Education and Professional Development* (pp. 297–306). Hershey, PA: IGI Global. doi:10.4018/978-1-5225-1067-3.ch016

Calongne, C. M., Stricker, A. G., Truman, B., & Arenas, F. J. (2017). Cognitive Apprenticeship and Computer Science Education in Cyberspace: Reimagining the Past. In A. Stricker, C. Calongne, B. Truman, & F. Arenas (Eds.), *Integrating an Awareness of Selfhood and Society into Virtual Learning* (pp. 180–197). Hershey, PA: IGI Global. doi:10.4018/978-1-5225-2182-2.ch013

Carneiro, A. D. (2017). Defending Information Networks in Cyberspace: Some Notes on Security Needs. In M. Dawson, D. Kisku, P. Gupta, J. Sing, & W. Li (Eds.), Developing Next-Generation Countermeasures for Homeland Security Threat Prevention (pp. 354-375). Hershey, PA: IGI Global. https://doi.org/ doi:10.4018/978-1-5225-0703-1.ch016

Carvalho, W. F., & Zarate, L. (2021). Causal Feature Selection. In A. Azevedo & M. Santos (Eds.), *Integration Challenges for Analytics, Business Intelligence, and Data Mining* (pp. 145-160). IGI Global. https://doi.org/10.4018/978-1-7998-5781-5.ch007

Chase, J. P., & Yan, Z. (2017). Affect in Statistics Cognition. In *Assessing and Measuring Statistics Cognition in Higher Education Online Environments: Emerging Research and Opportunities* (pp. 144–187). Hershey, PA: IGI Global. doi:10.4018/978-1-5225-2420-5.ch005

Chatterjee, A., Roy, S., & Shrivastava, R. (2021). A Machine Learning Approach to Prevent Cancer. In G. Rani & P. Tiwari (Eds.), *Handbook of Research on Disease Prediction Through Data Analytics and Machine Learning* (pp. 112–141). IGI Global. https://doi.org/10.4018/978-1-7998-2742-9.ch007

Cifci, M. A. (2021). Optimizing WSNs for CPS Using Machine Learning Techniques. In A. Luhach & A. Elçi (Eds.), *Artificial Intelligence Paradigms for Smart Cyber-Physical Systems* (pp. 204–228). IGI Global. https://doi.org/10.4018/978-1-7998-5101-1.ch010

Cimermanova, I. (2017). Computer-Assisted Learning in Slovakia. In D. Tafazoli & M. Romero (Eds.), *Multiculturalism and Technology-Enhanced Language Learning* (pp. 252–270). Hershey, PA: IGI Global. doi:10.4018/978-1-5225-1882-2.ch015

Cipolla-Ficarra, F. V., & Cipolla-Ficarra, M. (2018). Computer Animation for Ingenious Revival. In F. Cipolla-Ficarra, M. Ficarra, M. Cipolla-Ficarra, A. Quiroga, J. Alma, & J. Carré (Eds.), *Technology-Enhanced Human Interaction in Modern Society* (pp. 159–181). Hershey, PA: IGI Global. doi:10.4018/978-1-5225-3437-2.ch008

Cockrell, S., Damron, T. S., Melton, A. M., & Smith, A. D. (2018). Offshoring IT. In M. Khosrow-Pour, D.B.A. (Ed.), Encyclopedia of Information Science and Technology, Fourth Edition (pp. 5476-5489). Hershey, PA: IGI Global. https://doi.org/ doi:10.4018/978-1-5225-2255-3.ch476

Coffey, J. W. (2018). Logic and Proof in Computer Science: Categories and Limits of Proof Techniques. In J. Horne (Ed.), *Philosophical Perceptions on Logic and Order* (pp. 218–240). Hershey, PA: IGI Global. doi:10.4018/978-1-5225-2443-4.ch007

Dale, M. (2017). Re-Thinking the Challenges of Enterprise Architecture Implementation. In M. Tavana (Ed.), *Enterprise Information Systems and the Digitalization of Business Functions* (pp. 205–221). Hershey, PA: IGI Global. doi:10.4018/978-1-5225-2382-6.ch009

Das, A., & Mohanty, M. N. (2021). An Useful Review on Optical Character Recognition for Smart Era Generation. In A. Tyagi (Ed.), *Multimedia and Sensory Input for Augmented, Mixed, and Virtual Reality* (pp. 1–41). IGI Global. https://doi.org/10.4018/978-1-7998-4703-8.ch001

Dash, A. K., & Mohapatra, P. (2021). A Survey on Prematurity Detection of Diabetic Retinopathy Based on Fundus Images Using Deep Learning Techniques. In S. Saxena & S. Paul (Eds.), *Deep Learning Applications in Medical Imaging* (pp. 140–155). IGI Global. https://doi.org/10.4018/978-1-7998-5071-7.ch006

De Maere, K., De Haes, S., & von Kutzschenbach, M. (2017). CIO Perspectives on Organizational Learning within the Context of IT Governance. *International Journal of IT/Business Alignment and Governance, 8*(1), 32-47. https://doi.org/doi:10.4018/IJITBAG.2017010103

Demir, K., Çaka, C., Yaman, N. D., İslamoğlu, H., & Kuzu, A. (2018). Examining the Current Definitions of Computational Thinking. In H. Ozcinar, G. Wong, & H. Ozturk (Eds.), *Teaching Computational Thinking in Primary Education* (pp. 36–64). Hershey, PA: IGI Global. doi:10.4018/978-1-5225-3200-2.ch003

Deng, X., Hung, Y., & Lin, C. D. (2017). Design and Analysis of Computer Experiments. In S. Saha, A. Mandal, A. Narasimhamurthy, S. V, & S. Sangam (Eds.), Handbook of Research on Applied Cybernetics and Systems Science (pp. 264-279). Hershey, PA: IGI Global. doi:10.4018/978-1-5225-2498-4.ch013

Denner, J., Martinez, J., & Thiry, H. (2017). Strategies for Engaging Hispanic/Latino Youth in the US in Computer Science. In Y. Rankin & J. Thomas (Eds.), *Moving Students of Color from Consumers to Producers of Technology* (pp. 24–48). Hershey, PA: IGI Global. doi:10.4018/978-1-5225-2005-4.ch002

Devi, A. (2017). Cyber Crime and Cyber Security: A Quick Glance. In R. Kumar, P. Pattnaik, & P. Pandey (Eds.), *Detecting and Mitigating Robotic Cyber Security Risks* (pp. 160–171). Hershey, PA: IGI Global. doi:10.4018/978-1-5225-2154-9.ch011

Dhaya, R., & Kanthavel, R. (2022). Futuristic Research Perspectives of IoT Platforms. In D. Jeya Mala (Ed.), *Integrating AI in IoT Analytics on the Cloud for Healthcare Applications* (pp. 258–275). IGI Global. doi:10.4018/978-1-7998-9132-1.ch015

Doyle, D. J., & Fahy, P. J. (2018). Interactivity in Distance Education and Computer-Aided Learning, With Medical Education Examples. In M. Khosrow-Pour, D.B.A. (Ed.), Encyclopedia of Information Science and Technology, Fourth Edition (pp. 5829-5840). Hershey, PA: IGI Global. https://doi.org/ doi:10.4018/978-1-5225-2255-3.ch507

Eklund, P. (2021). Reinforcement Learning in Social Media Marketing. In B. Christiansen & T. Škrinjarić (Eds.), *Handbook of Research on Applied AI for International Business and Marketing Applications* (pp. 30–48). IGI Global. https://doi.org/10.4018/978-1-7998-5077-9.ch003

El Ghandour, N., Benaissa, M., & Lebbah, Y. (2021). An Integer Linear Programming-Based Method for the Extraction of Ontology Alignment. *International Journal of Information Technology and Web Engineering*, *16*(2), 25–44. https://doi.org/10.4018/IJITWE.2021040102

Elias, N. I., & Walker, T. W. (2017). Factors that Contribute to Continued Use of E-Training among Healthcare Professionals. In F. Topor (Ed.), *Handbook of Research on Individualism and Identity in the Globalized Digital Age* (pp. 403–429). Hershey, PA: IGI Global. doi:10.4018/978-1-5225-0522-8.ch018

Fisher, R. L. (2018). Computer-Assisted Indian Matrimonial Services. In M. Khosrow-Pour, D.B.A. (Ed.), Encyclopedia of Information Science and Technology, Fourth Edition (pp. 4136-4145). Hershey, PA: IGI Global. doi:10.4018/978-1-5225-2255-3.ch358

Galiautdinov, R. (2021). Nonlinear Filtering in Artificial Neural Network Applications in Business and Engineering. In Q. Do (Ed.), *Artificial Neural Network Applications in Business and Engineering* (pp. 1–23). IGI Global. https://doi.org/10.4018/978-1-7998-3238-6.ch001

Gardner-McCune, C., & Jimenez, Y. (2017). Historical App Developers: Integrating CS into K-12 through Cross-Disciplinary Projects. In Y. Rankin & J. Thomas (Eds.), *Moving Students of Color from Consumers to Producers of Technology* (pp. 85–112). Hershey, PA: IGI Global. doi:10.4018/978-1-5225-2005-4.ch005

Garg, P. K. (2021). The Internet of Things-Based Technologies. In S. Kumar, M. Trivedi, P. Ranjan, & A. Punhani (Eds.), *Evolution of Software-Defined Networking Foundations for IoT and 5G Mobile Networks* (pp. 37–65). IGI Global. https://doi.org/10.4018/978-1-7998-4685-7.ch003

Garg, T., & Bharti, M. (2021). Congestion Control Protocols for UWSNs. In N. Goyal, L. Sapra, & J. Sandhu (Eds.), *Energy-Efficient Underwater Wireless Communications and Networking* (pp. 85–100). IGI Global. https://doi.org/10.4018/978-1-7998-3640-7.ch006

Gauttier, S. (2021). A Primer on Q-Method and the Study of Technology. In M. Khosrow-Pour D.B.A. (Eds.), *Encyclopedia of Information Science and Technology, Fifth Edition* (pp. 1746-1756). IGI Global. https://doi.org/10.4018/978-1-7998-3479-3.ch120

Ghafele, R., & Gibert, B. (2018). Open Growth: The Economic Impact of Open Source Software in the USA. In M. Khosrow-Pour (Ed.), *Optimizing Contemporary Application and Processes in Open Source Software* (pp. 164–197). Hershey, PA: IGI Global. doi:10.4018/978-1-5225-5314-4.ch007

Ghobakhloo, M., & Azar, A. (2018). Information Technology Resources, the Organizational Capability of Lean-Agile Manufacturing, and Business Performance. *Information Resources Management Journal*, *31*(2), 47–74. doi:10.4018/IRMJ.2018040103

Gikandi, J. W. (2017). Computer-Supported Collaborative Learning and Assessment: A Strategy for Developing Online Learning Communities in Continuing Education. In J. Keengwe & G. Onchwari (Eds.), *Handbook of Research on Learner-Centered Pedagogy in Teacher Education and Professional Development* (pp. 309–333). Hershey, PA: IGI Global. doi:10.4018/978-1-5225-0892-2.ch017

Gokhale, A. A., & Machina, K. F. (2017). Development of a Scale to Measure Attitudes toward Information Technology. In L. Tomei (Ed.), *Exploring the New Era of Technology-Infused Education* (pp. 49–64). Hershey, PA: IGI Global. doi:10.4018/978-1-5225-1709-2.ch004

Goswami, J. K., Jalal, S., Negi, C. S., & Jalal, A. S. (2022). A Texture Features-Based Robust Facial Expression Recognition. *International Journal of Computer Vision and Image Processing*, *12*(1), 1–15. https://doi.org/10.4018/IJCVIP.2022010103

Hafeez-Baig, A., Gururajan, R., & Wickramasinghe, N. (2017). Readiness as a Novel Construct of Readiness Acceptance Model (RAM) for the Wireless Handheld Technology. In N. Wickramasinghe (Ed.), *Handbook of Research on Healthcare Administration and Management* (pp. 578–595). Hershey, PA: IGI Global. doi:10.4018/978-1-5225-0920-2.ch035

Hanafizadeh, P., Ghandchi, S., & Asgarimehr, M. (2017). Impact of Information Technology on Lifestyle: A Literature Review and Classification. *International Journal of Virtual Communities and Social Networking*, 9(2), 1–23. doi:10.4018/IJVCSN.2017040101

Haseski, H. İ., Ilic, U., & Tuğtekin, U. (2018). Computational Thinking in Educational Digital Games: An Assessment Tool Proposal. In H. Ozcinar, G. Wong, & H. Ozturk (Eds.), *Teaching Computational Thinking in Primary Education* (pp. 256–287). Hershey, PA: IGI Global. doi:10.4018/978-1-5225-3200-2.ch013

Hee, W. J., Jalleh, G., Lai, H., & Lin, C. (2017). E-Commerce and IT Projects: Evaluation and Management Issues in Australian and Taiwanese Hospitals. *International Journal of Public Health Management and Ethics*, 2(1), 69–90. doi:10.4018/IJPHME.2017010104

Hernandez, A. A. (2017). Green Information Technology Usage: Awareness and Practices of Philippine IT Professionals. *International Journal of Enterprise Information Systems*, 13(4), 90–103. doi:10.4018/IJEIS.2017100106

Hernandez, M. A., Marin, E. C., Garcia-Rodriguez, J., Azorin-Lopez, J., & Cazorla, M. (2017). Automatic Learning Improves Human-Robot Interaction in Productive Environments: A Review. *International Journal of Computer Vision and Image Processing*, 7(3), 65–75. doi:10.4018/IJCVIP.2017070106

Hirota, A. (2021). Design of Narrative Creation in Innovation: "Signature Story" and Two Types of Pivots. In T. Ogata & J. Ono (Eds.), *Bridging the Gap Between AI, Cognitive Science, and Narratology With Narrative Generation* (pp. 363–376). IGI Global. https://doi.org/10.4018/978-1-7998-4864-6.ch012

Hond, D., Asgari, H., Jeffery, D., & Newman, M. (2021). An Integrated Process for Verifying Deep Learning Classifiers Using Dataset Dissimilarity Measures. *International Journal of Artificial Intelligence and Machine Learning*, 11(2), 1–21. https://doi.org/10.4018/IJAIML.289536

Horne-Popp, L. M., Tessone, E. B., & Welker, J. (2018). If You Build It, They Will Come: Creating a Library Statistics Dashboard for Decision-Making. In L. Costello & M. Powers (Eds.), *Developing In-House Digital Tools in Library Spaces* (pp. 177–203). Hershey, PA: IGI Global. doi:10.4018/978-1-5225-2676-6.ch009

Hu, H., Hu, P. J., & Al-Gahtani, S. S. (2017). User Acceptance of Computer Technology at Work in Arabian Culture: A Model Comparison Approach. In M. Khosrow-Pour (Ed.), *Handbook of Research on Technology Adoption, Social Policy, and Global Integration* (pp. 205–228). Hershey, PA: IGI Global. doi:10.4018/978-1-5225-2668-1.ch011

Huang, C., Sun, Y., & Fuh, C. (2022). Vehicle License Plate Recognition With Deep Learning. In C. Chen, W. Yang, & L. Chen (Eds.), *Technologies to Advance Automation in Forensic Science and Criminal Investigation* (pp. 161-219). IGI Global. https://doi.org/10.4018/978-1-7998-8386-9.ch009

Ifinedo, P. (2017). Using an Extended Theory of Planned Behavior to Study Nurses' Adoption of Healthcare Information Systems in Nova Scotia. *International Journal of Technology Diffusion*, 8(1), 1–17. doi:10.4018/IJTD.2017010101

Ilie, V., & Sneha, S. (2018). A Three Country Study for Understanding Physicians' Engagement With Electronic Information Resources Pre and Post System Implementation. *Journal of Global Information Management*, 26(2), 48–73. doi:10.4018/JGIM.2018040103

Ilo, P. I., Nkiko, C., Ugwu, C. I., Ekere, J. N., Izuagbe, R., & Fagbohun, M. O. (2021). Prospects and Challenges of Web 3.0 Technologies Application in the Provision of Library Services. In M. Khosrow-Pour D.B.A. (Ed.), *Encyclopedia of Information Science and Technology, Fifth Edition* (pp. 1767-1781). IGI Global. https://doi.org/10.4018/978-1-7998-3479-3.ch122

Inoue-Smith, Y. (2017). Perceived Ease in Using Technology Predicts Teacher Candidates' Preferences for Online Resources. *International Journal of Online Pedagogy and Course Design*, 7(3), 17–28. doi:10.4018/IJOPCD.2017070102

Islam, A. Y. (2017). Technology Satisfaction in an Academic Context: Moderating Effect of Gender. In A. Mesquita (Ed.), *Research Paradigms and Contemporary Perspectives on Human-Technology Interaction* (pp. 187–211). Hershey, PA: IGI Global. doi:10.4018/978-1-5225-1868-6.ch009

Jagdale, S. C., Hable, A. A., & Chabukswar, A. R. (2021). Protocol Development in Clinical Trials for Healthcare Management. In M. Khosrow-Pour D.B.A. (Ed.), *Encyclopedia of Information Science and Technology, Fifth Edition* (pp. 1797-1814). IGI Global. https://doi.org/10.4018/978-1-7998-3479-3.ch124

Jamil, G. L., & Jamil, C. C. (2017). Information and Knowledge Management Perspective Contributions for Fashion Studies: Observing Logistics and Supply Chain Management Processes. In G. Jamil, A. Soares, & C. Pessoa (Eds.), *Handbook of Research on Information Management for Effective Logistics and Supply Chains* (pp. 199–221). Hershey, PA: IGI Global. doi:10.4018/978-1-5225-0973-8.ch011

Jamil, M. I., & Almunawar, M. N. (2021). Importance of Digital Literacy and Hindrance Brought About by Digital Divide. In M. Khosrow-Pour D.B.A. (Ed.), *Encyclopedia of Information Science and Technology, Fifth Edition* (pp. 1683-1698). IGI Global. https://doi.org/10.4018/978-1-7998-3479-3.ch116

Janakova, M. (2018). Big Data and Simulations for the Solution of Controversies in Small Businesses. In M. Khosrow-Pour, D.B.A. (Ed.), Encyclopedia of Information Science and Technology, Fourth Edition (pp. 6907-6915). Hershey, PA: IGI Global. doi:10.4018/978-1-5225-2255-3.ch598

Jhawar, A., & Garg, S. K. (2018). Logistics Improvement by Investment in Information Technology Using System Dynamics. In A. Azar & S. Vaidyanathan (Eds.), *Advances in System Dynamics and Control* (pp. 528–567). Hershey, PA: IGI Global. doi:10.4018/978-1-5225-4077-9.ch017

Kalelioğlu, F., Gülbahar, Y., & Doğan, D. (2018). Teaching How to Think Like a Programmer: Emerging Insights. In H. Ozcinar, G. Wong, & H. Ozturk (Eds.), *Teaching Computational Thinking in Primary Education* (pp. 18–35). Hershey, PA: IGI Global. doi:10.4018/978-1-5225-3200-2.ch002

Kamberi, S. (2017). A Girls-Only Online Virtual World Environment and its Implications for Game-Based Learning. In A. Stricker, C. Calongne, B. Truman, & F. Arenas (Eds.), *Integrating an Awareness of Selfhood and Society into Virtual Learning* (pp. 74–95). Hershey, PA: IGI Global. doi:10.4018/978-1-5225-2182-2.ch006

Kamel, S., & Rizk, N. (2017). ICT Strategy Development: From Design to Implementation – Case of Egypt. In C. Howard & K. Hargiss (Eds.), *Strategic Information Systems and Technologies in Modern Organizations* (pp. 239–257). Hershey, PA: IGI Global. doi:10.4018/978-1-5225-1680-4.ch010

Kamel, S. H. (2018). The Potential Role of the Software Industry in Supporting Economic Development. In M. Khosrow-Pour, D.B.A. (Ed.), Encyclopedia of Information Science and Technology, Fourth Edition (pp. 7259-7269). Hershey, PA: IGI Global. doi:10.4018/978-1-5225-2255-3.ch631

Kang, H., Kang, Y., & Kim, J. (2022). Improved Fall Detection Model on GRU Using PoseNet. *International Journal of Software Innovation*, *10*(2), 1–11. https://doi.org/10.4018/IJSI.289600

Kankam, P. K. (2021). Employing Case Study and Survey Designs in Information Research. *Journal of Information Technology Research*, *14*(1), 167–177. https://doi.org/10.4018/JITR.2021010110

Karas, V., & Schuller, B. W. (2021). Deep Learning for Sentiment Analysis: An Overview and Perspectives. In F. Pinarbasi & M. Taskiran (Eds.), *Natural Language Processing for Global and Local Business* (pp. 97–132). IGI Global. https://doi.org/10.4018/978-1-7998-4240-8.ch005

Kaufman, L. M. (2022). Reimagining the Magic of the Workshop Model. In T. Driscoll III, (Ed.), *Designing Effective Distance and Blended Learning Environments in K-12* (pp. 89–109). IGI Global. https://doi.org/10.4018/978-1-7998-6829-3.ch007

Kawata, S. (2018). Computer-Assisted Parallel Program Generation. In M. Khosrow-Pour, D.B.A. (Ed.), Encyclopedia of Information Science and Technology, Fourth Edition (pp. 4583-4593). Hershey, PA: IGI Global. doi:10.4018/978-1-5225-2255-3.ch398

Kharb, L., & Singh, P. (2021). Role of Machine Learning in Modern Education and Teaching. In S. Verma & P. Tomar (Ed.), *Impact of AI Technologies on Teaching, Learning, and Research in Higher Education* (pp. 99-123). IGI Global. https://doi.org/10.4018/978-1-7998-4763-2.ch006

Khari, M., Shrivastava, G., Gupta, S., & Gupta, R. (2017). Role of Cyber Security in Today's Scenario. In R. Kumar, P. Pattnaik, & P. Pandey (Eds.), *Detecting and Mitigating Robotic Cyber Security Risks* (pp. 177–191). Hershey, PA: IGI Global. doi:10.4018/978-1-5225-2154-9.ch013

Khekare, G., & Sheikh, S. (2021). Autonomous Navigation Using Deep Reinforcement Learning in ROS. *International Journal of Artificial Intelligence and Machine Learning, 11*(2), 63–70. https://doi.org/10.4018/IJAIML.20210701.oa4

Khouja, M., Rodriguez, I. B., Ben Halima, Y., & Moalla, S. (2018). IT Governance in Higher Education Institutions: A Systematic Literature Review. *International Journal of Human Capital and Information Technology Professionals, 9*(2), 52–67. doi:10.4018/IJHCITP.2018040104

Kiourt, C., Pavlidis, G., Koutsoudis, A., & Kalles, D. (2017). Realistic Simulation of Cultural Heritage. *International Journal of Computational Methods in Heritage Science, 1*(1), 10–40. doi:10.4018/IJCMHS.2017010102

Köse, U. (2017). An Augmented-Reality-Based Intelligent Mobile Application for Open Computer Education. In G. Kurubacak & H. Altinpulluk (Eds.), *Mobile Technologies and Augmented Reality in Open Education* (pp. 154–174). Hershey, PA: IGI Global. doi:10.4018/978-1-5225-2110-5.ch008

Lahmiri, S. (2018). Information Technology Outsourcing Risk Factors and Provider Selection. In M. Gupta, R. Sharman, J. Walp, & P. Mulgund (Eds.), *Information Technology Risk Management and Compliance in Modern Organizations* (pp. 214–228). Hershey, PA: IGI Global. doi:10.4018/978-1-5225-2604-9.ch008

Lakkad, A. K., Bhadaniya, R. D., Shah, V. N., & Lavanya, K. (2021). Complex Events Processing on Live News Events Using Apache Kafka and Clustering Techniques. *International Journal of Intelligent Information Technologies*, *17*(1), 39–52. https://doi.org/10.4018/IJIIT.2021010103

Landriscina, F. (2017). Computer-Supported Imagination: The Interplay Between Computer and Mental Simulation in Understanding Scientific Concepts. In I. Levin & D. Tsybulsky (Eds.), *Digital Tools and Solutions for Inquiry-Based STEM Learning* (pp. 33–60). Hershey, PA: IGI Global. doi:10.4018/978-1-5225-2525-7.ch002

Lara López, G. (2021). Virtual Reality in Object Location. In A. Negrón & M. Muñoz (Eds.), *Latin American Women and Research Contributions to the IT Field* (pp. 307–324). IGI Global. https://doi.org/10.4018/978-1-7998-7552-9.ch014

Lee, W. W. (2018). Ethical Computing Continues From Problem to Solution. In M. Khosrow-Pour, D.B.A. (Ed.), Encyclopedia of Information Science and Technology, Fourth Edition (pp. 4884-4897). Hershey, PA: IGI Global. doi:10.4018/978-1-5225-2255-3.ch423

Lin, S., Chen, S., & Chuang, S. (2017). Perceived Innovation and Quick Response Codes in an Online-to-Offline E-Commerce Service Model. *International Journal of E-Adoption*, *9*(2), 1–16. doi:10.4018/IJEA.2017070101

Liu, M., Wang, Y., Xu, W., & Liu, L. (2017). Automated Scoring of Chinese Engineering Students' English Essays. *International Journal of Distance Education Technologies*, *15*(1), 52–68. doi:10.4018/IJDET.2017010104

Ma, X., Li, X., Zhong, B., Huang, Y., Gu, Y., Wu, M., Liu, Y., & Zhang, M. (2021). A Detector and Evaluation Framework of Abnormal Bidding Behavior Based on Supplier Portrait. *International Journal of Information Technology and Web Engineering*, *16*(2), 58–74. https://doi.org/10.4018/IJITWE.2021040104

Mabe, L. K., & Oladele, O. I. (2017). Application of Information Communication Technologies for Agricultural Development through Extension Services: A Review. In T. Tossy (Ed.), *Information Technology Integration for Socio-Economic Development* (pp. 52–101). Hershey, PA: IGI Global. doi:10.4018/978-1-5225-0539-6.ch003

Mahboub, S. A., Sayed Ali Ahmed, E., & Saeed, R. A. (2021). Smart IDS and IPS for Cyber-Physical Systems. In A. Luhach & A. Elçi (Eds.), *Artificial Intelligence Paradigms for Smart Cyber-Physical Systems* (pp. 109–136). IGI Global. https://doi.org/10.4018/978-1-7998-5101-1.ch006

Manogaran, G., Thota, C., & Lopez, D. (2018). Human-Computer Interaction With Big Data Analytics. In D. Lopez & M. Durai (Eds.), *HCI Challenges and Privacy Preservation in Big Data Security* (pp. 1–22). Hershey, PA: IGI Global. doi:10.4018/978-1-5225-2863-0.ch001

Margolis, J., Goode, J., & Flapan, J. (2017). A Critical Crossroads for Computer Science for All: "Identifying Talent" or "Building Talent," and What Difference Does It Make? In Y. Rankin & J. Thomas (Eds.), *Moving Students of Color from Consumers to Producers of Technology* (pp. 1–23). Hershey, PA: IGI Global. doi:10.4018/978-1-5225-2005-4.ch001

Mazzù, M. F., Benetton, A., Baccelloni, A., & Lavini, L. (2022). A Milk Blockchain-Enabled Supply Chain: Evidence From Leading Italian Farms. In P. De Giovanni (Ed.), *Blockchain Technology Applications in Businesses and Organizations* (pp. 73–98). IGI Global. https://doi.org/10.4018/978-1-7998-8014-1.ch004

Mbale, J. (2018). Computer Centres Resource Cloud Elasticity-Scalability (CRECES): Copperbelt University Case Study. In S. Aljawarneh & M. Malhotra (Eds.), *Critical Research on Scalability and Security Issues in Virtual Cloud Environments* (pp. 48–70). Hershey, PA: IGI Global. doi:10.4018/978-1-5225-3029-9.ch003

McKee, J. (2018). The Right Information: The Key to Effective Business Planning. In *Business Architectures for Risk Assessment and Strategic Planning: Emerging Research and Opportunities* (pp. 38–52). Hershey, PA: IGI Global. doi:10.4018/978-1-5225-3392-4.ch003

Meddah, I. H., Remil, N. E., & Meddah, H. N. (2021). Novel Approach for Mining Patterns. *International Journal of Applied Evolutionary Computation*, *12*(1), 27–42. https://doi.org/10.4018/IJAEC.2021010103

Mensah, I. K., & Mi, J. (2018). Determinants of Intention to Use Local E-Government Services in Ghana: The Perspective of Local Government Workers. *International Journal of Technology Diffusion*, *9*(2), 41–60. doi:10.4018/IJTD.2018040103

Mohamed, J. H. (2018). Scientograph-Based Visualization of Computer Forensics Research Literature. In J. Jeyasekar & P. Saravanan (Eds.), *Innovations in Measuring and Evaluating Scientific Information* (pp. 148–162). Hershey, PA: IGI Global. doi:10.4018/978-1-5225-3457-0.ch010

Montañés-Del Río, M. Á., Cornejo, V. R., Rodríguez, M. R., & Ortiz, J. S. (2021). Gamification of University Subjects: A Case Study for Operations Management. *Journal of Information Technology Research*, *14*(2), 1–29. https://doi.org/10.4018/JITR.2021040101

Moore, R. L., & Johnson, N. (2017). Earning a Seat at the Table: How IT Departments Can Partner in Organizational Change and Innovation. *International Journal of Knowledge-Based Organizations*, 7(2), 1–12. doi:10.4018/IJKBO.2017040101

Mukul, M. K., & Bhattaharyya, S. (2017). Brain-Machine Interface: Human-Computer Interaction. In E. Noughabi, B. Raahemi, A. Albadvi, & B. Far (Eds.), *Handbook of Research on Data Science for Effective Healthcare Practice and Administration* (pp. 417–443). Hershey, PA: IGI Global. doi:10.4018/978-1-5225-2515-8.ch018

Na, L. (2017). Library and Information Science Education and Graduate Programs in Academic Libraries. In L. Ruan, Q. Zhu, & Y. Ye (Eds.), *Academic Library Development and Administration in China* (pp. 218–229). Hershey, PA: IGI Global. doi:10.4018/978-1-5225-0550-1.ch013

Nagpal, G., Bishnoi, G. K., Dhami, H. S., & Vijayvargia, A. (2021). Use of Data Analytics to Increase the Efficiency of Last Mile Logistics for Ecommerce Deliveries. In B. Patil & M. Vohra (Eds.), *Handbook of Research on Engineering, Business, and Healthcare Applications of Data Science and Analytics* (pp. 167–180). IGI Global. https://doi.org/10.4018/978-1-7998-3053-5.ch009

Nair, S. M., Ramesh, V., & Tyagi, A. K. (2021). Issues and Challenges (Privacy, Security, and Trust) in Blockchain-Based Applications. In A. Tyagi, G. Rekha, & N. Sreenath (Eds.), *Opportunities and Challenges for Blockchain Technology in Autonomous Vehicles* (pp. 196–209). IGI Global. https://doi.org/10.4018/978-1-7998-3295-9.ch012

Naomi, J. F. M., K., & V., S. (2021). Machine and Deep Learning Techniques in IoT and Cloud. In S. Velayutham (Ed.), *Challenges and Opportunities for the Convergence of IoT, Big Data, and Cloud Computing* (pp. 225-247). IGI Global. https://doi.org/10.4018/978-1-7998-3111-2.ch013

Nath, R., & Murthy, V. N. (2018). What Accounts for the Differences in Internet Diffusion Rates Around the World? In M. Khosrow-Pour, D.B.A. (Ed.), Encyclopedia of Information Science and Technology, Fourth Edition (pp. 8095-8104). Hershey, PA: IGI Global. https://doi.org/ doi:10.4018/978-1-5225-2255-3.ch705

Nedelko, Z., & Potocan, V. (2018). The Role of Emerging Information Technologies for Supporting Supply Chain Management. In M. Khosrow-Pour, D.B.A. (Ed.), Encyclopedia of Information Science and Technology, Fourth Edition (pp. 5559-5569). Hershey, PA: IGI Global. doi:10.4018/978-1-5225-2255-3.ch483

Negrini, L., Giang, C., & Bonnet, E. (2022). Designing Tools and Activities for Educational Robotics in Online Learning. In N. Eteokleous & E. Nisiforou (Eds.), *Designing, Constructing, and Programming Robots for Learning* (pp. 202–222). IGI Global. https://doi.org/10.4018/978-1-7998-7443-0.ch010

Ngafeeson, M. N. (2018). User Resistance to Health Information Technology. In M. Khosrow-Pour, D.B.A. (Ed.), Encyclopedia of Information Science and Technology, Fourth Edition (pp. 3816-3825). Hershey, PA: IGI Global. doi:10.4018/978-1-5225-2255-3.ch331

Nguyen, T. T., Giang, N. L., Tran, D. T., Nguyen, T. T., Nguyen, H. Q., Pham, A. V., & Vu, T. D. (2021). A Novel Filter-Wrapper Algorithm on Intuitionistic Fuzzy Set for Attribute Reduction From Decision Tables. *International Journal of Data Warehousing and Mining*, *17*(4), 67–100. https://doi.org/10.4018/IJDWM.2021100104

Nigam, A., & Dewani, P. P. (2022). Consumer Engagement Through Conditional Promotions: An Exploratory Study. *Journal of Global Information Management*, *30*(5), 1–19. https://doi.org/10.4018/JGIM.290364

Odagiri, K. (2017). Introduction of Individual Technology to Constitute the Current Internet. In *Strategic Policy-Based Network Management in Contemporary Organizations* (pp. 20–96). Hershey, PA: IGI Global. doi:10.4018/978-1-68318-003-6.ch003

Odia, J. O., & Akpata, O. T. (2021). Role of Data Science and Data Analytics in Forensic Accounting and Fraud Detection. In B. Patil & M. Vohra (Eds.), *Handbook of Research on Engineering, Business, and Healthcare Applications of Data Science and Analytics* (pp. 203–227). IGI Global. https://doi.org/10.4018/978-1-7998-3053-5.ch011

Okike, E. U. (2018). Computer Science and Prison Education. In I. Biao (Ed.), *Strategic Learning Ideologies in Prison Education Programs* (pp. 246–264). Hershey, PA: IGI Global. doi:10.4018/978-1-5225-2909-5.ch012

Olelewe, C. J., & Nwafor, I. P. (2017). Level of Computer Appreciation Skills Acquired for Sustainable Development by Secondary School Students in Nsukka LGA of Enugu State, Nigeria. In C. Ayo & V. Mbarika (Eds.), *Sustainable ICT Adoption and Integration for Socio-Economic Development* (pp. 214–233). Hershey, PA: IGI Global. doi:10.4018/978-1-5225-2565-3.ch010

Oliveira, M., Maçada, A. C., Curado, C., & Nodari, F. (2017). Infrastructure Profiles and Knowledge Sharing. *International Journal of Technology and Human Interaction*, *13*(3), 1–12. doi:10.4018/IJTHI.2017070101

Otarkhani, A., Shokouhyar, S., & Pour, S. S. (2017). Analyzing the Impact of Governance of Enterprise IT on Hospital Performance: Tehran's (Iran) Hospitals – A Case Study. *International Journal of Healthcare Information Systems and Informatics, 12*(3), 1–20. doi:10.4018/IJHISI.2017070101

Otunla, A. O., & Amuda, C. O. (2018). Nigerian Undergraduate Students' Computer Competencies and Use of Information Technology Tools and Resources for Study Skills and Habits' Enhancement. In M. Khosrow-Pour, D.B.A. (Ed.), Encyclopedia of Information Science and Technology, Fourth Edition (pp. 2303-2313). Hershey, PA: IGI Global. https://doi.org/ doi:10.4018/978-1-5225-2255-3.ch200

Özçınar, H. (2018). A Brief Discussion on Incentives and Barriers to Computational Thinking Education. In H. Ozcinar, G. Wong, & H. Ozturk (Eds.), *Teaching Computational Thinking in Primary Education* (pp. 1–17). Hershey, PA: IGI Global. doi:10.4018/978-1-5225-3200-2.ch001

Pandey, J. M., Garg, S., Mishra, P., & Mishra, B. P. (2017). Computer Based Psychological Interventions: Subject to the Efficacy of Psychological Services. *International Journal of Computers in Clinical Practice, 2*(1), 25–33. doi:10.4018/IJCCP.2017010102

Pandkar, S. D., & Paatil, S. D. (2021). Big Data and Knowledge Resource Centre. In S. Dhamdhere (Ed.), *Big Data Applications for Improving Library Services* (pp. 90–106). IGI Global. https://doi.org/10.4018/978-1-7998-3049-8.ch007

Patro, C. (2017). Impulsion of Information Technology on Human Resource Practices. In P. Ordóñez de Pablos (Ed.), *Managerial Strategies and Solutions for Business Success in Asia* (pp. 231–254). Hershey, PA: IGI Global. doi:10.4018/978-1-5225-1886-0.ch013

Patro, C. S., & Raghunath, K. M. (2017). Information Technology Paraphernalia for Supply Chain Management Decisions. In M. Tavana (Ed.), *Enterprise Information Systems and the Digitalization of Business Functions* (pp. 294–320). Hershey, PA: IGI Global. doi:10.4018/978-1-5225-2382-6.ch014

Paul, P. K. (2018). The Context of IST for Solid Information Retrieval and Infrastructure Building: Study of Developing Country. *International Journal of Information Retrieval Research, 8*(1), 86–100. doi:10.4018/IJIRR.2018010106

Paul, P. K., & Chatterjee, D. (2018). iSchools Promoting "Information Science and Technology" (IST) Domain Towards Community, Business, and Society With Contemporary Worldwide Trend and Emerging Potentialities in India. In M. Khosrow-Pour, D.B.A. (Ed.), Encyclopedia of Information Science and Technology, Fourth Edition (pp. 4723-4735). Hershey, PA: IGI Global. https://doi.org/ doi:10.4018/978-1-5225-2255-3.ch410

Pessoa, C. R., & Marques, M. E. (2017). Information Technology and Communication Management in Supply Chain Management. In G. Jamil, A. Soares, & C. Pessoa (Eds.), *Handbook of Research on Information Management for Effective Logistics and Supply Chains* (pp. 23–33). Hershey, PA: IGI Global. doi:10.4018/978-1-5225-0973-8.ch002

Pineda, R. G. (2018). Remediating Interaction: Towards a Philosophy of Human-Computer Relationship. In M. Khosrow-Pour (Ed.), *Enhancing Art, Culture, and Design With Technological Integration* (pp. 75–98). Hershey, PA: IGI Global. doi:10.4018/978-1-5225-5023-5.ch004

Prabha, V. D., & R., R. (2021). Clinical Decision Support Systems: Decision-Making System for Clinical Data. In G. Rani & P. Tiwari (Eds.), *Handbook of Research on Disease Prediction Through Data Analytics and Machine Learning* (pp. 268-280). IGI Global. https://doi.org/10.4018/978-1-7998-2742-9.ch014

Pushpa, R., & Siddappa, M. (2021). An Optimal Way of VM Placement Strategy in Cloud Computing Platform Using ABCS Algorithm. *International Journal of Ambient Computing and Intelligence*, *12*(3), 16–38. https://doi.org/10.4018/ IJACI.2021070102

Qian, Y. (2017). Computer Simulation in Higher Education: Affordances, Opportunities, and Outcomes. In P. Vu, S. Fredrickson, & C. Moore (Eds.), *Handbook of Research on Innovative Pedagogies and Technologies for Online Learning in Higher Education* (pp. 236–262). Hershey, PA: IGI Global. doi:10.4018/978-1-5225-1851-8.ch011

Rahman, N. (2017). Lessons from a Successful Data Warehousing Project Management. *International Journal of Information Technology Project Management*, *8*(4), 30–45. doi:10.4018/IJITPM.2017100103

Rahman, N. (2018). Environmental Sustainability in the Computer Industry for Competitive Advantage. In M. Khosrow-Pour (Ed.), *Green Computing Strategies for Competitive Advantage and Business Sustainability* (pp. 110–130). Hershey, PA: IGI Global. doi:10.4018/978-1-5225-5017-4.ch006

Rajh, A., & Pavetic, T. (2017). Computer Generated Description as the Required Digital Competence in Archival Profession. *International Journal of Digital Literacy and Digital Competence*, 8(1), 36–49. doi:10.4018/IJDLDC.2017010103

Raman, A., & Goyal, D. P. (2017). Extending IMPLEMENT Framework for Enterprise Information Systems Implementation to Information System Innovation. In M. Tavana (Ed.), *Enterprise Information Systems and the Digitalization of Business Functions* (pp. 137–177). Hershey, PA: IGI Global. doi:10.4018/978-1-5225-2382-6.ch007

Rao, A. P., & Reddy, K. S. (2021). Automated Soil Residue Levels Detecting Device With IoT Interface. In V. Sathiyamoorthi & A. Elci (Eds.), *Challenges and Applications of Data Analytics in Social Perspectives* (Vol. S, pp. 123–135). IGI Global. https://doi.org/10.4018/978-1-7998-2566-1.ch007

Rao, Y. S., Rauta, A. K., Saini, H., & Panda, T. C. (2017). Mathematical Model for Cyber Attack in Computer Network. *International Journal of Business Data Communications and Networking*, 13(1), 58–65. doi:10.4018/IJBDCN.2017010105

Rapaport, W. J. (2018). Syntactic Semantics and the Proper Treatment of Computationalism. In M. Danesi (Ed.), *Empirical Research on Semiotics and Visual Rhetoric* (pp. 128–176). Hershey, PA: IGI Global. doi:10.4018/978-1-5225-5622-0.ch007

Raut, R., Priyadarshinee, P., & Jha, M. (2017). Understanding the Mediation Effect of Cloud Computing Adoption in Indian Organization: Integrating TAM-TOE- Risk Model. *International Journal of Service Science, Management, Engineering, and Technology*, 8(3), 40–59. doi:10.4018/IJSSMET.2017070103

Rezaie, S., Mirabedini, S. J., & Abtahi, A. (2018). Designing a Model for Implementation of Business Intelligence in the Banking Industry. *International Journal of Enterprise Information Systems*, 14(1), 77–103. doi:10.4018/IJEIS.2018010105

Rezende, D. A. (2018). Strategic Digital City Projects: Innovative Information and Public Services Offered by Chicago (USA) and Curitiba (Brazil). In M. Lytras, L. Daniela, & A. Visvizi (Eds.), *Enhancing Knowledge Discovery and Innovation in the Digital Era* (pp. 204–223). Hershey, PA: IGI Global. doi:10.4018/978-1-5225-4191-2.ch012

Rodriguez, A., Rico-Diaz, A. J., Rabuñal, J. R., & Gestal, M. (2017). Fish Tracking with Computer Vision Techniques: An Application to Vertical Slot Fishways. In M. S., & V. V. (Eds.), Multi-Core Computer Vision and Image Processing for Intelligent Applications (pp. 74-104). Hershey, PA: IGI Global. https://doi.org/doi:10.4018/978-1-5225-0889-2.ch003

Romero, J. A. (2018). Sustainable Advantages of Business Value of Information Technology. In M. Khosrow-Pour, D.B.A. (Ed.), Encyclopedia of Information Science and Technology, Fourth Edition (pp. 923-929). Hershey, PA: IGI Global. doi:10.4018/978-1-5225-2255-3.ch079

Romero, J. A. (2018). The Always-On Business Model and Competitive Advantage. In N. Bajgoric (Ed.), *Always-On Enterprise Information Systems for Modern Organizations* (pp. 23–40). Hershey, PA: IGI Global. doi:10.4018/978-1-5225-3704-5.ch002

Rosen, Y. (2018). Computer Agent Technologies in Collaborative Learning and Assessment. In M. Khosrow-Pour, D.B.A. (Ed.), Encyclopedia of Information Science and Technology, Fourth Edition (pp. 2402-2410). Hershey, PA: IGI Global. doi:10.4018/978-1-5225-2255-3.ch209

Roy, D. (2018). Success Factors of Adoption of Mobile Applications in Rural India: Effect of Service Characteristics on Conceptual Model. In M. Khosrow-Pour (Ed.), *Green Computing Strategies for Competitive Advantage and Business Sustainability* (pp. 211–238). Hershey, PA: IGI Global. doi:10.4018/978-1-5225-5017-4.ch010

Ruffin, T. R., & Hawkins, D. P. (2018). Trends in Health Care Information Technology and Informatics. In M. Khosrow-Pour, D.B.A. (Ed.), Encyclopedia of Information Science and Technology, Fourth Edition (pp. 3805-3815). Hershey, PA: IGI Global. doi:10.4018/978-1-5225-2255-3.ch330

Sadasivam, U. M., & Ganesan, N. (2021). Detecting Fake News Using Deep Learning and NLP. In S. Misra, C. Arumugam, S. Jaganathan, & S. S. (Eds.), *Confluence of AI, Machine, and Deep Learning in Cyber Forensics* (pp. 117-133). IGI Global. https://doi.org/10.4018/978-1-7998-4900-1.ch007

Safari, M. R., & Jiang, Q. (2018). The Theory and Practice of IT Governance Maturity and Strategies Alignment: Evidence From Banking Industry. *Journal of Global Information Management*, 26(2), 127–146. doi:10.4018/JGIM.2018040106

Sahin, H. B., & Anagun, S. S. (2018). Educational Computer Games in Math Teaching: A Learning Culture. In E. Toprak & E. Kumtepe (Eds.), *Supporting Multiculturalism in Open and Distance Learning Spaces* (pp. 249–280). Hershey, PA: IGI Global. doi:10.4018/978-1-5225-3076-3.ch013

Sakalle, A., Tomar, P., Bhardwaj, H., & Sharma, U. (2021). Impact and Latest Trends of Intelligent Learning With Artificial Intelligence. In S. Verma & P. Tomar (Eds.), *Impact of AI Technologies on Teaching, Learning, and Research in Higher Education* (pp. 172-189). IGI Global. https://doi.org/10.4018/978-1-7998-4763-2.ch011

Sala, N. (2021). Virtual Reality, Augmented Reality, and Mixed Reality in Education: A Brief Overview. In D. Choi, A. Dailey-Hebert, & J. Estes (Eds.), *Current and Prospective Applications of Virtual Reality in Higher Education* (pp. 48–73). IGI Global. https://doi.org/10.4018/978-1-7998-4960-5.ch003

Salunkhe, S., Kanagachidambaresan, G., Rajkumar, C., & Jayanthi, K. (2022). Online Detection and Prediction of Fused Deposition Modelled Parts Using Artificial Intelligence. In S. Salunkhe, H. Hussein, & J. Davim (Eds.), *Applications of Artificial Intelligence in Additive Manufacturing* (pp. 194–209). IGI Global. https://doi.org/10.4018/978-1-7998-8516-0.ch009

Samy, V. S., Pramanick, K., Thenkanidiyoor, V., & Victor, J. (2021). Data Analysis and Visualization in Python for Polar Meteorological Data. *International Journal of Data Analytics*, *2*(1), 32–60. https://doi.org/10.4018/IJDA.2021010102

Sanna, A., & Valpreda, F. (2017). An Assessment of the Impact of a Collaborative Didactic Approach and Students' Background in Teaching Computer Animation. *International Journal of Information and Communication Technology Education*, *13*(4), 1–16. doi:10.4018/IJICTE.2017100101

Sarivougioukas, J., & Vagelatos, A. (2022). Fused Contextual Data With Threading Technology to Accelerate Processing in Home UbiHealth. *International Journal of Software Science and Computational Intelligence*, *14*(1), 1–14. https://doi.org/10.4018/IJSSCI.285590

Scott, A., Martin, A., & McAlear, F. (2017). Enhancing Participation in Computer Science among Girls of Color: An Examination of a Preparatory AP Computer Science Intervention. In Y. Rankin & J. Thomas (Eds.), *Moving Students of Color from Consumers to Producers of Technology* (pp. 62–84). Hershey, PA: IGI Global. doi:10.4018/978-1-5225-2005-4.ch004

Shanmugam, M., Ibrahim, N., Gorment, N. Z., Sugu, R., Dandarawi, T. N., & Ahmad, N. A. (2022). Towards an Integrated Omni-Channel Strategy Framework for Improved Customer Interaction. In P. Lai (Ed.), *Handbook of Research on Social Impacts of E-Payment and Blockchain Technology* (pp. 409–427). IGI Global. https://doi.org/10.4018/978-1-7998-9035-5.ch022

Sharma, A., & Kumar, S. (2021). Network Slicing and the Role of 5G in IoT Applications. In S. Kumar, M. Trivedi, P. Ranjan, & A. Punhani (Eds.), *Evolution of Software-Defined Networking Foundations for IoT and 5G Mobile Networks* (pp. 172–190). IGI Global. https://doi.org/10.4018/978-1-7998-4685-7.ch010

Siddoo, V., & Wongsai, N. (2017). Factors Influencing the Adoption of ISO/IEC 29110 in Thai Government Projects: A Case Study. *International Journal of Information Technologies and Systems Approach*, *10*(1), 22–44. doi:10.4018/IJITSA.2017010102

Silveira, C., Hir, M. E., & Chaves, H. K. (2022). An Approach to Information Management as a Subsidy of Global Health Actions: A Case Study of Big Data in Health for Dengue, Zika, and Chikungunya. In J. Lima de Magalhães, Z. Hartz, G. Jamil, H. Silveira, & L. Jamil (Eds.), *Handbook of Research on Essential Information Approaches to Aiding Global Health in the One Health Context* (pp. 219–234). IGI Global. https://doi.org/10.4018/978-1-7998-8011-0.ch012

Simões, A. (2017). Using Game Frameworks to Teach Computer Programming. In R. Alexandre Peixoto de Queirós & M. Pinto (Eds.), *Gamification-Based E-Learning Strategies for Computer Programming Education* (pp. 221–236). Hershey, PA: IGI Global. doi:10.4018/978-1-5225-1034-5.ch010

Simões de Almeida, R., & da Silva, T. (2022). AI Chatbots in Mental Health: Are We There Yet? In A. Marques & R. Queirós (Eds.), *Digital Therapies in Psychosocial Rehabilitation and Mental Health* (pp. 226–243). IGI Global. https://doi.org/10.4018/978-1-7998-8634-1.ch011

Singh, L. K., Khanna, M., Thawkar, S., & Gopal, J. (2021). Robustness for Authentication of the Human Using Face, Ear, and Gait Multimodal Biometric System. *International Journal of Information System Modeling and Design*, *12*(1), 39–72. https://doi.org/10.4018/IJISMD.2021010103

Sllame, A. M. (2017). Integrating LAB Work With Classes in Computer Network Courses. In H. Alphin Jr, R. Chan, & J. Lavine (Eds.), *The Future of Accessibility in International Higher Education* (pp. 253–275). Hershey, PA: IGI Global. doi:10.4018/978-1-5225-2560-8.ch015

Smirnov, A., Ponomarev, A., Shilov, N., Kashevnik, A., & Teslya, N. (2018). Ontology-Based Human-Computer Cloud for Decision Support: Architecture and Applications in Tourism. *International Journal of Embedded and Real-Time Communication Systems*, *9*(1), 1–19. doi:10.4018/IJERTCS.2018010101

Smith-Ditizio, A. A., & Smith, A. D. (2018). Computer Fraud Challenges and Its Legal Implications. In M. Khosrow-Pour, D.B.A. (Ed.), *Encyclopedia of Information Science and Technology, Fourth Edition* (pp. 4837-4848). Hershey, PA: IGI Global. doi:10.4018/978-1-5225-2255-3.ch419

Sosnin, P. (2018). Figuratively Semantic Support of Human-Computer Interactions. In *Experience-Based Human-Computer Interactions: Emerging Research and Opportunities* (pp. 244–272). Hershey, PA: IGI Global. doi:10.4018/978-1-5225-2987-3.ch008

Srilakshmi, R., & Jaya Bhaskar, M. (2021). An Adaptable Secure Scheme in Mobile Ad hoc Network to Protect the Communication Channel From Malicious Behaviours. *International Journal of Information Technology and Web Engineering*, *16*(3), 54–73. https://doi.org/10.4018/IJITWE.2021070104

Sukhwani, N., Kagita, V. R., Kumar, V., & Panda, S. K. (2021). Efficient Computation of Top-K Skyline Objects in Data Set With Uncertain Preferences. *International Journal of Data Warehousing and Mining*, *17*(3), 68–80. https://doi.org/10.4018/IJDWM.2021070104

Susanto, H., Yie, L. F., Setiana, D., Asih, Y., Yoganingrum, A., Riyanto, S., & Saputra, F. A. (2021). Digital Ecosystem Security Issues for Organizations and Governments: Digital Ethics and Privacy. In Z. Mahmood (Ed.), *Web 2.0 and Cloud Technologies for Implementing Connected Government* (pp. 204–228). IGI Global. https://doi.org/10.4018/978-1-7998-4570-6.ch010

Syväjärvi, A., Leinonen, J., Kivivirta, V., & Kesti, M. (2017). The Latitude of Information Management in Local Government: Views of Local Government Managers. *International Journal of Electronic Government Research*, *13*(1), 69–85. doi:10.4018/IJEGR.2017010105

Tanque, M., & Foxwell, H. J. (2018). Big Data and Cloud Computing: A Review of Supply Chain Capabilities and Challenges. In A. Prasad (Ed.), *Exploring the Convergence of Big Data and the Internet of Things* (pp. 1–28). Hershey, PA: IGI Global. doi:10.4018/978-1-5225-2947-7.ch001

Teixeira, A., Gomes, A., & Orvalho, J. G. (2017). Auditory Feedback in a Computer Game for Blind People. In T. Issa, P. Kommers, T. Issa, P. Isaías, & T. Issa (Eds.), *Smart Technology Applications in Business Environments* (pp. 134–158). Hershey, PA: IGI Global. doi:10.4018/978-1-5225-2492-2.ch007

Tewari, P., Tiwari, P., & Goel, R. (2022). Information Technology in Supply Chain Management. In V. Garg & R. Goel (Eds.), *Handbook of Research on Innovative Management Using AI in Industry 5.0* (pp. 165–178). IGI Global. https://doi.org/10.4018/978-1-7998-8497-2.ch011

Thompson, N., McGill, T., & Murray, D. (2018). Affect-Sensitive Computer Systems. In M. Khosrow-Pour, D.B.A. (Ed.), Encyclopedia of Information Science and Technology, Fourth Edition (pp. 4124-4135). Hershey, PA: IGI Global. doi:10.4018/978-1-5225-2255-3.ch357

Triberti, S., Brivio, E., & Galimberti, C. (2018). On Social Presence: Theories, Methodologies, and Guidelines for the Innovative Contexts of Computer-Mediated Learning. In M. Marmon (Ed.), *Enhancing Social Presence in Online Learning Environments* (pp. 20–41). Hershey, PA: IGI Global. doi:10.4018/978-1-5225-3229-3.ch002

Tripathy, B. K. T. R., S., & Mohanty, R. K. (2018). Memetic Algorithms and Their Applications in Computer Science. In S. Dash, B. Tripathy, & A. Rahman (Eds.), Handbook of Research on Modeling, Analysis, and Application of Nature-Inspired Metaheuristic Algorithms (pp. 73-93). Hershey, PA: IGI Global. https://doi.org/doi:10.4018/978-1-5225-2857-9.ch004

Turulja, L., & Bajgoric, N. (2017). Human Resource Management IT and Global Economy Perspective: Global Human Resource Information Systems. In M. Khosrow-Pour (Ed.), *Handbook of Research on Technology Adoption, Social Policy, and Global Integration* (pp. 377–394). Hershey, PA: IGI Global. doi:10.4018/978-1-5225-2668-1.ch018

Unwin, D. W., Sanzogni, L., & Sandhu, K. (2017). Developing and Measuring the Business Case for Health Information Technology. In K. Moahi, K. Bwalya, & P. Sebina (Eds.), *Health Information Systems and the Advancement of Medical Practice in Developing Countries* (pp. 262–290). Hershey, PA: IGI Global. doi:10.4018/978-1-5225-2262-1.ch015

Usharani, B. (2022). House Plant Leaf Disease Detection and Classification Using Machine Learning. In M. Mundada, S. Seema, S. K.G., & M. Shilpa (Eds.), *Deep Learning Applications for Cyber-Physical Systems* (pp. 17-26). IGI Global. https://doi.org/10.4018/978-1-7998-8161-2.ch002

Vadhanam, B. R. S., M., Sugumaran, V., V., V., & Ramalingam, V. V. (2017). Computer Vision Based Classification on Commercial Videos. In M. S., & V. V. (Eds.), Multi-Core Computer Vision and Image Processing for Intelligent Applications (pp. 105-135). Hershey, PA: IGI Global. https://doi.org/ doi:10.4018/978-1-5225-0889-2.ch004

Vairinho, S. (2022). Innovation Dynamics Through the Encouragement of Knowledge Spin-Off From Touristic Destinations. In C. Ramos, S. Quinteiro, & A. Gonçalves (Eds.), *ICT as Innovator Between Tourism and Culture* (pp. 170–190). IGI Global. https://doi.org/10.4018/978-1-7998-8165-0.ch011

Valverde, R., Torres, B., & Motaghi, H. (2018). A Quantum NeuroIS Data Analytics Architecture for the Usability Evaluation of Learning Management Systems. In S. Bhattacharyya (Ed.), *Quantum-Inspired Intelligent Systems for Multimedia Data Analysis* (pp. 277–299). Hershey, PA: IGI Global. doi:10.4018/978-1-5225-5219-2.ch009

Vassilis, E. (2018). Learning and Teaching Methodology: "1:1 Educational Computing. In K. Koutsopoulos, K. Doukas, & Y. Kotsanis (Eds.), *Handbook of Research on Educational Design and Cloud Computing in Modern Classroom Settings* (pp. 122–155). Hershey, PA: IGI Global. doi:10.4018/978-1-5225-3053-4.ch007

Verma, S., & Jain, A. K. (2022). A Survey on Sentiment Analysis Techniques for Twitter. In B. Gupta, D. Peraković, A. Abd El-Latif, & D. Gupta (Eds.), *Data Mining Approaches for Big Data and Sentiment Analysis in Social Media* (pp. 57–90). IGI Global. https://doi.org/10.4018/978-1-7998-8413-2.ch003

Wang, H., Huang, P., & Chen, X. (2021). Research and Application of a Multidimensional Association Rules Mining Method Based on OLAP. *International Journal of Information Technology and Web Engineering*, *16*(1), 75–94. https://doi.org/10.4018/IJITWE.2021010104

Wexler, B. E. (2017). Computer-Presented and Physical Brain-Training Exercises for School Children: Improving Executive Functions and Learning. In B. Dubbels (Ed.), *Transforming Gaming and Computer Simulation Technologies across Industries* (pp. 206–224). Hershey, PA: IGI Global. doi:10.4018/978-1-5225-1817-4.ch012

Wimble, M., Singh, H., & Phillips, B. (2018). Understanding Cross-Level Interactions of Firm-Level Information Technology and Industry Environment: A Multilevel Model of Business Value. *Information Resources Management Journal*, *31*(1), 1–20. doi:10.4018/IRMJ.2018010101

Wimmer, H., Powell, L., Kilgus, L., & Force, C. (2017). Improving Course Assessment via Web-based Homework. *International Journal of Online Pedagogy and Course Design*, *7*(2), 1–19. doi:10.4018/IJOPCD.2017040101

Wong, S. (2021). Gendering Information and Communication Technologies in Climate Change. In M. Khosrow-Pour D.B.A. (Eds.), *Encyclopedia of Information Science and Technology, Fifth Edition* (pp. 1408-1422). IGI Global. https://doi.org/10.4018/978-1-7998-3479-3.ch096

Wong, Y. L., & Siu, K. W. (2018). Assessing Computer-Aided Design Skills. In M. Khosrow-Pour, D.B.A. (Ed.), Encyclopedia of Information Science and Technology, Fourth Edition (pp. 7382-7391). Hershey, PA: IGI Global. doi:10.4018/978-1-5225-2255-3.ch642

Wongsurawat, W., & Shrestha, V. (2018). Information Technology, Globalization, and Local Conditions: Implications for Entrepreneurs in Southeast Asia. In P. Ordóñez de Pablos (Ed.), *Management Strategies and Technology Fluidity in the Asian Business Sector* (pp. 163–176). Hershey, PA: IGI Global. doi:10.4018/978-1-5225-4056-4.ch010

Yamada, H. (2021). Homogenization of Japanese Industrial Technology From the Perspective of R&D Expenses. *International Journal of Systems and Service-Oriented Engineering, 11*(2), 24–51. doi:10.4018/IJSSOE.2021070102

Yang, Y., Zhu, X., Jin, C., & Li, J. J. (2018). Reforming Classroom Education Through a QQ Group: A Pilot Experiment at a Primary School in Shanghai. In H. Spires (Ed.), *Digital Transformation and Innovation in Chinese Education* (pp. 211–231). Hershey, PA: IGI Global. doi:10.4018/978-1-5225-2924-8.ch012

Yilmaz, R., Sezgin, A., Kurnaz, S., & Arslan, Y. Z. (2018). Object-Oriented Programming in Computer Science. In M. Khosrow-Pour, D.B.A. (Ed.), Encyclopedia of Information Science and Technology, Fourth Edition (pp. 7470-7480). Hershey, PA: IGI Global. doi:10.4018/978-1-5225-2255-3.ch650

Yu, L. (2018). From Teaching Software Engineering Locally and Globally to Devising an Internationalized Computer Science Curriculum. In S. Dikli, B. Etheridge, & R. Rawls (Eds.), *Curriculum Internationalization and the Future of Education* (pp. 293–320). Hershey, PA: IGI Global. doi:10.4018/978-1-5225-2791-6.ch016

Yuhua, F. (2018). Computer Information Library Clusters. In M. Khosrow-Pour, D.B.A. (Ed.), Encyclopedia of Information Science and Technology, Fourth Edition (pp. 4399-4403). Hershey, PA: IGI Global. doi:10.4018/978-1-5225-2255-3.ch382

Zakaria, R. B., Zainuddin, M. N., & Mohamad, A. H. (2022). Distilling Blockchain: Complexity, Barriers, and Opportunities. In P. Lai (Ed.), *Handbook of Research on Social Impacts of E-Payment and Blockchain Technology* (pp. 89–114). IGI Global. https://doi.org/10.4018/978-1-7998-9035-5.ch007

Zhang, Z., Ma, J., & Cui, X. (2021). Genetic Algorithm With Three-Dimensional Population Dominance Strategy for University Course Timetabling Problem. *International Journal of Grid and High Performance Computing, 13*(2), 56–69. https://doi.org/10.4018/IJGHPC.2021040104

About the Contributors

Surbhi Bhatia completed her PhD in Computer Science and Engineering in 2018 from Banasthali Vidyapith University, Vanasthali, India. She is currently Assistant Professor in the Department of Information Systems at King Faisal University, Hofuf, Saudi Arabia. She has authored/edited 3 books, holds 7 patents, and has more than 25 research publications. Her research interests including data mining, machine learning, database management systems, and computer languages: C, C++, Python.

Poonam Tanwar has 18 years of Teaching Experience working as associate Prof. in Manav Rachna International Institute of Research & Studies, Faridabad. She has published more than 50 research papers in various International Journals and Conferences. She has one copyright and filled 6 patents. She has edited 3 books and 2 in process. The book titled "Big Data Analytics and Intelligence: A Perspective for Health Care" in 2019 by Emerald, Natural Language processing and AI application for Industry 4.O by IGI Globe & Computational Intelligence & Predictive Analysis for Medical Science A Pragmatic Approach by Degurter. She was Guest Editor for Special issue of "Advancement in Machine Learning (ML) and Knowledge Mining (KM)" for International Journal of Recent Patents in Engineering (UAE) & one more is in process. She has been awarded woman researcher award by VDGOODS Academy Chennai. She has organized various Science & Technology awareness program for rural development. She received Certificate of RECOGNITION (Silver Category) for OUTSTANDING Contribution to Campus Connect Program for all academic years since 2011 to 2017 by INFOSYS, Chandigarh. Beside this she is Technical program committee member for various International Conferences Like ICIC 2018, ICFNN, Rome(Italy), European Conference on Natural Language Processing and Information Retrieval, Berlin(Europe) Etc.

Kuljeet Kaur received the B.Tech degree in computer science and engineering from Punjab Technical University, Jalandhar, India, in 2011 and the M.E. (Information Security) and Ph.D. (Computer Science and Engineering) degrees from Thapar Institute of Engineering and Technology (Deemed to be University), Patiala, India, in 2015 and 2018, respectively. She worked as a NSERC Postdoctoral Research Fellow at the École de technologie supérieure (ÉTS), Université du Québec, Montréal, Canada from 2018 till 2020. She is currently working as an Assistant Professor in the Electrical Engineering Department at ÉTS, Montreal and a Visiting Researcher in the School of Computer Science and Engineering (SCSE) at the Nanyang Technological University (NTU), Singapore. Her main research interests include Cloud Computing, Energy Efficiency, Smart Grid, Frequency Support, and Vehicle-to-Grid. Dr. Kaur has secured a number of research articles in top- tier journals such as IEEE Wireless Communications, IEEE TII, IEEE TCC, IEEE TVT, IEEE TMM, IEEE TSG, IEEE Systems Journal, IEEE IoT Journal, IEEE Communications Magazine, IEEE Wireless Communications, IEEE Network, IEEE PS, FGCS, JPDC, Springer PPNA, etc., and various International conferences including IEEE Globecom, IEEE ICC, IEEE PES GM, IEEE WCNC, IEEE Infocom Workshops, ACM MobiCom Workshops, ACM MobiHoc workshops, etc. During her PhD, she received two prestigious fellowships, i.e., INSPIRE fellowship from Department of Science & Technology, India (in 2015) and research scholarship from Tata Consultancy Services (TCS) (from 2016–2018). Dr. Kaur also received the IEEE ICC best paper award in 2018 at Kansas City, USA and 2019 Best Research Paper Award from Thapar Institute of Engineering and Technology, India. She serves as an Associate Editor of Wiley's Security and Privacy (SPY) and Journal of Information Processing Systems (JIPS), Springer's Human-centric Computing and Information Sciences (HCIS), and guest editor for special issues in IEEE Transaction on Industrial Informatics and IEEE Open Journal of the Computer Society. She is a website co-chair of N2Women community. She also serves as the Vice-Chair of the IEEE Montreal Young Professionals Affinity Group. She has also been a TPC Co-chair for IEEE Infocom 2020 and ACM MobiCom 2020 workshops on DroneCom. She is a member of IEEE, IEEE Communications Society, IEEE Computer, IEEE Women in Engineering, IEEE Software Defined Networks Community, IEEE Smart Grid Community, ACM, and IAENG.

* * *

Sapna Gambhir is a Senior IEEE member, Secretary WIE AG IEEE Delhi section for 2019-2021 and treasurer WIE AG IEEE Delhi section for the current session. She is an associate Professor of Computer Engineering Department in a State Government University with name J C Bose University of Science & Technology, YMCA, Faridabad (India). She has completed her Doctorate in Computer Engineering from Jamia Millia Islamia, Delhi in 2010. She has approx. 20 years of experience in academics and research & development. She has been awarded with "Best Woman Scientist Award" under Research Excellence and Academic Awards (REAA-2018) and "Best Teacher Award" from District Commissioner of Faridabad. She has published more than 80 research articles in peer-reviewed journal and conference. Two patents, out of which one is with USPTO and One is in Indian Patent Office (IPO) has been granted. She has already guided three Ph.Ds successfully as sole supervisor. Currently, three Ph.D scholars are doing their research under her guidance. She has also participated in UKIERI 2019 leadership program which is a collaborative initiative by Govt. of UK and India. She is a principal investigator of many research projects of government organizations. Her area of interest are wireless networks, Internet of Things, Mobile Adhoc Networks and medical imaging.

Sumita Gupta has completed her doctorate in Computer Engineering from JC Bose University of Science & Technology, YMCA Faridabad. She has total experience of 13 years including both Academia and Industry. She has teaching experience of 10 years during which published many papers in various national/ international conferences and journals indexed by reputed agencies. She worked as Patent Analyst for 2.7 years with Microsoft. Currently, she is working as an Assistant Professor at Amity School of Engineering & Technology, Amity University, Noida, India. Her current areas of interest are Database, Information Retrieval, Web Mining, Digital Libraries etc. She has guided various research projects, thesis and B.tech projects. She has organised various events like international conferences, FDPs, Training programmes and seminars. She is reviewer for various journals of national and International repute.

Reet Kaur Kohli is a second-year student at Amity University, pursuing B. Tech in Biotechnology with a specialization (hons.) in Bioinformatics. She has a keen interest in research in the fields of biotechnology, medical biotechnology and computational biology.

Senthilkumar M. is currently working as a Professor in the Department of Production Engineering at PSG College of Technology, Coimbatore. Obtained his B.E. Degree in Mechanical Engineering (1994), M.E. in Engineering Design (1996) from GCT Coimbatore and Ph.D. from Anna University Chennai. Has about 24 years of teaching experience and 1 year of industrial experience. His projects have also won many awards. He has been the Principal Investigator of many sponsored research projects. He has published 135 journal papers and about 50 conference papers. 13 PhD scholars have obtained their degrees under his guidance. He is currently serving as editor and reviewer for many leading international and national journals. Also, he is member in many national and international societies of engineering. He has been actively involved in consultancy works and specialized courses for many leading industries and academicians in the areas of design and vibration control. He has visited many countries (Portugal, United Kingdom, France, Swiss, Australia and Singapore) for joint research works. His fields of expertise include vibration control, composites, smart structures, etc.

Rosy Madaan is a PhD in Computer Engineering department from YMCA University of Science & Technology, Faridabad. She has completed her B.E. from M.D. University in CSE department in 2005. In 2010, she completed M.Tech., in Computer Engineering from YMCA University of Science & Technology, Faridabad. She has total of 10 years teaching experience. She has worked in various engineering colleges and currently she is working as an Associate Prof. in CSE department of MRIIRS. Her areas of interest are information retrieval, search engines, crawlers and question answering systems.

Ritu Punhani is an Assistance Professor in the Department of Information Technology at Amity University handled many responsibilities at the university level & Department level. She has conducted corporate training for the South African High Commission to train their employees on the concept of Software Project Management. Earned "Young Researcher" Award for research proposal "ISMS Process Maturity Standardization for Data Mining Industry", held at Central University of Rajasthan in collaboration with IIT Kharagpur, National School of Leadership (NSL) Pune, and International Association of Research Scholars (IARS). Published 27 research papers in the field of information technology, Book Chapters, and write books for MBA, M.Sc, and MCA courses. She has two copyrights and two patents in process.

Manikanta Reddy S. received B.Tech degree in Mechanical Engineering from Rajiv Gandhi University of Knowledge Technologies, in 2014, and the M.Tech degree from the Madanapalle Institute of Technology, Andhra Pradesh, in 2016. He has been a research candidate in the Department of Production Engineering, PSG College of Technology, Coimbatore, since 2018. His current research is concerned with damage detection in structural members using artificial intelligence techniques.

Manya Sangwan is Research scholar in Computer Engineering department at J.C. Bose University of Science & Engineering. Her research area involves Convolutional neural network, VGG16, Sequential.

Sreekanth T. G. received B.Tech degree in Mechanical Engineering from Kannur University (2014), M.E in Computer Integrated Manufacturing from PSG College of Technology in 2017 and and Ph.D. from Anna University Chennai in 2021.

Currently working as Assistant Professor at Department of Production Engineering, PSG College of Technology since June 2017.

Sunishtha Singh Yadav has research experience in the identification of functionally important single nucleotide polymorphisms (SNPs) in drug-metabolizing Cytochrome P450s biomarkers (CYPs) including CYP2C9, CYP2C19 & CYP2D6 and their effect on chemotherapeutic outcomes in patients. My research includes the identification of biomarkers and new therapeutic targets to predict the outcomes of chemo-radiotherapy in cancer patients. The area of my research includes Cancer epidemiology, CYP450s, Cell biology, Molecular Biology, Xenobiotics metabolism, Pharmacogenomics, and Pharmacogenetics.

Index

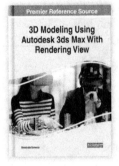

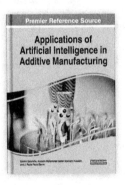
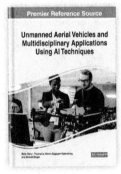

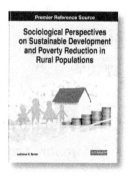

Printed in the United States
by Baker & Taylor Publisher Services